CW00750061

ALEXANDRE DUMAS
DICTIONARY OF CUISINE

A cookery book by the author of The Three Musketeers and The Count of Monte Cristo may seen an improbability. Yet Alexandre Dumas was an expert cook- his love of food was said to be equalled only by his love of women - and his Great Dictionary of Cuisine, written "to be read by worldly people and used by professionals" and published posthumously in 1873, it is a masterpiece in its own right.

This abridged version of the Dictionary is designed to be both useful and entertaining. A glance at the Index will show that there are hundreds of recipes - for sauces, soups, meat, fish , eggs, poultry and game - not all kitchen-tested with modern ingredients, but well within the scope of an experienced and imaginative cook.

THE KEGAN PAUL LIBRARY OF CULINARY ARTS

Editorial Advisor
Peter Hopkins

ALEXANDRE DUMAS'
DICTIONARY OF CUISINE

EDITED BY
LOUIS COLMAN

Routledge
Taylor & Francis Group

LONDON AND NEW YORK

First published in 2005 by
Kegan Paul Limited

Published 2013 by Routledge
2 Park Square, Milton Park, Abingdon, Oxfordshire OX14 4RN
711 Third Avenue, New York, NY 10017

Routledge is an imprint of the Taylor and Francis Group, an informa business

First issued in paperback 2015

© Kegan Paul, 2005

All Rights reserved. No part of this book may be reprinted or
reproduced or utilised in any form or by any electric, mechanical
or other means, now known or hereafter invented, including
photocopying or recording, or in any information storage or retrieval
system, without permission in writing from the publishers.

ISBN 978-0-7103-0839-9 (hbk)
ISBN 978-1-138-96647-5 (pbk)

British Library Cataloguing in Publication Data

Library of Congress Cataloging-in-Publication Data
Applied for.

Contents

The Dictionary

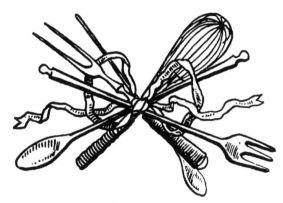

Editor's Introduction

Under a portrait of Alexandre Dumas in Katherine Bitting's great *Gastronomic Bibliography* the caption reads: "A noted author and gourmand who wrote novels and stories because he needed the revenue but produced his masterpiece, the *Grand Dictionnaire de Cuisine*, because he loved the work."

Bibliophile Jacob (Paul Lacroix, a contemporary of Dumas) commented knowledgeably: "Assuredly it is a great accomplishment to be a novelist, but it is no mediocre glory to be a cook. Novelist or cook, Dumas is a master, and the two vocations appear to go hand in hand, or, rather, to be joined in one."

Elizabeth Robins Pennell, herself neither hermit nor ascetic, said of the *Grand Dictionnaire* that it was "more exciting and thrilling than *Monte Cristo* or *Three Musketeers*. The anchorite in the desert could not dip into it without hailing the first camel, abandoning his dates and dry bread, and making straight for the nearest town in search of the materials for the master's dishes."

Culinary and gastronomic literature since the 1870s is full of references to Dumas' culinary skill and to his *Dictionary*. The latter is quoted and paraphrased as frequently as Dumas himself quotes and paraphrases others. Carrying the recognition of his authority perhaps to excess, a recent cookery book by a literary *avant-gardiste* credits Dumas' *Dictionary* with four recipes, none of which are to be found there. One of the most hard-working and ubiquitous of

I

culinary journalists quotes a nonexistent "headnote" from the *Dictionary* to make a point in the eternal Lobster Américaine vs. Lobster Armoricaine controversy. This is fame raised to the pitch of legend.

Almost unobtainable in French[1] and nonexistent in English, Dumas' *Great Dictionary* has had a continuing influence on culinary and gastronomic literature and practice for eighty-five years.

The circumstances that led to the writing of this book are related by Dumas in his dedicatory Letter to Jules Janin, beginning on p. 22. Janin was a well-known novelist, journalist, and dramatic critic. The manuscript was delivered to Dumas' publisher and friend, Alphonse Lemerre, in March 1870. It was only partly set in type when the Franco-Prussian War broke out, and publication was suspended. Dumas died the same year.

After the peace, D. J. Vuillemot, himself the subject of an article in this book (see p. 262), corrected and revised manuscript and galleys and saw the book through publication as *Le Grand Dictionnaire de Cuisine* in 1873. In 1882, the *Petit Dictionnaire de Cuisine* was published by Lemerre. It consisted of the recipes only. All the comments, history of and anecdotes on food and eating, and all the introductory matter were eliminated. This strictly utilitarian work was kept in print well into the twentieth century.

In the present edition the exigencies of modern publishing have happily coincided with modern requirements for a readable, useful, entertaining, and not over-redundant book. Mainly, recipes have been retained on the basis of their curiosity and usefulness, while the total bulk has been greatly reduced.

Here the reader will find recipes that impart a notion of the cooking of the periods covered, recipes that contain ideas that appear novel today, recipes that may never again be practical in original form but from which many others have sprung and will, subject to the imagination of the reader, spring.

While the recipes have been transcribed and translated without significant change, to preserve the atmosphere, the lusty enthusiasm,

[1]Except in abbreviated form.—ED.

and the fount of ideas of the original, obviously much had to be eliminated. Let me give examples to indicate the editorial principles followed. In the historical portions there has been considerable condensation. Several purple pages on the history of the barbarian invasion of Europe have been left out, but not the reference that makes a historical and culinary point. Some anecdotes that have become pointless in the course of eighty-five years have been omitted.

I have eliminated many, but not all, recipes dealing with ingredients — Mediterranean fish, for instance — unobtainable in England. However, in the case of fish, the recipes given are, for the most part, applicable to fish available nearly everywhere.

Recipes for bakery products have been largely eliminated. While a capon today may not be quite the same as it was to Dumas, because of developments in breeding and feeding, it is still essentially a capon, and an old rooster is still an aged cock. The same recipes hold. But many other ingredients, especially those used in baking, are completely different, though they still carry the same name. For exact measurements, imperative in baking, identical, standardized ingredients are essential. French flour in 1964 is completely different from English flour in 1964, and both are different from French flour in 1870.

Another editorial guide used here is obvious. This book, today, is not intended as a basic cookery book for an untaught bride. Innumerable new cookery books, for just this purpose, appear annually, and many standard ones are in wide circulation. Where a recipe of Dumas' is available in standard cookery books, it was considered expendable here.

No attempt has been made to adapt recipes in the sense of kitchen-testing with modern ingredients and restating the results. The basic culinary science is there. These recipes are the grandparents of those you see in current popular magazines. Making them readily available can revitalize the art of cooking, especially now, when the virtues of the turning spit, the charcoal grill, and even the smoke oven are coming back into use after so many years of neglect. Adaptation by the reader-cook can result in fifty recipes for each one given here. Each variation will have its usefulness, its virtues. Adaptations are easier now, with the availability of such machinery as automatic ovens, spits, and grills and of such ready-made products as glazes and basic sauces.

Ingredients may be added, subtracted, or substituted according to the judgment of the cook. Methods can be adapted, as in the case of a friend whose fridge serves to revive the principle of the "eternal kettle". She boils meat and bones and makes a bouillon, strains and freezes it, boils it when she next needs it for a sauce, throwing in any extra meat and bones that may be around and making up any depletion with water, freezes it again, and so on, forever. The results are magnificent, the basic broth being unrivalled for saucemaking.

Where crayfish are prescribed, shrimps or prawns may often be used. Where huge quantities of bacon are specified, they may be reduced by the cook. But use caution, especially when the bacon is required for barding. You can always skim or pour off the extra fat, as Dumas did. And, while the subject is up, perhaps meat should be larded more freely that it is today. (The *Dictionary* defines both "barding" and "larding"; see LARDING, p. 149.)

Dumas was old-fashioned — or, shall we say, conservative? — for his own times. Most of the recipes are from fifty to a hundred and fifty years older than the 1869 date of writing. As pointed out in editorial headnotes here and there, his nomenclature was far behind that of his own day. So was his apparatus for cooking. But it was adequate. The kitchen in which he worked was no kitchenette. It was a big room, with space not only for all his apparatus but enough to spare for all the appliances and gadgets you could find in your favourite magazine today, and elbowroom besides. Among the equipment were a mortar and pestle, not merely the small portable type used by the apothecary — though he had that, too — but also a stationary machine with the pestle handle running through fixed rings, operated by pulleys from the ceiling — a pile driver of a pestle.

In Dumas' day, gas stoves were commonly in use, but nowhere does he admit of their existence. He used the fireplace, the grill, the baking oven heated with coals, a crude (by standards of fifty years ago) oven and stove top — all fuelled with wood, charcoal, or, infrequently, coal — and a *bain-marie*. The spit was set in front of the fireplace, with the dripping pan beneath it, on notches set at appropriate distances from the fire. Elaborate machinery enabled the spit to be turned by hand.

I don't think you could readily find equipment today for cooking with "fire under and over", frequently prescribed in Dumas' recipes. This refers to a method in which the braising pot was set in coals or hot ashes. Over it was a special pot lid with raised edges and a long handle, set vertically into its centre, to lift it for basting. Hot coals were piled within the rim. Similar effects of even cooking, with browned or glazed top surface, can be obtained, with far greater convenience, in a modern oven.

Many of Dumas' recipes call for the use of a *four de campagne,* which can mean either an "under and over" container, or a sort of reflecting field oven for baking. Both have in their time been called Dutch ovens in this country. In New England the reflector was commonly used under the name of "tin kitchen". Internal evidence indicates Dumas had each in mind, at different times.

I don't think the spirit of Dumas' book is violated by eliminating much of this terminology and procedure, and substituting modern equivalents.

One last point about Dumas' culinary conservatism. To the joy of the reader, it was completely inconsistent. But one of the results is that familiar dishes — always with his individual touch — appear under unfamiliar names, and familiar names do not always represent familiar dishes. The element of surprise is always there. Even Dumas' contemporaries must have been delighted by his old-fashioned nomenclature. Perhaps tomorrow some of it will have swung full circle into favour again. The culinary art never stands still. Its past, present, and future are inexhaustible and inextricable; as Dumas says: "In cookery, all things are possible."

In this translation of the *Dictionary* there are no entries under the letters N, U, X and Y. This is one of the hazards of translation and of an alphabetical approach to organization. In the original French there are no entries under U or Y; X is represented by three lines on *xeres* (sherry), and Z by the same single entry you will find here. Entries under N translated into words with different initials — *navets* into turnips for example. For Q, Dumas resorted to *quartiers* (quarters) and *queues* (tails) of animals which have their own entries elsewhere.

Dumas' alphabetical organization makes delightful reading, but is not perfectly adapted for quick reference. A soup is as likely to be found under the name of its principal — or even minor — ingredient as under the heading soups. Therefore, to make this edition practicable and to avoid cross-references in the text, an index of recipes has been supplied.

Brief definitions of such terms as "fine spices", "four spices", and *"bain-marie"* have been supplied in the text under their own headings.

For reading this book, I suggest a comfortable chair in the living room, but not so comfortable as to discourage getting up for a go at the convenient kitchen.

A Few Words to the Reader

*F*rom birth man is instructed by his stomach to eat at least three times a day, to renew the strength he spends in labour or, as happens more often, in idleness. Eating is the great preoccupation of both primitive and civilized man. But the savage eats from need, the civilized man from desire.

This book is written for the civilized man. The savage has no need to whet his appetite.

There are three sorts of appetites:

1. Appetite that comes from hunger. It makes no fuss over the food that satisfies it. If it is great enough, a piece of raw meat will appease it as easily as a roasted pheasant or woodcock.

2. Appetite aroused, hunger or no hunger, by a succulent dish appearing at the right moment, illustrating the proverb that hunger comes with eating.

The third type of appetite is that roused at the end of a meal when, after normal hunger has been satisfied by the main courses, and the guest is truly ready to rise without regret, a delicious dish holds him to the table with a final tempting of his sensuality.

There are also three forms of gluttony.

First there is that gluttony which has been raised by the theologians to rank among the seven deadly sins. This is what Montaigne calls "the *science of the gullet", and it is well exemplified by Trimalchio and Vitellius.*

The greatest example of gluttony that has come to us from classical antiquity is that of Saturn, who devoured his children for fear they would dethrone him, and did not even notice that it was a paving stone he swallowed instead when it came to Jupiter's turn. He is forgiven, for in doing so he furnished Vergniaud with a fine simile: "The Revolution is like Saturn. It devours its own children."

Besides this sort of gluttony, which requires a strong stomach, there is what we might call the gluttony of delicate souls. Horace praised it, and Lucullus practised it. This is exemplified by the host who gathers together a few friends, never less numerous than the Graces, never more than the Muses, and does his utmost to distract their minds and cater to their tastes. The finest modern examples of this type of gluttony are men like Grimod de la Reynière and Brillat-Savarin.

Just as gluttony is an augmentative of gourmandism, its diminutive is epicurism. The glutton demands quantity, the epicure quality.

Our forefathers said, on seeing certain voracious faces: "Here is a man whose nose is pointed towards epicurism."

Those who insisted on being exact added: "Like St. James of the Hospital."

Whence came this saying, which at first sight appears rather incongruous? We shall tell you.

The portrait of St. James of the Hospital was painted on the door of the building bearing his name, near the Rue des Oies, which has since by corruption become the Rue aux Ours, a street on which the finest cookshops of Paris were to be found. And so, since the saint's face looked towards that street, it was said that his nose "was pointed towards epicurism".

In the same way, it was said of the statue of Queen Anne in London (a queen who was something of an epicure, especially in regard to champagne): "Like Queen Anne, who turns her back on the church to look at the wine merchant." And in fact, whether owing to chance or to the malice of the designer, Queen Anne did commit the impropriety, which can pass as a critique of her life, of turning her back on St. Paul's and keeping her royal smile for the great wine merchant whose establishment was on the opposite street corner.

The third form of gluttony, which I can only deplore, is that of those unfortunates who suffer from bulimia, a perpetual and insatiable hunger. They are neither gourmands nor gourmets; they are martyrs. It was doubtless during an attack of this disease that Esau sold his birthright to his brother Jacob for a mess of pottage.

Ancient Olympus apparently was not the home of gluttony. Its inhabitants ate nothing but ambrosia and drank only nectar. Rather, in this matter, man sets an example to the gods.

No one speaks of the feasts of Jupiter, Neptune, or Pluto. One does speak, however, of the feasts of Sardanapalus and of Belshazzar's feast. The expressions have become proverbial.

Poetry, painting and music have made Sardanapalus popular in France. He appears to us through the smoke and flame of his funeral pyre, sitting beside Myrrha on his throne and surrounded by his horses and slaves, who are being slaughtered to accompany him. And he is transfigured into the likeness of Hercules or Bacchus, those Oriental gods, rising to heaven on chariots of fire. This is the man who decreed that "whosoever invents a new dish shall be rewarded with a thousand gold pieces".

Belshazzar also serves as a point of comparison between ancient and modern gourmands. But it was his misfortune to run into a god who would not tolerate a combination of gourmandism and sacrilege. Had Belshazzar merely been a gourmand, Jehovah would not have interfered.

To distract himself while besieged in Babylon by Cyaxares and Cyrus, Belshazzar gave a great dinner for his courtiers and concubines. Everything was fine until he had the notion to call for the sacred vessels of gold and silver that Nebuchadnezzar had stolen from the Temple at Jerusalem. Scarcely had these vessels been profaned by sacrilegious lips when the palace was shaken by a clap of thunder and letters of fire appeared on the wall, spelling out those words which for twenty centuries now have been the terror of kings: Mene, mene, tekel, upharsin.

As when a sickness becomes serious one sends for the physician whom one mocked the night before, Belshazzar, terror-struck, sent for a young man about the palace who prophesied in his spare time for the amusement of the court. This was Daniel, who was studying to be a magician. No sooner had he seen the three words than he interpreted them, as though the language spoken by Jehovah were his mother tongue. They meant, he said: "God hath numbered thy kingdom, and finished it. Thou art weighed in the balances, and art found wanting. Thy kingdom is divided, and given to the Medes and Persians."

As a matter of fact, that very night Cyaxares and Cyrus took Babylon and put Belshazzar to death.

This was the same period that produced Milo of Crotona, that prodigious eater, whose town was a rival of Sybaris. One day the neighbours fought. Milo threw a lionskin over his shoulder, picked up a mace, put himself at the head of his compatriots, and in a single battle crushed the elite of the beautiful young men whose sleep was disturbed by the fold of a rose petal and who had caused all the cocks for a league around Sybaris to be slaughtered because their crowing disturbed their rest.

Milo's usual dinner included twenty-eight pounds of meat, twenty pounds of bread, and fifteen quarts of wine.

Man must sit to eat.

It took all the luxury and corruption of antiquity to bring first the Greeks, then the Romans, to eat reclined.

In Homer — and his heroes have fine appetites — the Greeks and Trojans eat sitting, and on separate seats. When Ulysses arrives at the palace of Alcinoüs, the king has a magnificent chair brought for him and tells his son Laodamas to make room for him.

The Egyptians, Apollodorus tells us, sat at table to eat.

Finally, the Romans sat at table until the end of the Second Punic War, 200 B.C.

It was the Greeks who set the example of this clumsy luxury. From time immemorial they lay on magnificent beds to eat their splendid feasts.

Herodotus tells of one such feast, as described to him by Thersander, one of the guests. It was given by Ortagenus the Theban a few days before the battle of Plataea. The remarkable thing is that he invited the Persian general Mardonius and fifty of the most important Persians. Fifty beds were set up in one room for this feast, with one Persian and one Greek on each bed. Now, the battle of Plataea was fought in 479 B.C. The fashion of lying on a bed to eat was therefore in vogue among the Greeks at least two hundred and twenty-nine years before it was adopted by the Romans.

Varro, the learned librarian, tells us that the number of guests at a Roman dinner was ordinarily three or nine — as many as the Graces, no more than the Muses. Among the Greeks, there were sometimes seven diners, in honour of Pallas. The sterile number seven was consecrated to the goddess of wisdom, as a symbol of her virginity. But the Greeks especially liked the number six, because it is round. Plato favoured the number twenty-eight, in honour of Phoebe, who runs her course in twenty-eight days. The Emperor Verus wanted twelve guests at his table in honour *of Jupiter, which takes twelve years to revolve around the sun. Augustus, under whose reign women began to take their place in Roman society, habitually had twelve men and twelve women, in honour of the twelve gods and goddesses.*

In France, any number except thirteen is good.

At ceremonial repasts, there was always one dish consisting of a hundred small birds such as ortolans, titlarks, robins, and swallows. Later this was improved upon. Only the tongues of birds which had talked or sung were served.

Each guest brought his own napkin to meals for which invitations were issued. Some of these were made of cloth of gold. Alexander Severus, less fastidious, had napkins of striped cloth made expressly for him. Trimalchio, the celebrated gourmand of whom Petronius sings, had cloth napkins, but woollen hand towels. Heliogabalus had some of painted cloth. Trebellius Pollio tells us that Gallienus used only cloth-of-gold tablecloths and napkins.

The Romans ate about the same meats that we do — beef, mutton, veal, kid, pork, lamb, barnyard fowl, chickens, pullets, ducks, capons, peacocks, flamingo, hens, cocks, pigeons — and many more than we do today, except for the turkey, which, though known under the name meleagris, *was more a curiosity than a food.*

We remember that in 390 B.C. it was the geese who saved the Capitol. Lucullus brought the pheasant, the cherry, and the peach to his compatriots from the Phasis.

The francolin (partridge) was their preferred bird, and their favourite francolins came from Ionia and Phrygia.

They ate our thrushes and blackbirds with delight, but only in the juniper-berry season.

All game was known to them: bear, boar, roe deer, fallow deer, rabbit, hare, partridge, and even the dormouse.

They were familiar with all the fish that to this day constitute the riches of the Mediterranean. The rich Romans had relays of slaves from the sea to Rome, to bring them live fish in buckets of water balanced on their heads. The most lavish host would show his guest the live fish he would later eat. The most beautifully coloured, such as the red mullet and the dolphin, were laid on marble tables where the voluptuaries watched their death agonies and the degradation of their colours.

The rich Romans had in their fresh- and salt-water aquariums pet fish which came at their call and ate from their hands. We recall the highly exaggerated anecdote told of Pollio, brother of Virgil's patron, who when Augustus was his dinner guest wanted to throw to his voracious eels a slave who had broken a glass bowl. Well-made glass was very rare in the time of Augustus. The slave escaped from the hands of those who were about to pitch him into the aquarium and threw himself at the Emperor's feet. Augustus, furious that a human life, even that of a slave, should be held cheaper than a bowl, ordered that every glass dish in Pollio's house be smashed, so that the slaves would not run the risk of being thrown to the eels for breaking them.

Sturgeon from the Caspian Sea was also highly esteemed by the Romans. And everyone knows the story of the magnificent turbot in regard to the sauce for which Domitian consulted the Senate and which by unanimous vote was served with a sauce piquante.

Athenaeus tells us that the most sought-after foods were the lampreys of Sicily, the stomachs of tunnies caught off the promontory of Pachynum, kids from the island of Melos, mullets from the Sciathus, cockles and prawns from Pelarum, sprats from Lipari, turnips from Mantinea, rape from Thebes, and beets from Ascra.

Now we can imagine what culinary fancies passed through the heads of men like Xerxes, Darius, Alexander, Mark Antony, Heliogabalus, when they found themselves masters of the world, unable even to estimate the extent of their riches.

When Xerxes spent a single day in a town, whether he dined or supped there, the impoverished inhabitants felt the consequences for a year or two, as though barrenness had struck the countryside.

Darius, when he went to dine in this or that town renowned for its good food, was often accompanied by twelve to fifteen thousand men. As a result, a single dinner or supper for Darius cost the town that had the honour to be his host more than a million francs [£70,000].

Thanks to Plutarch, Mark Antony's Alexandrian feasts have become classic. Cleopatra, whose host he was, despaired of matching such magnificence. She dissolved one of the pearls from her earrings in lemon juice and swallowed it. The pearl weighed twenty-four carats and was valued at six million sesterces. She was about to dissolve the other, but Antony prevented her.

Heliogabalus, that emperor who came from Syria and entered Rome on a chariot drawn by naked women, had a historian just to describe his meals. He never had a meal that cost less than sixty gold marks, which is fifty thousand francs in our money [or £3000]. He had pies made of the tongues of peacocks, nightingales, crows, pheasants, and parrots. Having heard that in Lydia there was a unique bird called the phoenix, he promised two hundred gold marks to anyone who brought it to him to eat. He fed his dogs, tigers and lions on pheasants, peacocks and partridges. He never drank from the same goblet twice, and all the goblets in his house were of pure gold or silver.

Heliogabalus made elaborate preparations for his own death, expecting that it would come in the midst of some uprising. He had a courtyard in his palace paved with porphyry so that he might throw himself down on it from a high place. He had a steel dagger fitted with a diamond-studded, carved gold hilt, to stab himself. He had especially spun a rope of gold and silk, to strangle himself. Surprised in the latrine by his assassins, he choked himself to death on the sponge that, to use Montaigne's expression, "the Romans used to wipe their behinds".

We have said that the first great and beautiful dinners were given by the Greeks. They used religious celebrations to justify their feasts. In fact, who could have invented them but a gay, witty, charming people, either completely idle or occupied with works of art, who left to their slaves the problems of providing the necessities of life? They dined on tables carved with that elevated taste which marked the Grecian artists. The beds on which they lay while feasting were decorated with tortoise shell, ivory and bronze. In some of them pearls and precious stones were encrusted. The mattresses were of purple embroidered with gold.

The cupbearers, fulfilling for the Greeks the tasks performed by Ganymede and Hebe for the gods, were young boys or beautiful young girls under orders to refuse nothing to the guests. Their faces were powdered and painted, their hair cut in ringlets. Their tunics of transparent stuff, belted with a ribbon, were tailored to fall about their feet, but they were pulled up over the belt so that the hem was raised to the knees.

It was in the course of these elegant dinners that Greek conversation took form — that conversation which has since been copied by all peoples, and of which ours, until the introduction of the cigar, was one of the liveliest imitations.

Polybius speaks of Archestratus, a citizen of Corinth, who is compared by the Marquis de Cussy to the great contemporary culinary artist known as Carême. Archestratus did not merely develop culinary theory. He contributed his genius to its practical application. He scoured the most fruitful countries of the world to examine the products of every clime. And from these travels he brought home to Athens all the culinary ideas of his time.

Athens, with its sugared wines, its fruits, its flowers, its pastries, and its desserts, never had what the Romans called the fine art of cooking. Rome ate better, and more substantially — which, strange as it seems, did not prevent it from matching Athens in wit.

The first cooks in Rome were Greeks, but towards the end of the Republic, in the days of Sulla, Pompey, Lucullus and Caesar, the Roman cuisine developed, especially in the direction of greater delicacy. The ravagers of the world who took the Roman standards to the north, south, east and west brought their cooks with them. And the cooks brought back to Rome the dishes they found, in all the countries they had visited, most worthy of the Roman table. Just as Rome had a Pantheon for all the gods, so it also had a temple for all the kinds of cookery.

Antony, especially pleased with his chef one day, had him come in at the dessert and presented him with a city of thirty-five thousand inhabitants.

The Romans invented the carving steward. Lucullus paid his up to twenty thousand francs [£1000] a year. Each guest was served by his own group of slaves. Each was individually perfumed. The flowers were renewed with every course. Heralds announced the quality of each wine served. Special officers practised the secret arts of reanimating flagging appetites.

It was only because of its ancient cuisine, Erasmus tells us, that Augustus bothered to rebuild Carthage.

One day the Emperor Claudius called his porters, stepped into his litter, and went posthaste to the Senate, as though he had a communication of the greatest urgency to make.

"Conscript Fathers!" he cried as he entered. "Tell me, would it be possible to live without salt pork?"

The astonished Senate, having deliberated, solemnly declared that life would indeed be deprived of one of its greatest delights if there were no salt pork.

Another day Claudius sat on his tribunal — for Claudius loved to render justice, just or unjust — to hear a most important matter. Elbow on table, chin in hand, he appeared to fall into a profound reverie. Suddenly he indicated that he wished to speak. The lawyer was silent. The litigants listened.

"Oh, my friends," said the Emperor, "how wonderful are meat pies! We shall have them for dinner."

God was good to this worthy emperor. He died as he had lived, a glutton. The immediate cause was indigestion caused by eating mushrooms, though it is also true that a poisoned feather was used to tickle his throat to make him vomit.

Cicero and Pompey once decided to drop in for dinner at Lucullus' villa at Naples, without giving him opportunity to prepare anything special. Arriving unexpectedly, they did not permit him to give any orders except that two more places be set at table.

Calling his major-domo, Lucullus merely said: "Two more covers in the Hall of Apollo."

But the major-domo knew that in the Hall of Apollo the minimum expenditure per guest was twenty-five thousand sesterces, or six thousand francs [£400]. So they had what Lucullus called "a little dinner" at six thousand francs per head.

Another day, by unbelievable chance, Lucullus had not invited anyone to share his table.

"I am alone," he said when his chef came to him for orders. The cook, thinking that a dinner costing ten or twelve thousand sesterces — that is, about twenty-five hundred francs [£150] — would do, acted accordingly. But after dinner Lucullus called him in and scolded him severely.

"But you were alone," the cook said, excusing himself.

"Precisely on those days when I am alone at table," Lucullus said, "you must take special pains. For then Lucullus is host to Lucullus."

This luxury grew and flourished until the end of the fourth century.

Then a great sound was heard from the far ends of unknown countries. From the north, the east, the south, with a great shout the innumerable hordes of barbarians rolled across the world. The incursions of the savage nations, which continued for nearly three centuries, cast darkest night over the ancient civilizations.

"When the world had no more cuisine, there was no literature, no high or lively wit, no more inspiration; the social idea did not exist," says Carême.

Happily, pages of the world's cookery book were scattered abroad. The wind threw fragments into the cloisters. There the flame of intelligence rose again. The monks tended it, and lighted new torches that threw their beams over the new society and made it productive. Genoa, Venice, Florence, Milan, and finally Paris, heirs to the noble passions of the art, became opulent cities and brought gastronomy back to life. There it had been extinguished, and there it was to be reborn.

Rome, most privileged of cities, has had two civilizations, both brilliant: its warrior history and its Christian history. After the luxury of its generals and emperors, it had the luxury of its cardinals and popes.

Through its commerce Italy regained the riches it once had conquered with its arms. As it had had its heathen gourmands, its Lucullus, Hortensius, Apicius, Antony and Pollio, it had also its Christian gourmands, its Leonardo da Vinci, Tintoretto, Titian, Paolo Veronese, Raphael, Boccio Bandinelli, Guido Reni. Until finally this new civilization could no longer be contained. It overflowed into France.

France was very backward in its cuisine. Only our excellent wines, though they had not attained the degree of perfection they have today, were superior to those of old Rome and new Italy. But by a happy chance, in the midst of the dispersion of peoples and the inundation of barbarians, the convents had remained places of refuge in which the sciences, arts, and tradition of cookery lay hidden. But cookery had turned from pagan to Christian and suffered a division into meat and meatless.

The luxury of the table that we find in the paintings of Paolo Veronese, especially in his Marriage at Cana, came to France with Catherine de Médici, and continued to grow during the reigns of Francis II, Charles IX, and Henry III.

Linen, especially fine linen, made its appearance late in France. Cleanliness does not presage civilization. It results from it. Our lovely ladies of the thirteenth and fourteenth centuries, at whose feet Galaor, Amadis, and Lancelot of the Lake knelt, not only did not wear undergarments but, it must be admitted, did not even know about them. Tablecloths, already in use at the time of Augustus, had disappeared, and their white surfaces were not seen on our tables until the close of the thirteenth century, and then only for kings and princes.

Napkins did not come into use until forty years later, under the reign that followed.

Our first ancestors, the Celts, wiped their hands on the bales of hay that served them for seats. The Spartans put a piece of soft bread beside each guest for the same purpose. In Rheims, before the first table napkins came into use, hands were wiped on hanks of wool that were neither new nor newly washed.

In 1792, at the time of Lord Macartney's voyages, the Chinese still used nothing but two little pieces of wood to bring their food to their mouths. The fork and spoon were just about absent from France until the sixteenth century, and their use was not widespread until the last century.

St. Peter Damian relates with horror that the sister of Romain Archile, who had married one of the sons of Pietro Orseolo, Doge of Venice, instead of eating with her fingers used golden forks and spoons to lift food to her mouth — which he regards as an effect of insensate luxury that must call down divine wrath upon her head and her husband's head. Both, in fact, died of the plague.

Knives had been in use long before forks, because they were necessary to cut meats that could not be torn apart with the fingers.

As for glasses, they were known to the Romans, as the story I have told about Pollio shows. Today, the curious traveller who visits Pompeii can see for himself that the use of glass was common among them. But after the barbarian invasion glasses were known only by tradition.

From the days of Phaedrus to Aristotle, about four centuries before Christ, wine was kept in earthenware amphorae, which held about twenty quarts, or in goatskins, from which it evaporated so much that it was necessary to scrape the skins and dissolve the coagulated liquid before it could be imbibed. In Spain it is still kept in goatskins, which give it an abominable flavour. The Spaniards, however, consider this as appetizing as the flavour of our Burgundy and Bordeaux. And in France there was no such thing as a bottle before the fourteenth century.

As for spices, which today provide the major condiments for all our sauces, they began to be a little commoner in France when Christopher Columbus discovered America and Vasco da Gama the passage of the Cape of Good Hope. But in 1163 they were still so rare and precious that the Abbé of Saint-Gilles in Languedoc, having a great favour to ask of Louis the Young, could think of no better way to propitiate him than to send bags of spices with his plea. Presents given to judges were called spices [épices], and this expression still survives.

In countries almost surrounded by the sea, like France, salt was used *in the most ancient times as a seasoning for meat and vegetables. Pepper, on the other hand, has been known for no more than a hundred and fifteen or twenty years. M. Poivre, a native of Lyons, brought it from the Île de France, in Cochin China. Before that, it sold for its weight in gold. Spice dealers who were so fortunate as to have a few ounces proclaimed themselves "Spice and Pepper Merchants" on their shop signs. Apparently, pepper was not that rare among the ancient Romans, for three thousand pounds of it were included in the tribute levied upon Rome by Alaric.*

The intellectual faculties seem to have soared in an enduring exaltation under the influence of spices. Is it to spices that we owe Ariosto, Tasso, and Boccaccio? Is it to spices that we owe Titian's masterpieces? I am tempted to believe it.

It was especially under Henry III that the elegant delicacies of the Florentine and Roman tables flourished in France. The tablecloth was folded and curled like a lady's collar from the time of Francis I. Already silver-plated luxury had passed all bounds, and it took an ordinance of Philip the Fair to curb it. Under his successors further ordinances unsuccessfully attempted to impose further limits on it.

In the early sixteenth century, under Louis XII and Francis I, dinner was at ten o'clock in the morning and supper at four. In the seventeenth century, dinner was at noon, supper at seven. If anyone, in this connection, wants to see something quite curious, and learn of great numbers of dishes that have been lost and forgotten, let him read the Memoirs of Héroard *the physician, whose task it was to record the lunches and dinners of Louis XIII.*

In those days pages, and sometimes the mistress of the house and her daughters, brought silver basins to the guests to wash their hands. This done, everyone sat at table, and after eating each went to an adjoining room to wash his hands again. If the master wished to show special honour to a guest, he sent his own full glass to him. In Spain today, when the mistress of the house wishes to indicate her favour, she touches her lips to the glass and sends it to you to drink her health.

Our forefathers said that to live in health it was necessary to get drunk once a month.

Commerce, establishing itself along the shores from the Bay of Bengal to Dunkirk, completely changed the routing of the spices that came to us from India, while those that came from America crossed the Atlantic. Italian commerce languished then, and bit by bit disappeared. Scientific, and especially culinary, discoveries no longer came to us from the Venetians, Genoese, and Florentines, but from the Portuguese, the Germans, and the Spaniards. Bayonne, Mainz, and Frankfurt sent us their hams; Strasbourg smoked its sausages and bacon for us; Amsterdam sent us its little herrings, and Hamburg its beef.

At this point coffee made its appearance in France. A Moslem priest had noticed that the goats in Yemen which ate the berries of a certain plant growing in that country were happier, gayer, and livelier than the others. He roasted the berries, ground them, made an infusion from them, and discovered coffee as we know it.

Despite Mme de Sévigné's prophecy, coffee continued to be the high spot of every dessert in the reign of Louis XIV.

Cabarets or taverns, prototypes of the cafés, had long been in existence, and began to soften our ways. Eating in the same room, often at the same table, Frenchmen learned to live like brothers and friends.

In the reign of Louis XIV the cuisine was elaborate, sumptuous, and fairly subtle. At the Condé table one began to surmise how delicate it could become.

To the suppers of the Regent Philip of Orléans, to the cooks he developed and treated and paid so royally, we are indebted for the excellent cuisine of the eighteenth century. This simple and at the same time know-ledgeable cuisine, which we have today in a complete and perfected form, moved forward in a tremendous, rapid, unhoped-for fashion. Full of verve, far from obscuring wit, it whipped it into life. French conversation, a model for all Europe, found its perfection at table, from midnight to one in the morning, between the pear and the cheese.

The conversation ranged from the great questions of the day to those of preceding centuries, and was developed at table with profundity, reason, and light by Montesquieu, Voltaire, Diderot, Helvétius, d'Alembert, and others like them, the while refinements of cookery spread from the Condés, the Soubises, the Richelieus, and the Talleyrands, and — what enormous progress! — one could dine as well in a restaurant for twelve francs as in Talleyrand's home and better than at Cambacérès'.

A word on those useful establishments, whose chefs sometimes vied with men like Beauvilliers and Carême. In Paris they have existed no longer than eighty to a hundred years. They cannot, therefore, credit their nobility to their antiquity. Restaurants are directly descended from the cabaret-taverns. At all times there were shops where wine was sold and shops where food was served. Those which sold wine were called cabarets. Those which sold food were called taverns.

The profession of wine merchant is one of the oldest that survives in the capital. Boileau cites statutes for them from 1264, but the merchants were not organized into corporate bodies for another three hundred and fifty years. At that time they were divided into four classes, hostelers, cabaretkeepers, taverners, and sellers of wine by the pot. These last sold wine retail but did not keep taverns. The wine they sold could not be consumed on the premises. There was an opening in the grille before their establishments through which the customer passed his empty pot and withdrew it after it had been filled. Of this custom all that remains today is the grille that constitutes part of the wine merchant's store front.

The cabaretkeepers were permitted to serve drinks in their own establishments, and food as well, but they were expressly forbidden to sell wine in bottles. They were obliged to use standard pint pots. In the eleventh century, lords, monks, and kings did not consider it beneath their dignity to sell by the pot or at retail the wine produced on their estates. To make a quick profit they abused their absolute authority by ordering the cabarets of the city closed down until all their own wine was sold.

It was towards the middle of the last century that one Boulanger established the first restaurant in Paris, on the Rue des Poules. Over his door was the legend: Venite omnes, qui stomacho laboris, et ego restaurabo vos — "Come, all ye that labour on your stomach, and I shall restore you."

The establishment of restaurants in Paris marked great progress indeed. Before they were invented, strangers were at the mercy of the cooking of the innkeepers, which was generally bad. There were some hotels serving a table d'hôte, but with few exceptions they offered only the barest essentials. Of course there were the cookshops, but they served only whole cuts, and if one wished to dine with a friend, one had to buy a whole leg of lamb, a whole turkey, or a whole chine of beef.

Finally, a genius came along who understood that if one diner asked for a chicken wing, another could not fail to appear who wanted the drumstick. Variety of dishes, definite prices, care given to service would bring success to the first who established all three qualities.

The Revolution, which destroyed so many things, created new restaurantkeepers. The stewards and chefs of the great lords, left without employment by the immigration of their masters, turned philanthropic and bethought themselves to share the fruits of their culinary science with the public.

At the time of the first Bourbon restoration, in 1814, the restaurant-keeper took a great step. Beauvilliers appeared in his dining rooms dressed like a gentleman, sword at side.

Among the restaurantkeepers who wielded the sceptre in the kitchen we must mention one Méot. He sold consommé, fresh eggs, and chicken au gros sel, serving them on little marble tables like those in the cafés today. In my youth I still heard talk of the succulent dinners Méot served, and of the brisk, engaging air of his wife at the cashier's desk. Méot had been chef to the Prince de Condé — that is to say, Vatel's successor.

After Paris, the city with the most restaurants is San Francisco. It has restaurants from every country, even China.

Today there is little difference between the cookshops and the restaurants, and it was long the custom, at the end of the last century and the beginning of this, to go to a cookshop for oysters and fish soup. And this made sense, for often one dines better at Maire's, Philippe's, or Magny's than at the finest restaurants in Paris.

Here are some of the restaurantkeepers whose names the gourmands of the last century and the beginning of this one have remembered with gratitude: Beauvilliers, Méot, Robert, Rose, Borel, Legacque, the Véry Brothers, Neveux, and Baleine.

Those of today are Verdier of the Maison d'Or, Bignon, Brébant, Riche, the Café Anglais, Peter's, Véfour, the Frères Provençaux.

If I omit any celebrities, may they forgive me. It is an oversight.

ALEXANDRE DUMAS

DEDICATION
A Letter to Jules Janin

You and I were born at the meeting of two centuries, two years apart, I believe – I in 1802 and you in 1804 or 1805. As a result, neither of us ever knew – except by reputation – the most famous gastronomes of the last century.

The most famous table of those days was kept by Talleyrand.

Bouché, or Bouche-sèche, who was trained in the Condé household and whose good food was renowned for tastiness and impressiveness, was given full charge of the Prince's kitchens. It was he who created those large diplomatic dinner parties which have become classic and will always be imitated. The Prince had complete confidence in him, left him completely free in his expenditures, and accepted everything he did as good. Bouché died in the Prince's service. Carême dedicated the *Pâtissier royal*, one of his finest books, to him.

Much has been said about Talleyrand's table, but many of the things said do not have the virtue of being exactly true.

Talleyrand was one of the first to realize that a wholesome, well-thought-out cuisine would improve the health and prevent serious diseases. In fact, his health during the last forty years of his life is a powerful argument in favour of this opinion.

All of Europe that was illustrious in politics, learning, and art, great generals, ministers, diplomats, and poets, sat at Talleyrand's table, and not one failed to recognize that it was here that the finest hospitality was dispensed. The Revolution had killed all the great lords, the great tables, the great manners. Talleyrand re-established all that. Thanks to him France's reputation for magnificence and hospitality went around the world once more.

At eight o'clock every morning, Talleyrand spent an hour with his cook, discussing the dishes for dinner. This was the only meal he ate, for in the morning all he had before getting to work was three or four cups of camomile tea.

Here is the illustrious cook Carême's opinion of Cambacérès' cuisine, which, it seems, has often been mistakenly praised:

I have written several times that Cambacérès' kitchens never merited their great reputation. I shall repeat certain details, and cite a few more, to clarify the picture of that villainous house.

M. Grand'Manche, chef of the kitchens of the archchancellor, was a learned practitioner and an honourable man, whom we all esteem. Having been called in by him for the great affairs at the Prince's house, I was able to appreciate his work, and I can consequently say a little about it. The Prince occupied himself with his table every morning, expending minute care — but only to discuss and decrease its expense. He showed, in the highest degree, that worry and concern over details which marks the miser. At every service, he took note of the dishes that had not been eaten, or only partly eaten. Next day he composed his dinner from these vile leftovers. Heavens! What a dinner! I do not mean that leftovers cannot be used. I do mean they cannot yield the dinner of a prince and an eminent gastronome. This is a delicate point. The master has nothing to say about it, nothing to see. Only the ability and probity of the cook are concerned. Leftovers must be employed only with caution, ability, and, above all, silence.

The household of the Prince de Talleyrand, which is the first in Europe, in the world, and in history, operates according to those principles. They are principles of taste. They were the principles of every great gentleman I ever served: Lord Castlereagh, George IV, the Emperor Alexander, etc.

The archchancellor [Cambacérès] received innumerable presents in the form of food from the departments, especially the finest birds. All these were stuffed into a vast larder of which the Prince himself had the key. He took note of the provisions and the day of their arrival, and he alone gave orders for their use. Frequently, by the time he gave the order, the provisions were spoiled. Food never appeared at his table until it was at least stale.

Cambacérès was never a gourmand in the true, learned sense of the word. He was born a big, even a voracious, eater. Can it be believed that his favourite dish was hot meat-ball pie, a heavy, insipid, stupid dish? One day, when the good Grand'Manche wanted to replace the meat balls with quenelles of poultry, cockscombs and cock's kidneys, will you believe it, the Prince turned red with anger and demanded his old-fashioned meat balls that were tough enough to break one's teeth. He found them delicious. For hors d'oeuvres, he was often served a bit of warmed-over pastry crust, and the butt of a ham that had seen service all week appeared on his table. And his able cook, who never had the great sauces! Not even that cook's assistant a bottle of Bordeaux! What parsimony! What a pity! What a house!

How different was the great, dignified dwelling of the Prince de Bénévent [Talleyrand]! Complete confidence, completely justified, in the chef, one of the most illustrious practitioners of our day, M. Bouché. Only the most sanitary and the finest products were employed. Everything was ability, order, splendour. Talent was happy there, and highly placed. The chef governed the stomach. Who knows but what he influenced the charming, active, or great thoughts of the minister. Forty-eight-course dinners were given in the halls on the Rue de Varenne. I have designed them and I have seen them served. What a man was M. Bouché! What great tableaux he created! Who has not seen them has seen nothing!

Neither Cambacérès nor Brillat-Savarin ever knew how to eat. Both of them loved strong, vulgar foods. They simply filled their stomachs. That is letter-perfect truth. Savarin was a big eater and it seems to me he talked very little and with difficulty. He had a heavy air, and looked like a parish priest. At the end of his meal, he was absorbed with his digestion. I have seen him sleep.

Let's finish the picture. Brillat-Savarin was neither a gastronome nor a gourmet. He was just a vigorous eater. He was tall, and because of his heavy bearing, his vulgar manners, and his clothing, which was always ten to twelve years behind the fashion, he was called the drum major of the Court of Cassation.

Suddenly, twelve years after his death, we inherited one of the most charming books on gastronomy one could dream of, his *Physiology of Taste.*

Grimod de la Reynière was one of the heroes of that period. An accident when he was very young deprived him of his hands. By dint of ingenuity and perseverance, he made of the remaining stumps organs nearly as supple as hands themselves. As a youth he was very elegant. His health was sound, his stomach stanch. He died at the age of eighty. His nephew, the Count d'Orsay, presented me to him. He kept us to dinner, and gave us one of the best I ever ate. That was about 1834 or 1835.

It was said that at Louis XVIII's dinners, even when he dined tête-à-tête with M. d'Avray, the King exhausted the mysteries of the most recherché luxury. Chops were not merely grilled. They were grilled between two other chops. The diner himself opened this marvellous censer, which poured forth its juices and most delicate perfumes. Ortolans stuffed with truffles were cooked in the stomachs of partridges, so that His Majesty sometimes hesitated for moments between the delicate bird and the perfumed vegetable.

There was a tasting jury for the fruits that were to be served at the royal table, and M. Petit-Radel, librarian of the Institute, was peach taster. One day a gardener from Montreuil, having by artful grafts obtained the most beautiful variety of peaches, wished to offer them in homage to Louis XVIII. But first he had to pass the tasting jury. He presented himself, therefore, at the library of the Institute, bearing a plate with four magnificent peaches, and asked for M. Petit-Radel.

He had some difficulty getting in. The librarian was engaged in some pressing work. The gardener insisted, asking only that he be permitted to pass the plate, the peaches, and his forearm through the door.

At the sound of this operation, M. Petit-Radel reopened his eyes, which had closed beatifically over a Gothic manuscript. At sight of the peaches, which seemed to advance on him of their own volition, he uttered a cry of joy, and cried out twice: "Come in! Come in!"

The gardener announced the purpose of his visit, and the jubilation of a gastronome spread itself over the savant's face. Lounging in his armchair with legs crossed and hands joined, he prepared himself with a gentle adjustment, a sensual movement of the shoulders, for the important judgment required of him.

The gardener asked for a silver knife. He picked up one of the peaches and cut it in quarters, put one on the point of the knife, and gaily presented it to M. Petit-Radel, saying: "Taste the juice."

Eyes closed, forehead impassive, full of the importance of his function, M. Petit-Radel silently tasted the juice.

Anxiety was already appearing in the gardener's eyes when, after two or three minutes, the judge's half opened.

"Good! Very good, my friend," were the only words he could say.

Immediately the second slice was offered, but the gardener said, with slightly more assurance: "Taste the flesh!"

Same silence, same serious mien of the learned gourmand. But this time the movements of his mouth were more evident, for he was chewing. Finally, he nodded.

"Ah! Very good! Very good!" said he.

Perhaps you think the superiority of the peach was established and everything was said? No.

"Taste the aroma!" said the gardener.

The aroma was found worthy of the flesh and the juice. Then the gardener, who had progressed little by little from a supplicant to a triumphant attitude, presented the last piece and, with a pride and satisfaction that he did not seek to hide, said: "Now. Taste the whole!"

It is superfluous to say that this last slice had the same success as its predecessors. M. Petit-Radel, his eyes moist with emotion, a smile on his lips, took the gardener's hands in his own as effusively as he would an artist's.

"Ah, my friend," he said, "it is perfect. Allow me to express my sincere compliments. Beginning tomorrow your peaches will be served at the King's table."

Louis XVIII had no illusions. He saw gourmandism fading away, and it saddened him.

"Doctor," he said one day to Corvisart,[1] "gastronomy is disappearing, and with it the last of the old civilization. It is the organized professions — the physicians, for example — who should put forth every effort to prevent the dissolution of society. At one time France was full of gastronomes, because it was full of groups whose members have now been annihilated or dispersed. There are no more farmers-general, no more abbés, no more white monks. All that is left of gastronomy resides in you, the physicians, who are

[1]Brillat-Savarin quotes himself as saying this to Corvisart.—ED.

predestined gourmands. You should uphold more firmly the burden with which destiny has charged you. You should attempt to emulate the Spartans at Thermopylae."

Louis XVIII, a delicate eater, had profound contempt for his brother, Louis XVI, a gross one who when he ate did not accomplish an intellectual, reasoned action, but a completely brutal one. When Louis XVI was hungry, he had to eat. On August 10th, when he went to the Convention to ask asylum, he was put in a box — I won't say the stenographer's box, because there were no stenographers at that time, but at least the box of the man responsible for an account of the proceedings. Scarcely was he seated when hunger overtook him, and he demanded food on the instant!

The Queen argued with him, trying to avoid such an exhibition of gluttony and thoughtlessness. He would not listen to reason. He was brought a roast chicken, into which he bit immediately, apparently indifferent to the grave discussions of life and death around him. What did it matter? He was eating, therefore he was alive. And he continued to eat until not a shred of chicken nor a crumb of bread remained.

This tendency of his towards insatiable hunger was so well known that Camille Desmoulins was able to spread the story, an odious calumny at such a moment, that he was arrested because he would not pass through Sainte-Menehould without eating the famous pigs' feet of that town. But everyone knows that Louis XVI was not arrested at Sainte-Menehould but at Varennes, and that pigs' feet had nothing to do with this arrest.

The long reign of Louis XV was monotonous in a culinary sense. Only Richelieu introduced a little variety into those unchanging perfumes, flowers, and fruits. He invented *boudins* à la Richelieu, and *bayonnaise*, which our restaurateurs obstinately call *Mahonaise* [mayonnaise] on the ground that it was invented the day before or the day after the capture of General Mahon.

It is true that Béchamel sauce and chops Soubise were also invented in his reign.

The Regency was a charming period in France. For seven or eight years one lived to drink, love, eat. Then one fine evening the Regent was talking with Mme de Falaris, his little crow, as he called her. His head was heavy, and he laid it on the shoulder of the beautiful courtesan, saying: "Do you believe in hell, sweetheart?"

"If I go, I hope to find you there," she said.

He did not answer. He was there already.

The Regent dead, M. le Duc succeeded him. He was a one-eyed villain from the wrong side of the House of Condé. He had received from nature that sum of virtues which prevents a prince from being hanged, not because he is an honest man but because he is a prince. He and his mistress, daughter of the tax farmer Pléneuf, took about a year to eat up what money remained in the coffers of France. Then, when there was no more money, they began to eat France itself.

One ate a great deal under the Regency of M. le Duc, but one did not eat well.

In our own day, a hundred louis was an ambition to which the most ambitious dared not aspire. My own salary at its highest, when I resigned[1] on August 8th, 1830, amounted to 166.66 francs a month. How much did you earn then, my dear Janin? You cannot have been rich, either. How, on four or five francs a day, could one think about gastronomy? It was necessary to think of what was most pressing. Before eating, we had to think about existing.

Of all our close circle of friends, my dear Janin, scarcely any but you and I survive. And we were never real drinkers or real eaters. The others are dead. The joyous cloth of 1830 has become a winding sheet in 1869. We shall always eat, but we will not dine, and especially we will not sup.

Around 1844 or 1845 I was seized with remorse that I was failing to keep up my custom of serving suppers. My friends were just about all the wits of the period: talented painters, fashionable musicians, popular singers. I arranged for a table of fifteen places, and I extended a permanent invitation to fifteen friends to get together at my home between eleven and midnight every Wednesday. I asked them to let me know three or four days in advance when they could not come, so that I could fill their places.

These suppers generally consisted of a pie made from some game, a roast, a fish, and a salad. I should, of course, have put the fish ahead of the roast.

At that time I still went hunting, and three or four partridges,

[1] Dumas had been appointed assistant librarian to the Duke of Orleans.—ED.

a hare, and a couple of rabbits provided meat for the pie on which Julien exercised his unfailing art. I had invented an oil dressing for fish that was a great success. Duval furnished me roasts that were practically quarters of beef.

Finally, I made a salad that satisfied my guests so well that when Ronconi, one of my most regular guests, could not come he sent for his share of the salad, which was taken to him under a great umbrella when it rained so that no foreign matter might spoil it.

"How," you will ask me, my dear Janin, who are so strong in theory and so weak in practice, "how could you make a salad one of the important dishes for your supper?"

It is because my salad was not just a salad like any other salad.

It is the task of the master or the mistress of the house, if they are worthy of such priestly duty, to attend personally to the seasoning of all salads. It must be done an hour before the salad bowl is to be broached. The salad should be turned over three or four times during that hour.

Here is the definition of salad, or rather of salads, given by the *Dictionary of French Cooking*, the best book on this important subject that I know:

Salads

Salads are composed of potherbs to which are added a few aromatic herbs and seasoning of salt, white pepper, oil, vinegar, and sometimes mustard or soya sauce.

Salads vary according to the season. Towards the end of autumn one starts to eat the chicories. Ordinarily, no garnishing herbs are added to this type of salad. It is sufficient to put a piece of stale bread rubbed with garlic in the bottom of the bowl, which is sufficient to season the salad.

As you see, I have emphasized *garnishing herbs*. A less exact and learned manual would have said no *garnish*, for its author would probably not have known that all herbs are divided into three categories:

Potherbs, of which there are six: sorrel, lettuce, chard, orach, spinach, and purslane. They are used to make soups, meatless stuffings, and teas. Our own advice is to use them mainly in teas.

Seasoning herbs, of which there are ten, not including bay, which you can't count because it is a tree: parsley, tarragon, chervil, scallions, shallots, savory, fennel, thyme, sweet basil, and tansy.

Garnishing herbs, of which there are twelve: upland cress, water cress, chervil, tarragon, burnet, samphire, buckshorn plantain, dwarf basil, purslane, fennel, garden-balm, and chives.

The piece of stale bread rubbed with garlic that the *Dictionary of French Cooking* recommends for the seasoning of chicory is called a *capon*. Where did it get this name? The most profound etymological research has cast no light on the problem. I have been obliged to cast about among the probabilities, which are as follows:

The capon as poultry originated in Caux, or in the province of Maine, while the capon as a crust of bread rubbed with garlic originated in Gascony.

Now, a Gascon is by nature both poor and vain. The idea must have occurred to some Gascon, perhaps to d'Artagnan, to call a crust of bread rubbed with garlic a capon, so that when anyone asked him whether he had dined well he could truthfully answer: "Superbly! I had a capon and a salad."

Which, taken literally, is a pretty good dinner for a Gascon.

As for me, I am very fond of the cuisine of Provence, and have made a special study of it, particularly of its home cooking. And in spite of the Roman prohibition against entering the temple of Cybele after eating garlic, in spite of any hatred for the odour of garlic, in spite of the rule of King Alfonso of Castile that prohibited the eating of garlic by the knights of the order he created in 1330, I remain of the medical opinion of Raspail, and the culinary opinion of Durand, both of whom recommend the use of garlic as a savoury and healthful substance.

You are no doubt familiar with all the salads, from escarole to romaine lettuce. But in the extraordinary case that you care for that quaint herb called *chicory*, I'll give you advice that may seem strange at first but that you will agree, after you take it, is really excellent. That is to mix in violet petals, and sprinkle it with two or three pinches of the Florentine iris used in sachets to perfume linen.

Let's get back to that salad I served in my home, of which Ronconi took such care to get his portion. It was a salad of great imagination, composite order, with five principal ingredients:

Slices of beet, half-moons of celery, minced truffles, rampion with its leaves, and boiled potatoes.

Before going any further, let us mention that it is a common error to assume that salt and pepper are dissolved in vinegar, and consequently to begin seasoning a salad by sprinkling it with a spoonful or two of salted and peppered vinegar.

Chaptal was the first, in France — he borrowed the idea from Northern Europe — to saturate the salad with oil, salt, and pepper before adding vinegar. This method, which we recommend for informal salads, has the double advantage of distributing the salt and pepper more evenly, and of collecting the excess vinegar in the bottom of the salad bowl. Chaptal, whose previous services to France during his ministry had been recognized by the title of Count, was recompensed for the services he rendered the table by the phrase that passed into the culinary vocabulary: salad seasoned à la Chaptal. Without coveting any such precious reward, I shall tell you how I season my salad.

First I put the ingredients into the salad bowl, then overturn them on to a platter. Into the empty bowl I put one hard-boiled egg yolk for each two persons — six for a dozen guests. These I mash with oil to form a paste, to which I add chervil, crushed tuna, macerated anchovies, Maille mustard, a large spoonful of soya, chopped gherkins, and the chopped white of the eggs. I thin this mixture by stirring in the finest vinegar obtainable. Finally, I put the salad back into the bowl, and my servant tosses it. On the tossed salad I sprinkle a pinch of paprika, which is the Hungarian red pepper.

And there you have the salad that so fascinated poor Ronconi.

These suppers went on for about a year. It was about that time that *The Three Musketeers* was being published in *Le Siècle*. The novel, as we know, was quite successful. Scarcely was publication completed when the director of the Théâtre Ambigu asked me to make a drama out of it. The success of the play was as great as the novel's.

The Duc de Montpensier attended the opening performance, and during an intermission invited me into his loge. Although the play was carefully mounted, it was not by a great deal as perfectly staged as the Théâtre Historique later did it. The Duc deplored the fact that I had presented in so small a theatre a play for which, he said, the Opéra would scarcely have been large enough. He asked me why I had chosen the Ambigu. I answered that we had no choice as to which theatre should present our plays, that we gave them to the directors who asked for them.

"But," I added, "if Your Highness will get the licence for me, I shall build a theatre, and I shall show you how a play should be presented."

"Well," said he, "let's not just drop it. I'll do all I can to help you."

I shook my head.

"Why do you do that?" he asked.

"Oh, I don't mean Your Highness won't do all he can. But the King will not grant me the licence."

"Why not?"

"Because he considers me a literary and political demagogue."

"This is not the King's business. It's M. Duchâtel's. At the next court ball I'll dance twice with Mme Duchâtel and I'll arrange the whole thing with her."

Two or three weeks later, I received a letter from M. Duchâtel, inviting me to call on him at the ministry.

We talked for more than half an hour about my project and how I envisioned it. I saw that M. Duchâtel did not understand at all, and I perceived that if the Duc de Montpensier was to be success-ful he had more than one ill-will to conquer on the way.

One day the Duc sent me word that the licence had been granted. I ran to thank M. Duchâtel, who asked me sarcastically where we planned to build our theatre. I told him, which was the truth, that I had put down forty thousand francs for an option to buy the Hotel Foulon at six hundred thousand. He asked where we would find the money to build. I answered that we had already found it, and gave him the name of the banker with whom we had a deposit of fourteen hundred thousand francs.

"Well," said M. Duchatel, "when does the building start?"

"Tomorrow, sir."

"And we shall have the pleasure of your first production?"

"In all probability a year from today."

"And it will be called?"

"*La Reine Margot.*"

The curious thing is that everything happened just as I had said, to the day.

I kept my word. The Théâtre Historique competed with the greatest successes of the period. If the mounting of my plays did not overshadow all previous attempts, at least it competed successfully at times even with the Opéra.

One fine day, as happens to all thrones not well founded, everything cracked. The young dynasty disappeared in three days, just as the old dynasty had done.

If history deigned to deal with such matters, I could tell how the theatre was not excluded from this great catastrophe. As a result of the troubles, all business was suspended, and nearly all the theatres were closed. I had made many enemies through my successes with books and in the theatre. By a judgment that remained incomprehensible to the lawyers, and even to the judges themselves, I was condemned to pay four hundred thousand francs of the debts of the Théâtre Historique.

The four hundred thousand francs were paid in fifteen years.

In my contract with Michel Lévy, I had retained the right to write a cookery book and to sell it to whomever I pleased. Broken by the forced labour that for fifteen years had averaged a production of not less than three volumes a month, my imagination enervated, my head aching, completely ruined but having no more debts, I resolved to seek a momentary rest by writing this book, which I anticipated as a diversion.

Alas, my friend, when one wants to do things differently from others, often without doing better, nothing is diversion. Everything is work.

For the last year and a half, in weakened physical condition and sustained only by moral power, I have been obliged to seek temporary periods of rest and of sea air to provide me with the strength I need. I have successively been at Fécamp, eighteen months ago; a year ago at Le Havre; six months ago at Maisons-Lafitte; finally, I have just returned from Roscoff, where I had counted on writing this work out of my own memories, but have been able to do it only at the cost of exhausting labour and research.

Here it is.

Yours,
ALEXANDRE DUMAS

ONE MORE
WORD
TO
THE PUBLIC

WHEN I DECIDED to write this book, and in a weary moment thought of it as the crowning of a literary work comprising four or five hundred volumes, I must confess I was a bit embarrassed, not as to the content, but as to the form I should give this work.

However I might approach it, more would be expected of me than I was in a position to give. If I wrote with wit and imagination like Brillat-Savarin in the *Physiology of Taste,* no professional cook would pay any attention to it.

If I wrote a purely practical book like the *Cuisinière Bourgeoise,* worldly people would say: was it worth while that Michelet should say there had been no more able dramatic architect since Shakespeare, and for Ourliac to say that he had not merely the spirit of France but the spirit of Gascony besides – to have him write an eight-hundred-page book to tell us that whereas rabbit should be skinned alive, a hare should be hung!

That was not my aim. I wanted to be read by the worldly ones and used by the professionals.

Early in this century, Grimod de la Reynière had published an *Almanach des Gourmands,* which was pretty successful. But it was a book on gastronomy, not of recipes.

34

But since I had travelled much – in Italy and Spain, where you eat badly; in the Caucasus and in Africa, where you can starve – I was tempted to show how you can eat better in the first and one way or another in the second.

I deliberated a long time, and finally came to a conclusion:

To take from the classic cookery books that are now in the public domain, such as the *Dictionary* by the author of the *Memoirs of the Marquise de Créqui* and Beauvilliers' *L'Art du Cuisinier*, from the elder Durand, of Nîmes, and from the voluminous dispensatories of the time of Louis XIV and XV, all the recipes that have won a place on the best tables. To borrow from Carême, that apostle of the gastronomes, everything his publishers, Mm. Garnier, will allow me to take. To check the witty writings of the Marquis de Cussy and appropriate his best inventions. To reread Elzéar Blaze and, by adding my hunting instincts to his, try to invent something new in preparing quail and ortolans. To add to all this unknown dishes gathered from the ends of the earth, and the least known and liveliest anecdotes on the cooking of peoples and on the peoples themselves. To write the physiology of all the edible animals and plants that are worth the trouble.

In this way my book, containing both wit and learning, will not frighten the practical cook, and will perhaps merit reading by serious men and by not-so-serious women whose fingers will not be too wearied in turning pages derived sometimes from de Maistre and sometimes from Laurence Sterne.

This much determined, I start quite naturally with the letter A.

P.S. Let's not forget to mention, for that would be ungrateful, that for certain recipes I have consulted the great restaurateurs of Paris and even of the provinces, such as the Café Anglais, Verdier, Magny, the Frères Provençaux, Pascal, Grignon, Peter's, Véfour, Véry, and especially my old friend Vuillemot.

Their names are given wherever their work has been used. Here I give them thanks.

A. D.

*Man does not live on what he eats
but on what he digests.*

The Dictionary

ABSINTHE. A perennial plant with bitter leaves, found everywhere in Europe. In the North, a wine called vermouth is made from it.

There are two varieties, the Roman and the Pontic, also known as marine absinthe. Absinthe that grows along the shore or high in the mountains is fine to eat. To the latter we owe the special flavour of animals that have fed upon it, highly esteemed by gourmands and known as *pré-salé* [salt-meadow].

Though its dispensers boast that the beverage called absinthe will strengthen the stomach and aid digestion, and though the Salerno school recommends absinthe for seasickness, it is impossible not to deplore its ravages among our soldiers and poets over the past forty years. There is not a regimental surgeon who will not tell you that absinthe has killed more Frenchmen in Africa than the *flitta*, the yataghan, and the guns of the Arabs put together.

Among our Bohemian poets absinthe has been called "the green Muse". Several, and unfortunately not the poorest, have died from its poisoned embraces. Hégésippe Moreau, Amédée Roland, Alfred de Musset, our greatest poet after Hugo and Lamartine — all succumbed to its disastrous effects.

De Musset's fatal passion for absinthe, which may have given some of his verses their bitter flavour, caused the dignified Academy to descend to punning. It seems that de Musset frequently found himself in no condition to attend the academic sessions. Which prompted one of the forty Immortals to say that "he absinthes himself a bit too much".

But absinthe has a competent defender in the author of the *Memoirs of the Marquise de Créqui*, who claims that a glass of candy absinthe can only aid the digestion. Here is his recipe:

Candy Cream of Absinthe. Eight quarts of brandy; 2 pounds of tips of absinthe leaves; zest of 4 oranges or lemons; 7 pounds of sugar; 1 gallon of river water. Distill the brandy, absinthe, and zests in a *bain-marie* [for which you use the river water], and reduce to 4 quarts. Add the sugar. When it has melted, stir and filter.

Absinthe is forbidden in all military barracks.

ACANTHUS. A plant celebrated in the history of the fine arts. Its very large, pleasingly shaped leaves were used to crown Corinthian columns.

Vitruvius tells of the introduction of acanthus leaves as ornaments. A young Corinthian girl having died just before a marriage she had looked forward to, her desolate nurse put various objects the girl had loved into a basket and placed it on her grave, covering it with a large tile to preserve the contents from the weather. It happened that an acanthus root was buried directly under the basket. The following spring the acanthus sprouted, its great leaves surrounding the basket, their tips curled around the tile. Callimachus, passing by, observed the lovely effect and decided to use it in the decoration of the Corinthian column.

The acanthus is fairly common in Greece, Italy, Spain, and southern France. But except in Greece and Arabia, where the leaves are eaten raw, it is not used for food.

ACETO-DOLCE. Fruits and pieces of vegetables pickled in vinegar, with new wine cooked down to the consistency of syrup added afterwards. The best *aceto-dolce* [literally, "sweet and sour"] is made with quartered quinces, to which is added syrup made from new muscat-grape wine or honey.

AMBERGRIS. Let us quote from the illustrious Professor Brillat-Savarin:

It is well for everyone to know that though ambergris, used as a perfume, may be harmful to those with delicate nerves, taken internally it is an exhilarating and sovereign tonic. Our ancestors made great use of it in their cooking and were none the worse.

Maréchal de Richelieu, of glorious memory, constantly chewed pastilles made of ambergris. As for me, on those days when I feel the weight of years, when I think with difficulty and feel myself oppressed by some unknown power, I take a piece of ambergris as big as a bean, crush it with sugar, and drink it in a big cup of chocolate. I have always found it worked wonders. With this tonic, life becomes easier, thought progresses with facility, and I do not suffer from the insomnia that would inevitably follow if I took a cup of coffee to achieve the same results.

One day I went to visit one of my best friends (M. Rubat). I was told he was ill, and in fact I found him by his fire in his dressing gown in an attitude of complete depression. His appearance frightened me. His face was pale, his eyes unnaturally bright, and his lower lip drooped, exposing the teeth in his lower jaw. The effect was hideous.

I inquired anxiously into the cause of this sudden change. He hesitated, but after I had pressed him, he said, blushing, "My friend, you know that my wife is jealous, and that this madness of hers has given me some very bad times. For several days she has had a frightful fit of it, and in trying to prove to her that she has lost none of my affection, and that there has been no diversion from the conjugal tribute, I have put myself in this condition."

"So you forgot," I told him, "that you're forty-five years old and that jealousy is a disease without a remedy. Don't you know that furens quid femina possit?" I said a few more ungallant things, because I was angry.

"Let's see," I continued; "your pulse is faint, irregular, slow. What are you going to do?"

"The doctor has just left," he said. "He thinks I have a nervous fever and has ordered a bleeding. He's sending the surgeon."

"The surgeon!" I cried. "Keep him away, or you're dead! Chase him

away as you would a murderer, and tell him I have taken possession of you, body and soul. Besides, does your doctor know what brought on your illness?"

"Alas, no! False shame prevented me from making a complete confession to him."

"Well, you must ask him to call again. I'm going to prepare you a potion suitable for your condition. Meanwhile, drink this."

I gave him a glass of water saturated with sugar, which he drank with the confidence of an Alexander and the trust of a charcoal burner.

Then I left him and ran home to prepare a potion, which will be found in the Variétés [*Part 2 of the* Physiology], *together with the various methods I used to speed up the process. For in such a case a few hours can cause irreparable damage.*

I soon returned with my potion and found him better already. The colour was coming back into his cheeks, his eyes were less bright, but his lip still drooped like a frightful deformity.

The doctor soon reappeared. I told him what I had done, and the patient made his confession. The doctoral brow at first took on a severe aspect. But soon, looking at us with an ironic air, he said to my friend:

"You should not be surprised that I didn't guess at an illness that becomes neither your age nor your condition, and you were much too modest in hiding its cause, which can only do you honour. But I must scold you for having exposed me to an error that might have proved fatal. However," he continued, with a bow in my direction, which I returned with interest, *"my colleague has advised you correctly. Take his soup, and if, as I think, the fever leaves you, breakfast tomorrow on a cup of chocolate into which two egg yolks have been mixed."*

With these words, he took his hat and cane and left us very much tempted to be gay at his expense.

I gave my patient a big cup of my elixir of life soon after. He drank it avidly and wanted more, but I insisted he wait for two hours, and gave him another before I left.

Next day he had no fever and was almost well. He breakfasted as instructed, continued the potion, and the day after was able to attend to his usual occupations. But the rebellious lip did not stiffen again until after the third day.

Soon afterwards the whole affair became known, and all the ladies whispered together about it. Some of them admired my friend, most were sorry for him, and all glorified the professor of gastronomy.

Here is the recipe for the elixir, which it would be a pity not to leave to posterity:

Take 6 large onions, 3 carrots, a handful of parsley. Chop fine and brown with a piece of good fresh butter. Add 2 ounces of sugar candy, ⅓ ounce of crushed ambergris, a piece of toast, and 3 quarts of water. Boil for 45 minutes, adding water from time to time to maintain the full quantity of 3 quarts.

While this is going on, kill, pluck, and clean an old rooster, which you will pound, flesh and bones, in a mortar with an iron pestle. Chop up 2 pounds of prime beef. Mix the meats and add a sufficient quantity of salt and pepper. Put into a pot over a hot fire and stir, adding butter every once in a while so it won't stick, until it is heated through and browned.

Add the bouillon little by little, stirring. When it is all mixed, boil briskly for 45 minutes, again adding hot water from time to time to keep up the liquid quantity.

The operation is finished now, and we have a potion whose effect is assured whenever the patient, though exhausted by any such cause as we have indicated, has at least kept his stomach in functioning condition.

To use it, give the patient 1 cup every 3 hours the first day until he goes to sleep. The following days, just 1 cup in the morning and 1 at night, until the whole is consumed. Meanwhile, keep the patient on a light but nourishing diet, such as chicken legs, fish, sweet fruits, and jams. It seldom becomes necessary to make a second batch. Towards the fourth day, the patient can resume his usual occupations and must try to be wiser in the future, if at all possible.

By leaving out the ambergris and the sugar, this same method may be used to improvise a fine-tasting soup worthy of the table of a connoisseur. The old rooster may be replaced by 4 old partridges and the beef by leg of lamb. The preparation will not be any less delightful or efficacious.

The method of chopping the meat and browning it before adding water can be utilized whenever one is in a hurry. It is based on the fact that meats so prepared can be heated to a much higher temperature than they can in water. It can be used whenever one needs a meat soup but can't spend 5 or 6 hours waiting for it, which can frequently happen, especially in the country. Naturally, those who use this method will glorify the professor.

ANCHOVY. A sea fish smaller than the finger, without scales and with a big head and big black eyes, a very big mouth, silvery body, and rounded back. They are abundant off the shores of Provence, and it is from there that we get them salted. The grilled anchovy has a delicate flavour and is easy to digest. They are also pickled with salt and vinegar. The pickled anchovy appears on our tables only as an hors d'oeuvre, or when it is used for seasoning. It has stimulating qualities that facilitate digestion when used in moderation. It is used to stuff olives, and the Romans used it in making a garum sauce. These fish are caught at night along the shores of Italy, France, and Spain.

Anchovy Butter. Soak the salt out of your anchovies. Crush them in a mortar with cream. Put through a sieve. Mix with butter and serve as an hors d'oeuvre.

Anchovy Toast. Fry long, thin slices of bread in oil, put them on a platter, and pour over them a sauce made from virgin oil, lemon juice, coarse pepper, parsley, scallions, and chopped wild garlic. Half cover the slices with anchovy fillets washed in white wine.

ANDOUILLES (SAUSAGES). Pork Andouilles. Clean pork casings and cut them into pieces the length you will want to use them. Soak them in white wine with thyme, basil, and 2 cloves of garlic for 5 or 6 hours. Meanwhile, cut strips of fresh pork, pork fat, and casings. Mix, seasoning with salt, fine spices, crushed anise. Fill your casings, but not too full, or they might burst. Tie the ends and cook them in a pot in which they can lie straight, in half water and half milk, with a bouquet of parsley and scallions, a clove of garlic, thyme, basil, bay leaf, salt, pepper, and pork fat. When they are cooked, let them cool in this seasoning. Wipe them well, make a few cuts in them, grill, and serve.

Beef Andouilles. Treat your beef casings like the pork casings above. Take tripe and ox palates and cook until three quarters done. Cut these, and some calf udders and mild bacon, into strips. Mix in strips of onion cooked in butter or lard until almost done. Add 4 egg yolks, fine spices, salt. Stuff your casings and tie both ends. Cook them in a meat bouillon with 1 pint of white wine, a bouquet of parsley and scallions, a clove of garlic, bay leaf, basil, 3 cloves, salt, pepper, carrots, and onions. Finish and serve like the pork *andouilles* above.

ANISE. An aromatic plant of the family of Umbelliferae, abundant all over Europe, Egypt, and Syria, but especially in Italy and above all in Rome, where it is the despair of the foreigner who cannot escape its flavour or its aroma. They put it into their cakes and their bread. The Neapolitans put it into everything. In Germany it is the principal condiment in the bread served everywhere with an accompaniment of figs and diced pears. This is called pumpernickel. The name is derived from the exclamation of a horseman who, after tasting it, gave the rest to his horse, whose name was Nick, saying, "Bon pour Nick!" (Good for Nick), which, with the German accent, became *Pompernick.*

ANISETTE. Despite our national pride, we must admit that the best anisette in the world comes from Fokung's, in Amsterdam. The Bordeaux anisette comes a long way after that. The Fokung product should be drunk after coffee; the Bordeaux anisette is used for cooking.

APPLES. Apples may be eaten raw, in jams and marmalades, and many other ways. They make a fine cider — pleasant, generous, long-keeping. To make cider, two thirds tart and one third sweet apples are generally used.

According to Galen, apple juice bubbles and ferments in the stomach like wine in a vat. It is composed of very fine, indigestible particles that distribute themselves by way of the arteries to every part of the body. As a result, if many raw apples are eaten, their continued fermentation will damage the circulation of the blood and the major organs will suffer. Simon Pauli, a learned physician who was very fond of apples and ate them daily, says that for twenty-four years he suffered from strong palpitations of the heart, which he controlled by bleeding and by decreasing his intake of raw apples. He adds that when he ate many apples during an evening, he never failed to suffer once or twice during the night from insomnia and nightmares.

Solon, in an attempt to stop the extravagant expense of weddings, ordained that newlyweds should eat nothing but one apple each before going to the marriage bed; which was scarcely substantial comfort for the poor couples.

APRICOT. The tree that bears this fruit came to the Romans from Armenia. They called it *Prunus armeniaca*. At first only two varieties were known, but more have been developed. It derives from the peach and the plum, and is so early that there is seldom a spring when one does not hear it said: "There will be no apricots this year. The frost killed them all."

Besides the several varieties harvested in France, Chalon, on his voyage to Persia, ate excellent apricots with a red flesh and a delicious flavour. They were known as *tocmchams*, which means "eggs of the sun". Damascus, in Syria, is the home of the finest apricots. The people there make excellent apricot jams, which they eat with bread.

Among the varieties of apricots, we must not overlook those of Santo Domingo and the French West Indies. They grow on a fine sixty- to seventy-foot tree, with oval leaves and a broad, thick, pyramidal crown. The white flowers, an inch and a half in diameter, have a lovely perfume. Its fruit is as big as a person's head. The thick rind encloses a fleshy pulp and a large seed. It is sweet, aromatic, and very good. It is served sliced and sluiced with sugared wine. It is important to remove the two outer skins and the pulp next the pit, which are bitter. This fruit is heavy and remains long on the stomach. The spirits of wine distilled from its flowers, sugared, makes an aromatic liquor known as *eau de créole*.

The author of the *Memoirs of the Marquise de Créqui* [de Cour-champs], from whom we have taken those below, gives some fine recipes for apricots. This charming gastronome was a rival of Brillat-Savarin and of de Cussy, and was frequently at war with them over gastronomical questions of the greatest importance. Nurtured in the culinary tradition of the last half of the last century and the first of this, he is the man who above all must be consulted on matters of sweet entremets and all dainty dishes.

Apricots are used to flavour sherbets and ices. They make excellent pies, fritters, tarts, custards, jams, and preserves.

Apricot Flan à la Metternich. Line a piepan with short paste. Peel, pit, and halve 12 early apricots. Pick carefully, and pit, 40 late cherries. Arrange the fruit symmetrically on your pastry, each half apricot separated by cherries. Sprinkle with powdered sugar. Bake. Take the kernels of the cherry pits and half the apricot kernels and grind them in a marble mortar with a metal pestle — wooden ones tend to retain the flavour of the food for which they were last used. Add sugar, then mix with fresh sweet cream to the consistency of a cooked egg-yolk sauce. Pour this on your flan when it comes out of the oven. Take care it does not spill over the sides. Serve warm but not hot.

Apricot Cream. Cook 12 apricots with ¾ cup of sugar. Put through a strainer. Let them cool. Add a small glass of four-fruit ratafia[1] or of cherry brandy, or a white wine with a light flavour. Mix in 8 egg yolks. Put through a strainer once more. Add sugar to taste. Pour into a mould, or into individual small pots you can use at the table. Cook in a *bain-marie*. The recipe for this excellent cream is taken from a manuscript dispensatory of the time of Louis XIV.

Compote of Grilled Apricots à la Breteuil. Split and sugar selected ripe apricots and grill them over charcoal. Avoid using a coal fire, as the fumes from the dripping juices would impart a nauseating flavour to your fruit. Remember this when you grill pears and apples, also. Put your grilled apricot halves into a fruit jar and pour over them a boiling syrup in which apricots and raspberries have been cooked and which has been strained and reheated. This will make a perfect compote that will not tax the most sensitive stomach.

ARTICHOKE. Formerly this plant grew only in Italy. Now our gardeners have acclimatized it, and we have white, green, red, and sweet artichokes. The white, purple, and green are the tastiest. The very small variety is eaten raw.

Artichokes à la Barigoule. Take medium-sized, tender artichokes. Trim, remove the choke, blanch. Mix chopped parsley with 1 ounce of butter and 1 ounce of grated bacon for each artichoke. Stuff your artichokes with this preparation, tie them up so they will keep their shape, cover with bacon slices, and bake slowly. Serve with a sauce italienne to which you have added 1 glass of white wine, reduced to its original consistency.

Sauce for Boiled Artichokes. Crush the yolk of a hard-boiled egg with 1 tablespoonful of vinegar, salt, pepper, finely chopped garnishing herbs, and a finely chopped shallot. Add 2 tablespoonfuls of oil. Mix and serve.

[1]Plum, peach, apricot and almond liqueur.—ED.

Stuffed Artichokes. Parboil your artichokes in water. Trim, remove the choke, fill with a stuffing of chopped meat, parsley, and scallions. Finish cooking. Serve with a mixture of *fines herbes*, oil, and lemon juice.

Artichokes à la Grimod de la Reynière. Chop onions coarsely and fry in butter to a good colour. Season with salt and spices and set aside to cool in the butter. Boil artichoke bottoms; drain. Fill the hollow with the onions, cover with fresh bread crumbs, sprinkle with grated cheese, and bake to a good colour. Serve without sauce.

ASPARAGUS. There are three varieties, white, violet, and green. The white is the earliest. Its flavour is mild and pleasant, but it has little substance. The violet is the thickest and most substantial. The green is thinner, but more of it is edible. It has a fine flavour. In Italy, where taste is stranger than refined, the wild asparagus is preferred. The best way to prepare asparagus is by steaming. The Romans had a saying when they wanted something done quickly. "Do it," they said, "in less time than it takes to cook asparagus."

Wash your asparagus, cutting the bottoms to make them of equal length, tie them in bundles, and cook them in salted water, keeping them crisp. Serve them hot on a folded napkin, which absorbs the water. They may be eaten hot with oil or butter. Or they may be eaten cold with the sauce given above for boiled artichokes.

Asparagus en Petits Pois. Use very thin asparagus. Cut the tender part into small bits. Boil them only long enough to leave them crisp. Drain in a colander. Sauté with butter, salt, pepper, and *fines herbes*.

Asparagus Tips au Jus. Sauté asparagus tips in lard, add chopped parsley and chervil, salt, white pepper, nutmeg. Add consommé and simmer a little. Drain, sauce with the natural juice from roast lamb, and serve hot.

Fried Asparagus. Cut off the tough portions. Blanch in salted water, then plunge into cold water to retain colour. Drain. Flour and tie in bundles of 6 or 7. Dip in beaten egg and deep-fry.

Scrambled Eggs with Asparagus Tips. One day when you have chicken bouillon, try this. Mix asparagus tips into your beaten eggs, and for every 6 eggs add ½ glass of bouillon. Then scramble your eggs as usual. You will see how extraordinarily smooth the bouillon makes your eggs.

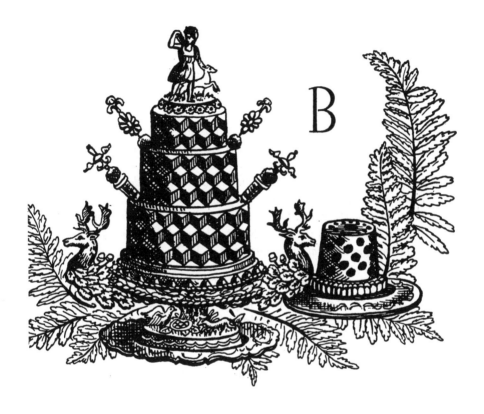

BABIRUSA. A sort of wild boar only recently seen in Europe. There are specimens in the Jardins des Plantes. Pliny said of it: "In the Indies there is a sort of wild boar that has two horns like a calf's and tusks like an ordinary wild boar."

"Good Lord, darling!" said a lády to her husband at the zoo. "What is that animal that has four horns instead of two?"

"Madam," said a passer-by, "it's a widower who has remarried," and passed by.

The babirusa is a dirty grey, with short, woolly hair and short ears. His hindquarters are higher than the front. His skin is thin, not lined with fat. The flesh is very pleasing to the taste. He is eaten like wild boar.

BACON. Pig flesh is generally heavy and indigestible, especially for people who don't exercise much. But when it is hardened with salt and dried with smoke, it is even more unhealthy. That is bacon. Bacon fat, besides, is usually rancid and acrid, can only have an evil effect on the stomach, and can excoriate the mouth and throat.

Bacon made from acorn-fattened pigs is generally firmer, and consequently better, than that from bran-fed animals.

BAIN-MARIE. Method of preparing certain sauces, which, placed directly on the heat, would thicken too quickly. The procedure is so well known it seems useless to explain it.

[*The twentieth-century cook may need to be reminded, however, that a* bain-marie *was a large pan of hot water into which other pots could be placed for indirect cooking. Or any similar arrangement for the same purpose. The direct ancestor of the double boiler. The words have been so translated in this book where that was appropriate.* — ED.]

BAKER, BAKERY. The profession of baking was entirely unknown to the ancients. They ate grain like other vegetable products, and even for a long time after they had discovered how to make flour by rubbing grain between two stones, they were still content to make it into a porridge.

Later, when they did make bread, it was prepared in each household separately and for each meal. The women had charge of this operation, and the greatest ladies did not disdain to put their hands into the dough. Besides, in those times, the refinements that gourmandism has demanded more and more as civilization developed were not called for. They made a sort of flat cake, or sometimes the sort of cake that takes flour, butter, eggs, saffron, and other ingredients. These were not baked in an oven, but on the hearth, either on hot stones or on a sort of grill, or in a kind of pie plate. Neither did they use salt, since this condiment had not yet been discovered.

The discovery that came hardest was the method of turning grain into flour. This was arduous labour, and crushing grain in a mortar with a pestle was so time- and energy-consuming that it was treated as a punishment. Slaves were condemned to this labour for the slightest infraction of rules. Then came hand mills, which made it less difficult but still very fatiguing.

As for baking bread in ovens, this came even later, and the profession of baking came with it.

The Greeks were the first to set up grain mills and ovens side by side. This was the first organization of a bakery. It was not until the sixth century after the founding of Rome that the Romans picked up the custom. At first their bakeries were all operated by Greeks. Little by little, however, they took on apprentices, who in turn became master bakers, and then the trade was organized into a hereditary corporation with several privileges. They had control of all premises used to grind flour, and all the apparatus, slaves, and animals of the bakeries. They were given land and inheritances, and everything was done to encourage and sustain their trade. So they could conduct business without interruption, they were exempted from all onerous duties. They had no holidays — a fact they did not always appreciate. Finally, the tribunals were open to them at all times so that any differences that might arise between them could be settled immediately.

On the other hand, they were submitted to certain obligations and restrictions, such as living together and intermarrying exclusively within their trade. If they married their daughters to comedians or gladiators, they were flogged and banished.

The Romans introduced the bakery to Gaul. They chose Mercurius Artius, called Artos in Greek, as their patron, and built him a temple whose ruins could still be seen a hundred years ago, with its marquetry floor, in a little village called Artas, near Grenoble, in the department of Isère.

There were bakers in France at the beginning of the monarchy. An ordinance of good King Dagobert — the same who is the hero of the song — dated 670,[1] informs us that the millers joined to their trade of grinding grain that of baking the bread for private individuals who bought their flour.

In their turn the operators of public ovens took over the commerce in flour and sold bread as well. Charlemagne, in the succeeding century, undertook to police the profession, which was becoming more and more important. In his capitularies, he ordained that the

[1]Dumas is in error. This Dagobert died in 638.—ED.

number of artisan bakers in each city should always be kept up, and that "they should make apprentices who could replace the masters in the business in case of great necessity." In addition, they were to keep their workplaces orderly and clean and their conduct beyond reproach. He instructed judges and other officers especially to see to the strict observance of this requirement.

St. Louis did more. In recognition of the services this profession rendered everyone, and to make these services available in a more stable fashion, he exempted bakers from military service. This was quite important in view of the fact that in those times of war all persons, unless specifically exempted, were obliged to go into the army when their lord gave the order.

Beginning in the eighth century and for several hundred years, a terrible malady, leprosy, spread and multiplied in France in frightful fashion. Bakers, their wives and their children, still privileged people, had the right to enter the Saint-Lazare hospital for treatment and cure, which was considered an enormous privilege in those days. To pay for this right, they each had to give the hospital a loaf of bread a week. Towards the end of the sixteenth century a denier was substituted for the loaf of bread.

The French word for baker, *boulanger*, says Ducange in his *History of Paris*, comes from the fact that in the beginning the bread they baked was formed into a ball (*boule*). The custom of making bread round continues in France. In the villages, where housewives bake their own bread, they always shape it so, but flatten it a little. But in some parts of the country it still retains its original globular form.

The bakers' guild today is one of the best and best organized institutions. No one can practice this profession without a licence from the prefect of police, and no licence is issued until it has been established that the applicant is of good moral character, that he has served an apprenticeship and knows his art. Besides, no baker, once he is licensed, may ever lack supplies. He must always have a month's flour in reserve, and his store must always have bread for sale.

In Paris today millions of pounds of bread are sold daily, made during the previous night by those strange, half-naked beings one glimpses through cellar windows, whose wild-seeming cries floating out of those depths always make a painful impression. In the morning, one sees these pale men, still white with flour, carrying a loaf under one arm, going off to rest and gather new strength to renew their hard and useful labour when night comes again. I have always highly esteemed the brave and humble workers who labour all night to produce those soft but crusty little loaves that look more like cake than bread.

BARAQUILLE. A sort of pastry. To prepare it, chop partridge and chicken breasts, veal sweetbreads, mushrooms, and raw truffles, and mix with butter and *fines herbes*. Case this in a very light pastry and bake.

BAVAROISE. A hot drink made by mixing syrup of maidenhair with tea. It can also be made with water or chocolate. It is sweet and soporific.

BEANS. Beans are eaten green in their pods; mature, with the pods removed, when they are called *flageolets*; and dried, when they are called Soissons beans, no matter where they come from. Since I am from the department of Aisne, I must necessarily appreciate my compatriots, and, in fact, until my last visit to Asia I would have said that beans actually from Soissons were the best in the world. But I feel obliged to recognize the fact that the beans from Trebizond are better.

Green Beans à la Bonne Fermière. Trim and wash very tender green beans. Boil. Drain well. Put into a pot with butter and chopped parsley and scallions. Sauté for a minute. Add a pinch of flour, salt, and good bouillon. Let boil until they have absorbed most of the liquid. Just before serving, add egg yolks mixed with milk, and a dash of verjuice or vinegar. When the sauce has thickened, serve.

Green or Yellow Beans. Slice lengthwise if they are very fat. Cook in salted water with a little butter. Put into a pot with butter and chopped parsley and scallions. Add a little of the cooking water. Thicken with cream and egg yolks, add the juice of a lemon, and serve.

Green Beans Lyonnaise. Cut onions into half slices and brown lightly in oil. Add the cooked beans, sprinkle with parsley and scallions, salt and pepper. Fry. Add a dash of vinegar before serving.

Green and White Beans à la Provençale. In a heavy skillet mix a few tablespoonfuls of oil with capers, anchovy fillets, crushed garlic. Add cooked beans, season with parsley, scallions, salt, coarse pepper. Sauté a few minutes. Turn out on to a platter. Pour a little vinegar into the pot, bring it to a boil, and pour over the beans.

Beans and Bacon à la Villageoise. The Duc d'Escars, de Cussy, d'Aigrefeuille, Grimod de la Reynière, and other men of experience have always agreed that this is the best way to eat dried beans.

Start off with a good stomach armed with a healthy appetite. Nothing will rob you of that but illness, or a lack of alimentary continence or of exercise. Rise early and go out in fine weather, on an empty stomach, for a ride or a walk. But since you are reading a cookery book, you must be in good health. Therefore: cook 3 pounds of dried beans with 1 pound of lightly salted bacon slices distributed evenly among the beans, and just enough water so you will not have to add or take away during the cooking. All the water and fat must be absorbed in the cooking, so the beans will be perfectly cooked and thickened, but not to make a porridge. That's all. (*Dictionnaire Général de la Cuisine Française.*)

Beans with Marrow. Cook dried beans in filtered rain water. Before they get cold, sauté them in 5 or 6 ounces of freshly melted marrow. Sprinkle with a good pinch of pepper, and just before serving add unripe seeded grapes blanched in salted water.

Scarlet Runner Beans à la Bourguignonne. Cook dried beans in a root-vegetable stock with a piece of fresh butter, a bouquet of aromatic herbs, and onions stuck with cloves. After 20 minutes of cooking, remove herbs and onions. Add ½ pint of red wine and a pinch of pepper. Garnish with little glazed onions and serve. Or you can garnish with crayfish tails, fish *rissoles*, carp or herring milt, marinated oysters, or fried mussels.

Beans with Cream. Cook dried beans in soft water with a little butter and season with nutmeg. When they are done, add heavy cream to thicken. Sprinkle with crisp pieces of fried celery.

Beans à l'Intendance. As above, using marrow instead of

butter, and a glass of Madeira instead of cream. Garnish with croutons dipped in Madeira, lightly salted, and flavoured with nutmeg before toasting.

Broad Beans (Favas). Broad beans are digestible when young, but they become heavy when they approach maturity and must not only be shelled but divested of their skins before eating.

Creamed Favas. Take small young beans. Do not skin. Blanch. Dip in cold water. Drain. Put into a pot with melted butter, pepper, chopped parsley, and summer savory. Heat, then add bouillon, a bit of sugar, and a bit of flour mixed with butter. Before serving, add 1 glass of cream, let reheat only to boiling point. Thicken with yolks of eggs.

Macédoine of Favas. Chop scallions, parsley, shallots, and mushrooms and put into hot butter a moment. Then add flour. Stir it in. Add bouillon, white wine, *bouquet garni*. Simmer. Add beans blanched as above, cubed and parboiled artichoke bottoms, salt, and pepper. After cooking, remove the bouquet, reduce the liquid, and serve.

BEAR. Few of our generation can have forgotten the sensation produced when my first book of *Travel Impressions* was published (in the *Revue des Deux Mondes* or the *Revue de Paris*), with the article on "The Bear Steak". There was a universal outcry against the daring narrator who had the audacity to state that there are places in civilized Europe where bear meat is eaten.

It would have been simpler for them to go to Chevet's in Paris and ask him for bear hams. He would have asked quite blandly whether they preferred a leg of bear from Canada or from Transylvania. And he would have provided whichever was desired. I could have given my readers the same advice at the time, but I certainly did not. It made my book talked about, and at that time, when I was just beginning my literary career, that was all I cared about.

But to my great astonishment, the person who should have been happiest about all the fuss, the innkeeper at Martigny, was furious. He wrote me indignant letters. He wrote to the papers demanding they print his statement that he had never served bear meat to any traveller. But his fury continued to rise as traveller after traveller arrived at his inn and asked him: "Have you any bear meat?"

If the idiot had thought of answering yes, he had, and then serving donkey meat, horse meat, mule meat, anything at all, as bear, he would have made a fortune.

Since then, our civilization has advanced. Bear meat is not to be found in every butchershop. But it can be procured without too much trouble.

Bear meat is now eaten everywhere in Europe. From the most ancient times, the front paws have been regarded as the most delicate morsel. The Chinese esteem them highly. In Germany, where the meat of the bear cub is much sought after, the front paws are a delicacy reserved for the very rich.

Here is the recipe for them as prepared in Moscow, St. Petersburg, and all over Russia, according to Urbain-Dubois, cook to Their Majesties of Prussia. The paws are bought skinned. They are washed, salted, put into a crock, and covered with a cooked vinegar marinade for 3 or 4 days. Cover the bottom of a pot with bits of bacon and ham and chopped vegetables. Arrange the paws on this and cover with the marinade and bouillon. Cover with slices of bacon. Cook gently for 7 or 8 hours, adding bouillon as required to keep them covered. Let cool in this liquid. Drain, wipe, and slice lengthwise into 4 pieces. Sprinkle with cayenne, dip in melted lard, bread, and grill gently for ½ hour. Serve on a platter with a reduced *sauce piquante* finished with 2 tablespoonfuls of currant jelly.

BEEF. I saw the birth of the *bifteck* (beefsteak) in Paris after the three-year occupation by the English in 1815. Before that, our cookery had been as far apart as our opinions. It was therefore with some trepidation that we saw the *bifteck* surreptitiously insinuate itself into our cuisine. However, since we are an eclectic and unprejudiced people, we soon perceived that although the Greeks bore this gift, it was not poisoned, and we handed the *bifteck* its certificate of citizenship. However, there is still a big difference between an English beefsteak and a French *bifteck*. We make ours from a fillet of the sirloin, while our neighbours cut theirs from the rump. But in England this part of the steer is much more tender than in France, because they feed their cattle better and slaughter them younger. They slice it about an inch thick, flatten it a bit, and fry it on special cast-iron skillets over coal rather than charcoal. The true *bifteck* fillet should be grilled over hot charcoal, and turned only once, to conserve the good juices that mix with the maître d'hôtel sauce.

The rump of English beef (and I eat it with renewed pleasure every time I go to England) is infinitely more savoury than the cut we use for *biftecks*. It must be eaten in an English tavern, sautéed with Madeira or anchovy butter or served on a bed of cress with vinegar. I would advise eating it with gherkins if any people in the whole world really knew how to prepare gherkins. As for French *bifteck*, it is best with maître d'hôtel sauce because the *fines herbes* and lemon dominate. However, I must make one observation: I see our cooks flatten their steaks on the kitchen table with the side of a cleaver. This I believe to be profoundly heretical. By doing so they squeeze out certain nutritive elements that could play an important role in mastication.

In general, the meat of ruminants is better in England than in France, because they are given particular attention in feeding and care. Nothing can compare with those whole roasted beef quarters that are trundled about on the miniature railways that separate the guests of an English tavern. Those pieces of beef, veined with fat, weighing up to a hundred pounds, from which one cuts one's chosen portion, have no peer for stimulation of the appetite. The English grow beef so fat the cattle seem to have lost the use of their legs and walk on their stomachs. The cattle breeders and feeders make the animals drink up to twenty gallons of water a day. As for their mutton, fed on grass much fresher than ours, it has a flavour we know not of.

Where English cooking is weak is in the sauce department. But large fish and butcher's meat are infinitely finer in London than in Paris.

Beef à l'Ecarlate. Let a rump of beef hang for 4 days or more, then bone it and lard with strips of bacon seasoned with parsley, chives, pepper, and spices. Rub with very dry salt that has been mixed with 1 to 1½ ounces of saltpeter. Put your beef, wrapped in cloth, into a crock with juniper berries, thyme, basil, scallions, garlic, a clove, and an onion. Cover and leave 8 days. Turn it over and leave it covered 3 or 4 days more. Remove and drain. Wrap in a fresh cloth and tie with string. Cook 4 hours without interruption in a kettle of boiling water seasoned with carrots, onions, and a *bouquet garni*. Let it cool in the water. Serve like ham, garnished with fresh parsley.

Beef à la Mode, à la Bourgeoise. Take, preferably, the centre cut of rump and lard with bacon. Put into a heavy covered pot with 2 carrots, 4 onions (1 with 2 cloves stuck in it), garlic, thyme, bay leaf, salt, and pepper. Pour over it a large glass of water, ½ glass of white wine or 1 tablespoonful of brandy, and cook slowly until tender (5 or 6 hours at least). Skim the fat off the gravy, then strain. Serve.

Sirloin. When your sirloin is fat and tender, cook it on the spit. For this purpose, trim it well, marinate it at least 12 hours in good oil with salt, pepper, bay leaf, and sliced onion. Cook it 1 hour, or even 2 if it is big. It is served in a sauce made from its own juice, with a dash of vinegar, shallots, salt, and pepper added. Or make a little *roux*, adding bouillon or gravy and water, salt, pepper, finely chopped gherkins, parsley, and shallots, and a dash of vinegar.

Sirloin Fillet à la Bourgeoise. Lard a sirloin fillet. Put pieces of fat into the bottom of a pot with onions, carrots, celery, and artichoke bottoms, and a *bouquet garni*. Lay your fillet on these vegetables, add 1 cup of bouillon from which all fat has been skimmed, and roast.

Sirloin Fillet with Cucumbers. Roast your fillet with cucumbers stuffed with chicken and marrow. This may be served with the addition of stuffed lettuce and creamed onions.

Sirloin à la Godard. Remove the large bone from the sirloin, but do not bone it entirely. Lard with thick strips of bacon properly seasoned and tie into a good shape. Put into a braising pot with a *bouquet garni*, onions, carrots, a bottle of Madeira and some good bouillon, salt, and pepper. Cook on a slow fire so that the liquid will be reduced almost to a glaze. At this point remove and serve with the following ragout:

Put 2 ladlefuls of meat glaze into a pot. Add the liquid from your braising, which you will have strained and from which you will have skimmed off all fat. Cook with a few sliced veal sweetbreads, mushrooms, quartered artichoke bottoms, some small hard-boiled eggs. Skim the fat off this ragout before using.

Sirloin Fillet with Conserves. Trim off all the fat, lard, and roast on the spit. In a pot, mix sliced pickled gherkins, pickled beets, onions, and cauliflower, preserved cherries, black currants, sorb apples, plums, etc., with a few skimming-spoonfuls of meat glaze and 1 of vinegar. Heat without boiling and put into the platter under your fillet.

Sirloin Fillet with Malaga. Trim as above. Lard well. Put in the bottom of your pot slices of bacon, a slice of veal rump, a slice of uncooked ham, carrots, onions, mushrooms, artichoke bottoms, and a *bouquet garni*, with the sirloin on top. Pour over it 2 glasses of Malaga and 2 or 3 ladlefuls of reduced bouillon, mixed. Cook over a slow fire 2 hours or more. Strain the liquid and pour over the meat to serve. I recommend this dish.

Tongue. Nearly all practising cooks who have written on the subject have stated that tongue is the finest-tasting part of any meat animal. They exclude beef tongue, although under Louis XII it was so highly esteemed that in certain parts of France there was a feudal prerogative under which the tongues of all cattle butchered belonged to the local lord.

Braised Beef Tongue. Remove the root from a fresh beef tongue. Soak it 2, 3, or more hours. Scrape it well with a knife. Blanch in a big pot with carrots and onions. Then cover it with bouillon and a glass of white wine. Add a few scraps of butcher's meat, poultry, and game to give it flavour. Bring to a boil, tightly cover, and set aside on a moderate heat. Simmer 4½ hours. Arrange on a platter with the vegetables cooked with it. Strain the liquid in which it was cooked, mix with 1 or 2 tablespoonfuls of espagnole sauce, and serve.

Beef Tongue Parmesan. Cook as above. Let cool in its own juice. Slice very thin. Put grated Parmesan cheese on the bottom of a deep dish, cover with a layer of tongue, and sprinkle with the liquid in which the meat was cooked. Make 3 or 4 more layers the same way, ending with 1 of Parmesan on top. Sprinkle with melted butter. Bake until the top cheese turns golden, and serve.

Tongue with Chopped Sauce. Soak the tongue twenty-four hours in fresh water, changing several times. Plunge a few times into boiling water, scrape off the skin, and trim. Lard with strips of bacon seasoned with salt, pepper, nutmeg, parsley, and chopped shallots, and prepare the following braising base:

Into a heavy pot put slices of bacon and a split calf's foot or a good piece of salt-pork rind, salt, pepper, parsley, scallions, thyme, bay leaf, clove, onions, and carrots.

Lay your tongue on this base and add 1 glass of white wine, ½ glass of brandy, 1 glass of water or bouillon. Cover with a piece of buttered paper, close the pot tightly with its lid. Cook 5 hours or longer over a slow fire. When the tongue is tender, split it lengthwise but not all the way through. Skim the fat from the braising liquid in which the tongue has cooked. Stir it into a *roux*. Reduce. Add chopped shallots and gherkins, parsley, mushrooms, and pepper. Boil 5 minutes. Pour over the tongue and serve.

Tongue Larded and Roasted. Prepare your tongue as above. Cook with 2 tablespoonfuls of bouillon, a few slices of bacon, a *bouquet garni*, 2 onions (with 2 cloves in 1 of them). When it is three quarters done, remove and let cool. Lard it with thick strips in the heavy part, thin in the rest, put on the spit, and roast for 1 hour. Serve with a *sauce piquante* to accompany.

Tripe à la Mode de Caen. Take a whole stomach, paunch and honeycomb, clean it well, parboil it, and put it into fresh water for 1 hour. Cut into pieces. Season with salt, pepper, four spices. Cut lean bacon into big dice and mix with the tripe. Cover the bottom of a large earthenware pot with sliced onions and carrots, a *bouquet garni*, garlic. On top of this place 12 blanched mutton feet, and 1 boned calf's foot. Put your tripe over this and then add 2 sliced carrots, a head of celery, and 12 whole leeks, which will keep the tripe properly moist while it cooks. Add a bottle of white wine, a good glass of cognac, 2 quarts of water, 8 ounces of beef marrow. Cover with buttered paper, then seal the pot with a paste made of flour and water. Bring to a boil, then simmer 12 hours. Remove the top layer of vegetables and serve very hot. (Vuillemot.)

Beef Foot Poulette. Blanch a beef foot. Soak 24 hours in cold water. Tie up the foot like a mummy with plenty of string, put into a kettle with lots of water, salt, coarse pepper, *bouquet garni*, carrots, onions with cloves stuck in them, and boil gently until the tendon breaks. Then loosen your string until the meat absorbs enough moisture to be soft.

Prepare a good allemande sauce, adding cut-up mushrooms and chopped parsley, lemon juice, and a good piece of fresh butter. Stir it smooth. Put your beef foot on a platter and pour your sauce over it. This is a very fine, pleasant dish. One foot will feed 6 hungry people.

Boiled Beef Persillade. On the bottom of a shallow casserole put fat from a beef roast, or clarified butter, and sprinkle with finely chopped parsley and chopped mushrooms, then fresh bread crumbs. On top of this put slices of cold boiled beef. Repeat. Add bouillon. Let simmer 45 minutes, adding bouillon if necessary. Skim off all fat. Serve with a ring of fried potatoes.

Boiled Beef Matelote à la Bourgeoise. Brown little onions in butter. Add 1 tablespoonful of flour. Let it brown a little. Add 1 glass of red wine, ½ glass of bouillon, a few mushrooms, salt, pepper, a bay leaf, a little thyme. Cook all together, pour over slices of boiled beef arranged in a shallow casserole and let the whole simmer ½ hour so that the sauce will penetrate the meat. Serve hot.

BEER. One of the most ancient and widespread of beverages. After wine it is certainly the best fermented liquor. It is more widely used than wine and is manufactured all over the world.

All over northern Europe a very substantial soup, healthier than most peasant fare, is made from beer. And the whole world knows that the national and indigenous soup of Russia is the same famous beer soup that Carême, when he was maître d'hôtel to the Emperor Alexander, served him at every meal when he was in Paris. Here is the recipe:

Beer Soup à la Berlinoise. Melt 5 ounces of butter in a pot, mix in 5 ounces of flour to make a light paste. Stir and cook a few seconds, but don't let it colour. Add and mix 3 quarts of light beer, pale or brown, and stir until it boils. Set aside 25 minutes before skimming. Put ½ glass of rum and ½ glass of white Rhine wine, a bit of preserved ginger, a piece of cinnamon, 3 ounces of sugar, and the zest of a lemon into a small pot, cover it, and keep it warm in a double boiler. After skimming your soup, thicken it with 15 raw egg yolks. Do not heat too much. Strain. Add 7 ounces of butter in little bits, then the rum infusion, strained. Serve in a tureen and send slices of toast to the table with it.

BEET. This plant contains more sugar than any other. At the time of the Continental blockade the chemists conceived the idea of substituting beets for sugar cane. I remember seeing, in 1812, a caricature showing the King of Rome with his nurse. The child was crying, and his nurse was offering him a beet, saying, "Suck it, my child. Your father says it is sugar." As with all great discoveries, this one that freed us from dependence on the colonies was greeted with derision. The people who worshipped Napoleon so long for his victories, which cost a third of our blood and a sixth of our territory, do not dream they owe beet sugar to him.

There are five varieties of beets: large red, small red, yellow, white, and the sugar beet. Beet leaves are mixed with sorrel to reduce their acidity. The big white leaves known as chard are highly esteemed. In winter, the little leaves that sprout from the root are eaten in salads. The root is cooked and pickled in vinegar.

The best way to cook beets is in the oven. First they should be washed in ordinary brandy. Then they are placed on grills in the brick oven, which is heated as for large loaves of bread. They are left in the oven until it cools, and the following morning cooked again the same way and at the same temperature. The beet is not really cooked until its skin is carbonized.

Beets are often eaten in salads with corn salad, celery, rampion. But the best combination is with glazed little white onions, slices of red-skinned potato, chunks of artichoke bottoms, steamed kidney beans, nasturtium flowers, and cress — which makes a salad that, for flavour, can rival Russian salad.

Beets may be served as hors d'oeuvres with olives and sardines, with a dressing of tarragon vinegar, oil, shallots, salt and pepper, topped with chopped hard-boiled eggs.

Beets à la Poitevine. Chop onions and brown in butter mixed with flour, add a pinch of four spices, and reheat sliced beets in this mixture. Just before serving, add $\frac{1}{2}$ tablespoonful of strong Orléans vinegar.

Creamed Beets. Cut cooked beets in thin slices and simmer them in béchamel sauce, to which you will have added a little coriander and nutmeg.

BISHOP. A beverage for which the English take credit. It is a mixture of orange juice, sugar, and light wine. It is very popular in Germany. If it is made with Bordeaux or Burgundy, it is a Bishop's drink. If it is made with an aged Rhine wine, it is a Cardinal's drink. But if you make it with Tokay, it is a Pope's drink.

BISQUE. Vincent de la Chapelle has said that a good bisque is the most royal of royal dishes. Grimod de la Reynière proudly proclaims it a food for princes and financiers. Brillat-Savarin says in his *Physiology of Taste* that if a shadow of justice remained in this world, cooked crayfish would be the object of divine worship.

Crayfish Bisque. Wash 50 crayfish. Put into a pot with a *mirepoix* composed of chopped carrots, sliced onions, a *bouquet garni*. Season with salt, pepper, and a touch of cayenne. Add a ladleful of consommé and a glass of Madeira. Stir and cook. Take out the meat from the crayfish tails, dice, and set aside. Cook 4 ounces of rice in consommé. Add the *mirepoix* and the crayfish carcasses. Crush them well in a mortar, add consommé, and press through a strainer. Add the liquid from the crayfish and heat, stirring constantly, but not to the boiling point. Strain again. Add a piece of fresh butter. Keep hot in a double boiler. Put the crayfish meat and small croutons fried in butter in the soup tureen, pour your soup over them, and serve very hot.

Crab Bisque. Boil 24 little crabs in salted water with onion, parsley, and sliced carrots. Let them cool in their juice. Drain them. Crush them in a mortar, adding a piece of soft bread the size of an egg or two tablespoonfuls of steamed rice. Add consommé. Press through a strainer, then warm in a *bain-marie*, adding more bouillon. This is best made with crabs that have a good proportion of roe or milt.

BOAR. The young wild boar, known in French as a *marcassin*, and in hunting terms as a *bête rousse*, may be prepared in every way the same as a full-grown boar. In olden times, hunters never killed them, but, having caught them, castrated them and let them loose. Thus "perfected", as they say of the choir boys in the Sistine Chapel, they grow bigger, more delicate, and less wild.

[*For boar's head, see* PORK: Pig's Head. — ED.]

Quarter of Young Wild Boar with Cherry Sauce. Take a fresh, tender, skinned quarter. Remove the bone from the upper end, and cut the butt bone square. Salt. Place in an earthenware vessel and pour over it 1 quart of warm cooked marinade. Leave it in the marinade 2 or 3 days. Drain. Wipe dry and place in a roasting pan with lard. Cover with greased paper and roast 45 minutes, basting frequently with the fat. Add a few tablespoonfuls of marinade and cook another ½ hour, continuing to baste. When it is well cooked on the outside, pour off the fat and cover the whole quarter with a thick coat of black bread, grated, dried, heated, and mixed with a little sugar and cinnamon and moistened with just enough red wine to make it workable. Sprinkle this layer with dried bread crumbs. Baste with the fat and leave in the oven another ½ hour. Serve on a platter, sending along with it the following sauce:

Cherry Sauce. Take 2 handfuls of dried cherries, the kind sold in Germany – that is, with the pits still in them. Soak them in water, then crush them thoroughly in a mortar. Add 1 glass of red wine, a piece of cinnamon stick, 2 cloves, a grain of salt, and a piece of lemon zest. Boil 2 minutes, then thicken with a little cornstarch mixed with water. Cover the pot and let it stand on the back of the stove 15 minutes. Strain.

This recipe is from M. Urbain-Dubois, cook to Their Royal Majesties of Prussia.

BOILED MEAT. President Hénault, dining at the table of Mme du Deffand, said that a chicken had been boiled too long, that it was like a honeycomb with nothing left but the wax, and madame agreed with him. Boiled meat is just cooked meat without its juice, said Mme de Créqui. There was an answer to give these illustrious gourmands:

"Have you eaten beef or chicken out of the eternal kettle?"

"No!"

"Well, taste it, and you will change your opinion."

"What is an eternal kettle?"

The eternal kettle is or, rather, was, since this illustrious gastronomic institution has long ceased to function, a receptacle that never left the fire, day or night. A chicken was put into it as a chicken was withdrawn, a piece of beef as a piece was taken out, and a glass of water whenever a cup of broth was removed. Every kind of meat that cooked in this bouillon gained rather than lost in flavour, for it inherited the juices that had been left in it by all the meat that preceded it, and in turn bequeathed some of its own. It was not necessary to leave meat in the kettle any longer than it required to cook. It lost none of its qualities.

Now that the eternal kettle is no more, we must content ourselves with a big piece of boiled beef.

Use a 12 to 15 pound rump, have it boned, and tie it properly for serving. Boil it in a bouillon you will have made the day before, into which you will put all the leftover meats from the roasts of the preceding day – chicken, turkey, rabbit, etc. Serve garnished *à la flamande*.[1]

BOUILLON. There is no good cooking without good bouillon. French cooking, the first of all cuisines, owes its superiority to the excellence of French bouillon. This excellence derives from a sort of intuition with which I shall not say our cooks, but our women of the people, are endowed.

Rivarol, leaving his soup plate three quarters full, used to say to the gourmands of Lübeck and Hamburg: "Gentlemen, there isn't a sicknurse or a charwoman in France who cannot make a better bouillon than the best cook in the Hanseatic League."

Similarly, you may travel around the world, but you will find no professional cook, whether *cordon rouge* or *cordon bleu*, who can make an omelet like the French housewife preparing dinner for her children.

There are five principles in meat from which bouillon derives its flavour. They are fibrin, gelatin, osmazome, albumin, and fat.

Fibrin is insoluble. Fibre makes up the tissue of meat. This is what you see when you look at meat. If meat is boiled a long time, what is left is pure fibre.

Gelatin diminishes with age. At ninety the bones are nothing but a sort of imperfect marble. That is what makes them so brittle. Bones are composed principally of gelatin and phosphate of lime.

Osmazome is the most flavourful part of meat, and is soluble in cold water. It is osmazome that gives goodness to soup. It is osmazome that forms meat *roux* in carmelizing. It is osmazome that makes roast-meat gravy. It is osmazome that gives savour to game.

[1] With cabbage or sauerkraut, and/or sausage.—ED.

Osmazome is especially abundant in full-grown, red-meat animals. There is little, if any, in lamb, suckling pig, pullet, and even in the white meat of full-grown poultry. It is because of this substance, then unknown, that the maxim on making good bouillon, "the pot must smile," was invented.

Albumin is found in the flesh and in the blood. It is like white of egg, and coagulates at a relatively low temperature. It forms the scum that one skims off the pot.

Fat is an oil insoluble in water. It forms between the cellular tissues and sometimes agglomerates in large masses in animals so predisposed, such as the pig, poultry, ortolans, and figpeckers.

If one wanted nothing but bouillon from a *pot-au-feu*, one could simply chop up meat, put into cold water, and heat it slowly to boiling. In this manner all the principal solubles would be drawn from the meat and in half an hour one would have a true consommé. We suggest this method when unexpected guests arrive and soup is needed in a hurry.

It is a mistake to think that poultry, unless it is old, will add anything to the osmazome of bouillon. But an old pigeon, a partridge, or a rabbit roasted in advance, a crow in November or December, add greatly to the flavour and aroma of a bouillon.

Now, we want from our *pot-au-feu*, besides bouillon, edible meat that can be eaten plain, boiled, the first day and reappear the next in another guise. So we shall show the way always to make good bouillon without ruining the meat.

Always take the biggest piece of meat practicable for your uses. The bigger, fresher, and thicker the piece of meat, the better the bouillon — not to mention economy in time and fuel. Do not wash the meat. This would take away some of its good juices. Take out the bone and tie up the meat well so it will not lose shape in cooking. Put 1 quart of water into the kettle for each pound of meat.

Heat your kettle slowly. This will release the albumin first. Later it will coagulate. As the albumin is lighter than water, it will rise to the surface, bringing with it any impurities that may be in your meat. Coagulated albumin in the form of white of egg is used to clarify other substances. The slower to come to a boil, the more scum. It should take at least 1 hour between the time you put your kettle on the fire and the time the scum gathers on the surface.

The scum should be removed the moment it is thick on the surface, otherwise the movement of the boiling water will precipitate it, clouding your bouillon. If the fire is even, it is not necessary to start all over to raise the scum, which must once more be removed. When the kettle is well skimmed and begins to bubble, add the vegetables, which consist of 3 carrots, 2 parsnips, 3 white turnips, a bunch of leeks and celery, tied together. Do not forget to add 3 big onions, 2 with a clove stuck in each, the third with a clove of garlic. In a second-rate kitchen, the bouillon is coloured with half a burnt onion, a piece of caramel, or a desiccated carrot. Don't forget to crack the bones (which you add to the bouillon) with a cleaver. These may be bought with the beef or they may come from yesterday's roast, but, in any case, the more broken up they are, the more gelatin they contribute.

It takes 7 hours of sustained simmering to give a bouillon the required quality. The pot should be covered to minimize evaporation. Think twice before adding water, though if your meat actually rises above the level of the bouillon it is necessary to add boiling water to cover it. The boiled beef coming out of the pot has lost half its weight.

According to Brillat-Savarin, there are four categories of persons who eat boiled beef:

First, those who eat it because their parents ate it and hope their own children will imitate them.

Second, the impatient, who abhor inactivity at the table and have the habit of avidly devouring the first thing put before them.

Third, the careless, who, not having received the sacred fire from heaven, consider meals mere necessary labour and put everything that may nourish them on the same level, sitting at table like an oyster on his rock.

Finally, those who are endowed with more appetite than they like to admit, who hasten to throw a first victim into their stomachs to appease the gastric fire that devours them, and to serve as a base for the various other foods they propose to send down later.

Let us go on, now, to the varieties of bouillon.

Bouillon Consommé à la Régence. Take a fresh piece of beef, a piece of breast of mutton, put them into a pan, and sear.

Then add, in a kettle, the saddles of hares, and a partridge or two, fill your kettle with bouillon, and simmer several hours.

Old-fashioned Bouillon Consommé. (Reduced by half, this can take the place of gravy in all sauces.) Trim all the fat from a shoulder of mutton, half roast it on the spit. Put it into your kettle with a good piece of beef and an old capon with plenty of meat on it, add a few carrots, onions, turnips, parsnips and a stalk of celery, cover with yesterday's bouillon, and proceed as above with simmering, vegetables, etc.

Modern Bouillon Consommé. Put into your kettle a good big slice of beef, a veal shin, a hen, an old rooster, a wild rabbit, or an old partridge. Add some bouillon, bring to a boil. Skim. Keep the bouillon level up. Add carrots, onions, celery, parsley, garlic, cloves. Simmer 5 hours. Strain through a cloth.

Bouillon Consommé. To make this sort of bouillon takes a lot of meat. When it is cold, it should jell. Usually it is made with the remains of game and other meats from a large dinner. Cover with ordinary bouillon and proceed as above. Do not salt.

To Keep Bouillon. Bring your bouillon to a boil, night and morning, over very high heat, and it will keep. (M. de Vuillemot adds: Put a piece of charcoal into your bouillon before boiling. This will keep it from souring.)

[**BOUQUET GARNI.** *A bunch of herbs — sprig of thyme, bay leaf, sprigs of parsley — tied together so it can be removed after the flavour has gone into the food with which it is cooked.* — ED.]

BURNET. A delicate aromatic herb whose leaves are used for seasoning.

This plant was at one time highly esteemed as astringent, diuretic, and healing. It also had the reputation of increasing the yield of milk. In the past few years it has been cultivated in the fields. This has its advantage, though the hay produced is really only good for sheep.

BUTCHERS AND BUTCHERSHOPS. The institution of the butchershop goes back to remote antiquity. Such establishments were set up as soon as it became possible to provide meat for sale on a continuing basis. At that time, they also served as slaughter-houses.

The Romans had separate abattoirs, called *lanionia*, and butcher-shops, called *macella*. At first these establishments were in different quarters, but finally they came together in one group, and a whole quarter was given over to them, which, after vendors of other comestibles had joined them, became known as *macellum magnum*. The growth of the Roman population soon required the establishment of two other great butcher markets, which rivalled the baths, the circus, and the amphitheatre in their magnificence. The Romans also had a special police force to examine meat, and prohibited the sale, under penalty of a heavy fine, of meat more than forty-eight hours killed in winter and twenty-four in summer.

From the earliest times of history in France, we find butcher-shops established in Paris on the Roman model. The butchers' guild already existed, headed by an elected chief. It was his duty to settle all differences that might arise in the guild, and he was answerable only to the provost of Paris in regard to the problems of the trade and the administration of property of the members. This property was owned in common by them all, excluding daughters, and if a family left no male heir its property reverted to the community.

For a long time there was only one butcher market in Paris. Its site is marked now only by the Tower of Saint-Jacques-la-Boucherie. Then another, the Boucherie du Parvis, was established. But its site was given, in 1212, by Philip Augustus, to the Bishop of Paris. Finally, the Templars, under charter from Philip the Bold, set up a butcher market near their establishment.

By an ordinance of Charles VI, dated 1418, any butcher who wanted to set up as a master butcher in Paris was obliged to give an *aboivrement* and a *past* — that is, a luncheon and a banquet. For the *aboivrement*, the new master butcher gave the head of the community a wax candle weighing about a pound and a half, and a cake made with eggs. To the wife of the head man, four big cuts of meat. To the provost of Paris, a pint of wine and four cakes. To the street commissioner of Paris and the provost of Fort-l'Évèque, to the parliamentary cellarer and concierge, half a pint of wine and two cakes each.

Higher tributes, in some cases up to sixty pounds of meat, were given to various officials for the *past*.

The various persons who had a right to this tribute were obliged to give a denier or two to the fiddler who played in the hall, when they sent to fetch what was owed them.

Some butchers became rich and rented their stalls at exorbitant prices. Parliament then decided that a court counsellor shouldpreside, once a year, at an adjudication of such grievances as might arise. Finally, Henry III, by letters patent in February 1587, united all the butchers of the city into one community, which he organized into a trade association, giving them statutes.

There were about 310 butchershops in Paris at the time of the Revolution of 1789, which brought plenty of trouble to the trade. In the general confusion, numerous persons set up to sell fresh meat wherever they were, even in cellars. The pernicious abuses that resulted were harmful to public health. A decree of 9 Germinal, Year VIII, declared that no one might practice the butchers profession without a permit from the prefect of police. Then on 8 Vendémiaire, Year XI, a decree re-established the guild of Paris butchers, set up a syndicate, and obliged each butcher, besides obtaining authorization from the prefect of police, to put up a bond of one, two, or three thousand francs, depending on the size of his shop. The imperial decree of February 8, 1811, was even more restrictive. It reduced the number of butchershops in the capital to three hundred, all shops over that number being bought out by the Poissy countinghouse out of the interest on the bonds it held. This countinghouse was a sort of bank that served as intermediary between the cattle vendors and the butchers, and made payments on behalf of the latter to the former up to the amount of the buyer's bond.

In the last fifty years, butchery has made immense progress. First, the abattoirs completely took over the slaughter of cattle by individual butchers. This had heretofore been done in the narrow Paris streets, creating frightful centres of infection detrimental to public health. The Montmartre abattoir, the Popincourt abattoir, and the Roule abattoir were first established. In a year or two they merged into a single one at Villette. It is there now, and to this immense and magnificent establishment all the retail butchers come to buy their daily supplies. The total increases daily and is now close to 900,000 pounds a day.

A few years back, shops selling horse meat were established in Paris. Certain interested hippophagi tried to make this meat popular. Banquets were given, and accounts of the menus put in the papers. Then fliers were distributed, offering good-quality horse meat cheap. But nothing came of it, and one by one the horse-meat shops disappeared. There can't be more than one or two now, in the poorest sections, their existence sustained only by the cheapness of their product.

For that matter, horse meat is not exactly bad. But it needs to be strongly seasoned, and above all to be approached without prejudice.

In Rome, as I have mentioned, there were butchershops on every street until they were all united in a single quarter. There were numerous such shops in the Forum, that great daily exhibition of the products of Rome and its environs. There was a butcher stall opposite the tribunal of the decemvirs, since it was from such a stall that Virginius snatched the knife with which he killed his daughter.

Perhaps it seems astonishing that Virginius, who was a centurion in the Roman army, should take a common butcher knife to kill the beautiful child whom Appius loved and planned to kidnap.

First of all, there are times when history is more picturesque than the romancers. History, in causing a foul blade used to kill the lowest animals to be plunged into this gracious creature, created a splendid opposition of the most elegant form to the basest weapon. And then it had to be so, since because of the constant quarrels it was forbidden to all citizens, even soldiers, to enter the Forum bearing arms. Virginius, though a centurion, had been obliged to submit to the law, and when he came to plead for his daughter, pleaded disarmed.

Alfieri, who has Virginia killed with a sword because, he says, it is nobler than a knife, should have known all this. The weapon is nobler, true. But in my opinion it is less dramatic. And the substitution argues an impermissible ignorance of the laws and customs of the times on the part of the author.

Butchers seem to have been fated to become illustrious under such circumstances as those related above and through their own acts as well. But always under bloody circumstances. Are they not men of blood, and do they not consequently love blood?

The active part taken by the butchers under Charles VI in the bloody quarrel between the Armagnacs and the Burgundians is well known. It is also known that Caboche, head of the butchers, became the chief of the Parisian people. The victorious Armagnacs destroyed their great butcher market and abolished their privileges. But their adversaries proved stronger in the end, and both butchers and market were re-established in their former glory.

BUTTER. Butter may be made from any kind of milk, but the fattest and richest is made from ewe's milk. In every country where I have travelled I have never failed to obtain fresh-churned butter. Wherever I went, I procured cow's, camel's, mare's, or ewe's milk. I filled a bottle with it three quarters full, stoppered it, and fastened it to my horse's neck. My horse did the rest. When I arrived at my destination, I unstoppered the bottle, and there was a piece of butter as large as my fist

Roast Butter à la Landais. Salt a ball of butter. Break 4 eggs and beat as for an omelet. Take very dry white bread and crumble it, adding a little salt. Roll the butter in the egg and then in the bread crumbs. Repeat the operation until all the eggs have been absorbed. Put on a spit. In the cooking, a *croustade* will be formed that may be served with oysters instead of bread. Drink old Barsac, but don't put it on the *croustade*. (Recipe from M. Vuillemot.)

CABBAGE. There are various types of cabbages, nearly all of them originating in Europe, where they are most widely used. In nearly every French province, cabbage is the mainstay of the peasants, who live chiefly on this vegetable, even though it has little nourishment, is windy, and spreads an evil odour. Cabbage was greatly venerated by the ancients, who swore by it just as the Egyptians rendered divine honours to the onion.

Cabbage with Bacon. An excellent plebeian dish. Cut a cabbage into quarters, blanch it. Put into a pot with bacon, sausages, cervelat, celery, onions, large carrots, bay leaf, and thyme. Cook slowly 1½ hours. To serve, remove the other vegetables, put your cabbage on a platter with the meats on top, and reduce the liquid and make into a sauce.

Stuffed Cabbage. Remove the stem and some of the inside of the cabbage from the bottom. Blanch. Drain. Spread the leaves carefully so as not to break them, and fill with a stuffing made from chicken, veal, beef marrow or cooked ham fat, truffles, mushrooms, parsley, scallions, salt, pepper, white of bread, 2 whole eggs, 2 or 3 extra yolks, a clove of garlic, all finely chopped and mixed. Close your cabbage carefully and tie with string so that the stuffing will not fall out. Put into a casserole.

Meanwhile, prepare a gravy from well-beaten slices of beef or veal that you will try out in a pan, add a little flour, let it colour, add good bouillon, season with *fines herbes* and slices of onion. Pour this mixture, half cooked, with the meat in it, over your cabbage and cook the whole together.

Serve the cabbage on a platter and pour over it a mushroom or veal-sweetbread ragout; surround with the gravy. Serve hot.

This dish can be made lenten by using fish instead of meat.

Cabbage à la Petite Russienne. Prepare as above, but use a stuffing made with coarsely chopped mushrooms, onions, parsley, salt, pepper, and grated nutmeg, thickened and mixed with semolina cooked in milk. Bake in the oven a long time. Serve with a butter and sour-cream sauce. (Royer's method.)

Cabbage en Garbure. Blanch and drain. Remove the thickest leaf ribs. Put a layer of cabbage leaves in the bottom of a soup pot, a layer of Gruyère cheese sliced thin, a layer of sliced bread. Repeat until you have enough. Season, cover with a good bouillon, and simmer for 1 hour. Serve as a thick soup or stew, with bouillon in another bowl. (Bordeaux cookery.)

Cabbage Loaf. Blanch a Savoy cabbage, dip in cold water, drain, take it apart, and remove the heavy ribs. Marinate the eye of a leg of veal with fine oil, parsley, scallions, shallots, garlic, mushrooms, coarse salt, pepper, and sliced ham. Spread cabbage leaves in the bottom of a pot, cover with slices of the veal and ham and a little of the marinade. Repeat this layering until you have a pile the size of a loaf of bread. Cook in a rich braising stock. When done, drain off the fat and serve with espagnole sauce.

Dutch Red Cabbage. This makes one of the finest side dishes. Peel and chop fine russet apples and onions. Remove the stem from your red cabbage and blanch. Cook all together with a good piece of butter, 1 tablespoonful of powdered sugar, a pinch of salt, pepper, and *bouquet garni*, for 5 or 6 hours. Add 1 glass of Bordeaux, remove the bouquet add a piece of butter, and when it is melted, serve.

CALAPÉ. An American name for a turtle stew cooked in the shell. This dish, which was the delight of my crew when we cruised between Africa and Sicily, has never seemed to me worthy to appear on a self-respecting table. I shall tell you how the turtles were caught and prepared.

In the calm weather of June and July a man was always perched on top of the mast as a lookout. When he saw a turtle, he called out and the small boat was launched immediately. Approaching very quietly as close as possible to the animal swimming on top of the water, our pilot would then slip into the water, swim up quietly, grab the turtle by its hind flippers, and turn it over. In this position it was helpless, unable to dive or turn over. The pilot slipped a line over the turtle's neck and, returning to the boat, helped tow the animal to the ship, where it was pulled aboard. The turtle was hung up by its hind flippers, the line around its neck pulled taut, and the head cut off with the stroke of a sword. After hanging for twelve hours, it was let down and put on its back. The flat belly shell was removed with a knife, care being taken not to cut into the entrails or the gall bladder. Keep only the meat and the liver. You will find two lobes of meat very much like veal in colour and flavour.

Cut the meat into pieces the size of a walnut, soak awhile, then cook on a slow fire for 3 or 4 hours in consommé with salt, pepper, cloves, bay leaf, and carrots. Meanwhile, prepare poultry quenelles seasoned with parsley, scallions, and anchovies. Simmer these in consommé. Put 3 or 4 glasses of dry Madeira in your turtle stew, add the quenelles and their liquid. Having cleaned the upper shell of your turtle, use it as a dish to serve the stew. From a turtle weighing from 120 to 180 pounds there will be enough to serve 50 persons.

CARÊME, MARIE-ANTOINE. This is a name that certainly did not seem predestined to acquire the gastronomic fame it now has. Since the death of Carême on January 12, 1833, many princes have lost their principalities and many kings have fallen from their thrones. Carême, by his genius king of cookery, has stood up, and no rival has obscured his glory. Like Theseus and Romulus, like all founders of empires, Carême was a sort of lost child. He was born in Paris in 1784, in a woodyard where his father was employed. There were fifteen children, and the father did not know how to feed them all.

One day, when Marie-Antoine was eleven years old, his father took him to the town gate for dinner. Then, leaving him in the middle of the street, he said to him: "Go, little one. There are good trades in this world. Let the rest of us languish in the misery in which we are doomed to die. This is a time when fortunes are made by those who have the wit, and that you have. Tonight or tomorrow, find a good house that may open its doors to you. Go with what God has given you and what I may add to that." And the good man gave him his blessing.

From that time on, Marie-Antoine never again saw his father and mother, who died young, nor his brothers and sisters, who were scattered over the world.

Night fell. The boy saw a lighted window and knocked on it. It was a cookshop whose proprietor's name has not been preserved in history. He took in the boy and put him to work next day.

At sixteen, he quit this dingy tavern and went to work as assistant to a restaurateur. His progress was rapid, and he already knew what he wanted to be. He went to work for Bailly, a famous pastrycook on the Rue Vivienne, who excelled in cream tarts and catered to the Prince de Talleyrand. From that moment he saw his future clearly. He had discovered his vocation.

"At seventeen," he says in his *Memoirs*, "I was chief pastrycook at Bailly's. He was a good master and took an interest in me. He gave me time off to study designs from prints. He put me in charge of preparing several set pieces for the table of the First Consul. I used my designs and my nights in his service, and he repaid me with kindness. In his establishment I began to innovate. The illustrious pastrycook Avice was then flourishing. His work aroused my enthusiasm, and knowledge of his methods gave me courage. I sought to follow without imitating him. I learned to execute every trick of my trade, and made unique, extraordinary pieces by myself. But to get there, young people, how many sleepless nights! I could not work on my designs and calculations until after nine or ten o'clock, and I worked three quarters of the night.

"I left M. Bailly with tears in my eyes and went to work for the successor of M. Gendron. I made it a condition that if I had opportunity to make an 'extra', I could have someone replace me. A few months later, I left the great pastryshops behind altogether, and devoted myself to preparing great dinners. It was enough to do. I rose higher and higher and earned a lot of money. Others became jealous of me, a poor child of labour, and I have often been the butt of attacks from little pastrycooks who will have far to climb to where I am now."

During the prodigality of the Directoire, Carême refined cooking into the delicate luxury and exquisite sensuality of the Empire. The Talleyrand household was served with wisdom and grandeur, Carême says. It gave an example to others and kept them in mind of basic principles.

The culinary director in this household was Bouché, or Bouche-sèche, who came from the Condé household, famous for its fine fare. So Talleyrand's cuisine was simply a continuation of the cuisine of the Condé household. Carême dedicated his *Patissier royal* to Bouché. It was there he made the acquaintance of Laguipière, the Emperor's cook, who died in the retreat from Moscow. Until that time, Carême had followed his art. After Laguipière, he learned to improvise. But practice did not satisfy him any longer. He wanted to go more profoundly into theory, to copy designs, to read and analyse scientific works and follow through with studies parallel to his profession. He wrote and illustrated a *History of the Roman Table*, but, unfortunately, both manuscript and drawings have been lost. Carême was a poet. He placed his art on the same level as all the others. And he was right to do so.

"From behind my stoves," he says, "I contemplated the cuisines of India, China, Egypt, Greece, Turkey, Italy, Germany, and Switzerland. I felt the unworthy methods of routine crumble under my blows."

Carême had grown up under the Empire, and you can imagine his distress when he saw it crash. He had to be forced to execute the gigantic royal banquet in the Plaine des Vertus in 1814. The following year, the Prince Regent called him to Brighton as his chef. He stayed with the English Regent two years. Every morning he prepared his menu with His Highness, who was a blasé gourmand. During these discussions he went through a course in gastronomic hygiene that, if printed, would be one of the classic books on cookery.

Bored with the grey skies of England, Carême returned to Paris but went back when the Prince Regent became King. From London he went to St. Petersburg as one of the Emperor Alexander's chefs, then to Vienna to direct a few great dinners for the Austrian emperor. He returned to London with Lord Stuart, the English ambassador, but soon quit to return to Paris to write and publish. He was constantly torn from his study of theory by calls from monarchs and congresses. His work shortened his life. "The charcoal is killing us," he said, "but what does it matter? The fewer the years, the greater the glory." He died before reaching the age of fifty, on January 12, 1833. He left disciples behind him, among them the excellent Vuillemot.

CARP. A pond and river fish. The Greeks and Romans do not mention it.[1] Delicious carp weighing from sixty to a hundred pounds are caught in the Rhine. Carp live for several hundred years. This was proved by carp put into the fishpond at Fontainebleau by Francis I. In a female carp eighteen inches long, Dr. Petit found 342,000 eggs. In the Middle East the Jews, to whom sturgeon caviar is forbidden, make caviar from carp roe. The biggest carp on record was taken in 1711. It weighed 140 pounds.

Carp caught in enclosed ponds often have a miry odour. To get rid of this, pour a glass of vinegar into a carp as it comes out of the water. It will immediately be covered with a sort of thick exudation, which comes off when you scale it. When the carp is dead, his flesh will be firm and taste as good as if it had been caught in live water.

Carp à la Danube. Make a stuffing with the boned meat of 2 soles and 1 pike, chopped fine with scallions and fine spices, salt, pepper, nutmeg, butter, and a little soft bread soaked in cream. Mix in egg yolks to get the right consistency and stuff your carp. Cook, over a slow fire, with white wine seasoned with salt, pepper, cloves, lime, *fines herbes*, and good fresh butter.

Carp à la Hussarde. Take a fine carp and open it as little as possible to clean it. Put into it butter mixed with *fines herbes* and seasoned to taste. Marinate with fine oil, *fines herbes*, thyme, and

---

[1]Dumas is mistaken. Carp is mentioned by both Athenæus and Aristotle.—ED.

basil. When it has picked up the flavour of the marinade, grill it and serve it with a remoulade sauce.

Carp Piémontaise. Clean, remove the gills, make cuts on both sides, and marinate for 2 hours in oil, salt, pepper, parsley, whole scallions, slices of onion, garlic, sliced shallots, thyme, basil, bay leaf. Grill it, basting from time to time with the marinade.

Lightly sauté mushrooms and truffles with butter, a *bouquet garni*, and a pinch of flour. Add some good gravy, half-cooked artichoke bottoms, little white onions, and ½ glass of champagne. When this ragout is cooked and the liquid reduced, mix in 3 egg yolks and cream, squeeze the juice of a lemon into it, and serve your carp on a platter with the ragout around it.

Carp à la Flamande. Having prepared your carp, lard it with thin strips of eel flesh seasoned with chopped *fines herbes*, fine spices, salt. Into a casserole put mushrooms, truffles, blanched white onions, a piece of butter, a bunch of all sorts of herbs chopped fine, a pinch of flour. Moisten with vegetable consommé and ½ glass of champagne. When your ragout is half cooked, lay your carp on it to finish cooking. If the sauce is not sufficiently reduced, put it on a hot fire until it is. Add capers. Serve the carp on a platter with the ragout around it.

Carp with Beer or à la Moscovite. Prepare your carp, cut it into 3 pieces. Put into a casserole with 1 bottle of good beer, 1 glass of brandy, a piece of butter mixed with flour, a bouquet of parsley, scallions, garlic, clove, thyme, bay leaf, basil, and sliced onions, salt, and pepper. Cook over a hot fire until the sauce is reduced. Take out the bouquet before serving.

Carp à la Bourguignonne. Dress your carp, keeping the blood aside in a bowl. Pour 1 glass of wine through the inside, letting it run into the blood. Put the carp on a platter, prick it well all over, rub with fine salt, and let stand 2 hours. Then put slices of onion into a fish-poacher, lay your carp on them, add a *bouquet garni* and a bottle of Burgundy. Cook on a slow fire.

When it is cooked, strain the liquid into the blood, add a piece of butter mixed with flour, and let this cook over a hot fire until well reduced. Add a chopped anchovy, nutmeg, and whole capers. Serve the carp on a platter with the sauce over it.

Carp on the Spit. Choose a fine milt carp, dress it as usual.

Fill it with a stuffing made from the milt, eel flesh, anchovies, mushrooms, chestnuts, bread crumbs, onions, sorrel, parsley, thyme, pepper, clove, and good fresh butter. Sew up the opening. Stick cloves and pieces of bay leaf into the fish. Wrap it in buttered paper and roast on the spit. Baste with butter mixed with verjuice or, better still, with hot milk and white wine. When it is ready, serve with a ragout of mushrooms, milt, truffles, morels, and other similar ingredients over it.

CARROTS. Home Style. Cut two fingers long and trim round. Cook 15 minutes in water. Drain. Continue cooking in a good bouillon with 1 glass of white wine, a bouquet of *fines herbes*, and a little salt. When they are done, add a little meat jelly to thicken the sauce.

Carrot Soup. Bring to a boil enough water for a big tureen of soup. Add 4 ounces of butter, salt, 1½ cup dried peas, 3 or 4 carrots cut into pieces. Cook. An hour before serving add such herbs as chervil, sorrel, etc., endive, a little parsley root, scallions, and onions. Cook all together.

CELERY. The ancients crowned themselves with celery at their feasts to neutralize the strength of wine. They called it *ache*. The Italian language took hold of this word and developed it into celery. "Let us fill our cups with wine of Massicus," says Horace, "and hasten to make ourselves crowns of celery and myrtle."

Celery Salad. Full, fresh, tender celery eaten as a salad, seasoned with aromatic vinegar, oil of Provence, and fine mustard, is truly delicious. It wakens the stomach, stimulates the appetite, and creates a verve that lasts for several hours.

Celery Ragout. Chop celery and cook as you would spinach. Season with salt, pepper, nutmeg, and some good bouillon. Serve with golden croutons. If you want to be greedy, top this dish with a few ortolans or breasts of red partridge. Try this. You will probably like it. (Dr. Roques' *Dictionary of Useful Plants*.)

Celery Bonne Femme. Clean. Remove all tough green leaves. Cut into pieces of equal length. Blanch. Drain. Put into a light *roux*, heat, and add bouillon, salt, pepper, nutmeg. When the celery is cooked, mix butter or gravy into the sauce.

Creamed Celery. Dice, blanch, drain. Heat in a pot with butter. Sprinkle with a bit of starch. Add consommé. Cook. Reduce the sauce. Stir into it raw egg yolks mixed with cream, and a little nutmeg. Serve garnished with croutons.

CELLAR. A carefully organized cellar must be both fresh and dry. The air must penetrate it only feebly. The sun, whose rays are worthy of man's homage outside, and which was first adored by the peoples of the earth as the god of the universe that gave birth to and nurtures all of nature's bounty, is fatal to a cellar. These precepts were observed even in antiquity. Here is what the celebrated architect and archaeologist Mazois has to say in describing Scaurus' cellar in ancient Rome:

"On the north side are the *cellae vinariae*, where all kinds of wines are kept. These cellars are lighted from the north, so that no ray of sunlight may heat the wine and, in so doing, cloud and weaken it. Care is taken that in this direction there should be no manure pile, tree roots, or any fetid thing. It is also distant from all baths, ovens, drains, cisterns, and reservoirs, for fear their proximity should alter the wine by giving it a bad odour. Scaurus, who cared more for his wine than for his reputation, voluntarily associates with the most corrupt men of Rome. But he will not permit anything that might corrupt his wine to approach the walls of his cellar. Once he considered divorcing his wife because she had visited his cellar when she was unwell. According to him, this might have soured his precious wines. He goes so far that he not only perfumes his containers with myrrh to give the wine a good flavour, but sprinkles it all over the environs.

"Scaurus' cellar is renowned. He managed to assemble in it three thousand amphorae of all the known varieties of wine. There are 195 different kinds, each requiring its own special care. Nothing is neglected. After study and observation, amphorae with too-rounded shapes were proscribed.

"Above the wine cellars are the storerooms for provisions, which are also lighted from the north so that the sun's rays will not penetrate to encourage insects that might devour the grain."

There is no limit to the number of wines that may be stored in a connoisseur's cellar, but a wise providence, founding itself on the science of the age at which wines should be drunk, links luxury to economy. Some wines should be stored in great quantity, many others only in sufficient number to take care of a few years' consumption. Unhappy the drinker who fills his cellar with barrels of Burgundy and champagne! These wines, which have a short life, should be drunk as soon as they have matured. Their degeneration is rapid. The Burgundy sours, the champagne becomes oily. In general, white wines are difficult to keep. They should be bought only as they are needed. But the Bordeaux, the wines of the South, and the Spanish wines may and should be kept a long time, since age is their chief merit. These should be stacked in huge piles, the youngest at the bottom so they will reappear only after they have been forgotten. Then they come to the table in bottles crusted with a triple coat of tartar, and if the host in noble pride calls out like Horace, "Here is a wine from the time of my birth, Mummius was consul," no sardonic laughter will go round from guest to guest, and his words will not be taken for a gasconade.

CÈPES FRANCS. A fairly large mushroom with a regular, drooping cap. The surface is dry, deeply grooved; the stems are swollen. The meat is white, light, has a pleasant aroma, and is of good quality. There are two principal varieties, those with reddish caps and those with black.

The reddish variety is dry in texture, but yields to the pressure of the fingers. Its flesh is delicate, well flavoured, and has an agreeable odour. It does not change colour on contact with the air. It is found in September and October in the environs of Paris. It can be preserved by drying, and restored with hot water. In Hungary sauces and cullises are made from it. It is warm and aphrodisiac in its effect. Never forget to cut this plant, and if it changes colour on contact with air, throw it away.

The black-capped cèpe is about four inches high. The cap is about two inches in thickness and in diameter. It turns a dark maroon. The flesh is dry, soft to the touch, finely perfumed, and has the finest mushroom flavour. It is more common in the northern and temperate parts of Europe, and is much sought after. It is treated just like the reddish cèpe.

This excellent mushroom is harvested in the greatest quantity in the South of France and around Bordeaux. But it is not dried there as it is in Geneva or in Italy, because it is believed to be excellent preserved in oil. It is therefore sold in tins.

Don't be deceived either by the printed statements or by any oral blandishments. The Bordeaux cèpes swell up with oil and become regular sponges that are impossible to restore to their original firmness. As a result, whether they are fried or grilled, they are still next to impossible to eat.

To prepare cèpes, cut off the stems and chop them up with parsley, bread crumbs, shallots, fresh butter, and a chopped clove of garlic. Make the whole into a paste seasoned with salt, pepper, and a little paprika. Spread this over the bottom surface of the caps, sprinkle with a few bread crumbs, and bake in a hot oven. (Recipe from Vuillemot.)

They can also be prepared *à la provençale*, sautéed in olive oil with parsley and chopped garlic. Brown them well, add a little meat glaze, and serve very hot.

CEPHALOPODS (OCTOPUS, CUTTLEFISH). The cephalopods are the highest-ranking molluscs.

Imagine a muscular sack, thick, soft, viscous, spherical in some varieties, cylindrical or tube-shaped in others, with colours that change like a chameleon's. Inside this sack, organs for aquatic respiration, a circulatory apparatus, a digestive tube including a stomach comparable to a bird's gizzard. On top of this a round head with two huge eyes, situated laterally, between which protrudes a little tube that represents not a nose, but the anus (in the middle of the face)! On top of everything and in the middle of this head put a mouth composed of circular lips, armed with two horny vertical jaws (a veritable parrot's beak) and furnished with a tongue covered with spikes. Finally, all around this mouth, plant a crown of fleshy, supple, vigorous, retractile appendages covered with suction disks.

Now you have an approximate idea of the cephalopods, so named by Cuvier because they have their feet on their heads, for the appendages we have just described are arms — or legs — take your pick, since they serve impartially for prehension and for locomotion.

One of these animals, described by Captain Frédéric Bouyer, commander of the frigate *Alecton*, as having been seen and captured between Madeira and Tenerife in 1862, measured sixteen to nineteen feet, not counting the eight arms, which were each nearly six and a half feet long. His mouth was over a foot and a half wide. The whole animal was estimated at four thousand pounds. The common poulp or cuttlefish of the Mediterranean is about two feet across.

This frightfully hideous mollusc is nevertheless eaten, especially in Naples. It is boiled and served with tomato sauce, or, more often, it is boiled and then fried. We ate one, called a *calmaro* in Italy, and discovered that it has a remarkable resemblance to fried calf's ear.

CERVELAT. A sort of short, fat sausage made of chopped pork seasoned with salt, pepper, and a clove of wild garlic. Pork cervelat has all the bad qualities of pig meat, and the manner in which it is prepared makes it even more indigestible. Cervelat is also made with fish. This is less indigestible, but the high proportion of spices used makes it anything but healthful, especially if it is eaten frequently.

Home-style Cervelat. Remove membranes and sinews from pork. Chop fine with an equal amount of bacon, add chopped parsley, scallions, thyme, basil, and fine spices. Mix thoroughly and form into flat oval cakes, wrap in casing, and tie both ends. Round sausages are prepared the same way, but poultry casings are used.

Hang your cervelat to smoke in the chimney for 3 days. Then cook in bouillon for 3 hours with salt, garlic, thyme, bay leaf, basil, parsley, and scallions. Let cool and serve as needed.

Milanese Cervelat. Chop and mix 6 parts lean pork to 1 part bacon, add salt and pepper, white wine, and pork blood. Mix and grind cinnamon and cloves and roll in this mixture long strips of pig's head meat, with which then lard the ground meat. Stuff into casings, cook, and serve.

Lyon Cervelat. Take equal quantities of lean pork, beef, and bacon. Chop the pork and beef very fine. Dice the bacon and mix it in evenly. Season with salt, ground pepper, broken pepper, and whole pepper, garlic, saltpetre, and shallots. Mix the whole thoroughly and set aside for 24 hours. Stuff into large casings, tie, and let stand in brine with saltpetre for 8 days. Hang in the chimney to dry. When they turn white they are dried enough. Tighten the strings and cover with a mixture of sage, thyme, and bay leaf, boiled in wine lees. When they are thoroughly dry again, wrap in paper and cover with dry ashes to keep.

Cervelat à la Bénédictine. Chop eel and carp meat with fresh butter, chopped parsley, shallots, garlic, and scallions. Stuff into fish casings, smoke 3 days, cook in white wine with onions and other root vegetables.

Truffles, pistachio nuts, chopped shallots or onions may be quickly sautéed on a hot fire and incorporated into the cervelat stuffings above.

[Note: *Portable smokehouses with 25- and 50-pound capacity are among the apparatus newly offered by specialty stores catering to the broiler-grill-barbecue-user trade.* — ED.]

CHERRY. A juicy, acid fruit. Eaten in small quantities, it contributes juices, alkaline salts, and sugary flesh to the stomach.

Cherry Soup. This is a fine, sweet side dish. Fry cubes of white bread in butter, then add the cherries and continue to sauté. Add water, sugar, kirsch, and serve.

German Cherry Soup. It is only for the record that we mention this execrable dish of crushed cherries and ground-up pits, ferociously spiced, drowned in wine, and served cold.

Cherry Compote. Cut off half the stems of your cherries and cook them in a sugar syrup. Flavour with raspberries and serve with their syrup.

CHICKEN. The inhabitants of the island of Cos taught the Romans the art of fattening poultry by keeping them closely penned in a dark place. The sumptuary laws of Rome proceeded against the poor chickens, however, forbidding the serving of any but plain and simple barnyard poultry.

Since we have no similar sumptuary law in France, I can tell you how to fatten a chicken and at the same time impart the finest flavour to it. It will turn into a fat pullet in three weeks or a month.

First feed your chickens heavily for a few days with ground barley, bran, and milk. Then put them in a dry, dark cage and keep them constantly provided with barley flour mixed with milk. Capons should be fed the same way. Buckwheat is favoured over barley by gourmets.

One day a friend visited Brillat-Savarin, who was convalescing and whose doctor had ordered him on a diet. He found the professor devouring a fat hen from Le Mans.

"Is that a diet for a sick man?" he asked indignantly.

"My friend," said Brillat-Savarin, "I am subsisting on barley and buckwheat only."

"And that hen?"

"She lived on it for two months. Now she gives me life in her turn. Ah! what a fine thing the Moors did for us when they sent us buckwheat! Nothing else makes a chicken so seductive, so fine, so exquisite!"

When I come across a field of buckwheat, I never tire of admiring this beneficent plant, which perfumes the whole countryside when it is in bloom. Its odour induces a sort of ecstasy in me. I imagine I am breathing the very essence of the chicken that one day will eat it.

Capon au Gros Sel. Eviscerate, pluck, and clean. Truss with feet tucked inside. Cover with slices of bacon. Cook in consommé. Drain, salt, sauce with reduced beef gravy, and serve with a separate dish of coarse salt.

Capon à la Cavalière. Poach 1 hour in bouillon with onions, carrots, celery, and a bouquet of herbs. Drain. Serve in crayfish purée, or tomato purée with anchovies, or *sauce Robert* with mustard, or béchamel sauce, made with cream, containing oysters, or sautéed mushrooms, etc.

Chicken Broiled on the Spit. Take a fat chicken, clean, cut off the wingtips, fill with butter mixed with lemon juice. Truss with the feet outside. Rub with lemon juice. Sprinkle with salt. Cover with thin slices of lemon from which you will have removed the seeds. Wrap in several thicknesses of paper. Roast about 1 hour. Serve with any sauce you wish.

Roast Chicken. Put about ¾ pound of butter, a little salt, the juice of a lemon, and a little nutmeg in a bowl and mix thoroughly with a wooden spoon. Use this mixture to stuff 2 fat pullets previously prepared for the oven. Truss and tie. Line the bottom of a roasting pan with slices of bacon. Put your pullets on these. Add 1 carrot, 1 onion with 2 cloves stuck in it, a bouquet of parsley and scallions, $\frac{1}{2}$ bay leaf, $\frac{1}{2}$ clove of garlic, a slice of ham, and a few scraps of veal. Peel a lemon to the flesh. Slice it thin, remove the seeds, put the slices on your pullets, which should lie breast up. Cover with slices of bacon. Add a ladleful of bouillon and $\frac{1}{2}$ glass of white wine. Cover. Roast in a moderate oven. When the pullets are done, untruss them, drain off the fat, and serve, on a platter, on truffle, highly-spiced espagnole, tomato, or any other sauce you prefer.

Oyster Sauce for the Above. Take 72 oysters, shuck, and put into a pot in their own liquid. Bring just to a boil. In another pot, put 4 large tablespoonfuls of reduced *velouté*. Drain your oysters and put them into the *velouté*. Bring just to a boil, add a pinch of chopped, blanched parsley, a piece of butter, and a pinch of coarse pepper. Just before serving, add the juice of a lemon, taste, and adjust your seasoning, then pour over the pullets.

Chicken with Tartar Sauce. Clean and prepare 2 pullets. Truss them with the feet inside. With the side of a cleaver, break the breastbones, flattening them. Break the thighbones. Heat them in a dish with butter, salt, and coarse pepper. Cover and bake. Fifteen minutes before serving, turn them in the butter and brown them on or under a grill, turning them several times so they take a good colour. Serve on a base of tartar sauce.

Fried Marinated Chicken. Cut 2 pullets into frying pieces. Marinate for 1 hour in an earthenware dish with slices of onion, sprigs of parsley, salt, coarse pepper, and the juice of 2 or 3 lemons. Drain. Flour in a bag. Have your deep fat or oil hot. Put the drumsticks in first, then the breast, the wings, the thighs, etc. When nicely browned, drain. If you wish, serve with six fried fresh eggs. Serve with a poivrade sauce.

Marinated Chicken. Cut up two broiled pullets. Marinate for $\frac{1}{2}$ hour in a cooked marinade. Drain. Dip into a fritter batter to which you have added beaten egg whites. Fry as above, the biggest pieces first. Drain, arrange, on a platter, on a bed of fried parsley.

Galantine of Chicken or Capon. Bone and skin 2 birds,

taking care to have as large an area as possible of skin without cuts or holes. Mix and chop the chicken meat very fine with a little bacon, a calf's udder, a few mushrooms, and truffles, soft white of bread soaked in cream, 3 or 4 raw egg yolks, *fines herbes*, fine spices, a little parsley and scallions, pepper, and salt.

Spread this forcemeat on the inside of the chicken skins. On top of this a layer of well-seasoned strips of bacon fat, then a layer of raw ham, another layer of bacon strips, a layer of green pistachios, and repeat until you have enough to fill the skin. Roll up, fold into a cloth, and tie at both ends.

Into a large pot put bacon strips, slices of beef well rubbed with *fines herbes*, fine spices, salt, pepper, onions, parsnips, and carrots. Lay your chickens on this and put similar seasonings on top. Cover and bake in a slow oven.

When cooked, drain well, unwrap, slice, and arrange on a platter. Arrange a truffle ragout on top so that the pieces of truffle are between the slices of galantine, and serve hot.

Chicken Livers à la Périgueux. Take 7 fat hen livers. Discard the gall and the portion of liver next to it. Stick slivers of truffles into them. Place them in a pan lined with bacon slices. Cover with a mirepoix sauce. If you have no mirepoix sauce handy, use instead 1 glass of white wine and 1 glass of consommé, a little salt, 1 carrot, 2 medium onions with a clove stuck in 1, a bouquet of parsley and scallions, ½ bay leaf, and ½ clove of garlic. Cover the livers with sliced bacon and a piece of paper. Cover and bake 22 minutes. Drain, arrange on a platter, and pour Périgueux sauce over them.

CHICK-PEAS. Are very nourishing, but hard to digest. They are usually made into a purée, or used in such dishes as olio and olla-podrida. The experiment has been made of roasting and grinding them to serve as a substitute for coffee, but nothing good ever came of that.

CHICORY. There are two sorts of chicory, which are typical of eighteen or twenty other varieties: wild chicory and cultivated chicory, commonly known as endive.

Wild chicory (dandelion), also called pissabed because of its power to stimulate urination, is eaten only very young and tender, in salads. We shall therefore refer you to the article on SALADS (p. 29) for its preparation.

Chicory à la Bonne Femme. Blanch in boiling water. Freshen in cold water. Drain. Break into leaves. Cook with butter and bouillon, thicken with flour. Serve with fried croutons.

Chicory au Grand Jus. Blanch, split in half, tie up. Put into a pot with sliced bacon, pepper, and mustard. Add bits of veal, beef, or mutton, onions, carrots, and a *bouquet garni*. Cover. Bake for 3 hours, covered. Press in a cloth to drain thoroughly. Arrange on a platter like a crown, and serve with your entree.

Creamed Chicory. Remove all the green leaves from the chicory, wash in several waters, drain, blanch in hot water with a handful of salt, and freshen in cold water. Chop up. Put into a casserole with butter. Cook for 15 minutes to reduce the moisture. Stirring, add slowly 2 glasses of cream. Add grated nutmeg and salt, and cook thoroughly.

CHIPOLATA. A little Spanish sausage. Also a preparation in which it is an important ingredient:

Take 24 each of carrots, turnips, roasted chestnuts, and onions. Cook in a sweetened consommé. Add some chipolatas and a few pieces of bacon. Put the whole into a pot with mushrooms, artichoke bottoms, sliced celery, and a few tablespoonfuls of white veal sauce. Reduce. Skim.

Use this to reheat poultry or veal, leftovers of brain, etc. Use also to garnish broiled meats or as a bed for serving capon or other barnyard fowl.

CHOCOLATE. It is believed that the word *chocolate* derives from the Mexican language: *choco*, a sound or noise, and *atl*, water, because the Mexican people beat it in water to make it foam. The ladies of the New World, it seems, are mad for chocolate. We are told that, not content to drink it every moment of the day at home, they sometimes have it brought to them in church. This habit brought down on them the censure of their confessors, who ended up, however, in taking their part and sharing their chocolate. Finally, Father Escobar, whose metaphysics were as subtle as his morality was accommodating, formally declared that chocolate made with water did not break any fast, thus proclaiming on behalf of his lovely penitents the ancient adage: *Liquidum non frangit jejunium.*

Brought to Spain in the seventeenth century, chocolate instantly become popular. The women, and especially the monks, eagerly took to this novel, aromatic drink, and soon it was all the fashion. Custom has not changed in this respect, and today throughout the Peninsula it is good form to offer chocolate on every occasion.

Chocolate came over the Pyrenees with Anne of Austria, wife of Louis XIII, the first to introduce it to France. Again with the aid of the monks, to whom their Spanish brethren sent samples as presents, it became very fashionable. In the early days of the Regency it became more popular than coffee, which, also newly imported, was regarded as a curiosity and a luxury, while chocolate, quite correctly, was considered a healthful and pleasant food.

Brillat-Savarin, in his excellent book, recommends chocolate as a tonic, a stomachic, and a digestive. He says that those who use it enjoy consistent good health, and he speaks of chocolate with ambergris as a sovereign remedy for those fatigued by any sort of labour. Let the illustrious gastronome speak for himself:[1]

"This is the proper place to speak of chocolate flavoured with ambergris, whose properties I have tested by a number of experiments, the results of which I am proud to present to my readers.

"Therefore, let every man who has drunk too deeply from the cup of sensuality; every man who has spent in labour an important part of the time he should have slept; every intelligent man who feels himself temporarily stupid; every man who finds the air damp and oppressive, time hanging heavily, and the atmosphere difficult to abide; every man tormented by a fixed idea that robs him of the ability to think — let all these, I say, administer to themselves a good pint of chocolate with sixty to seventy-two grains of ambergris to every four ounces. They will see how marvellous it is.

"In my private vocabulary, chocolate with ambergris is *chocolate of the afflicted*, because in each of the conditions I have described one feels an indefinable emotion, common to all, that resembles affliction."

CIDER. Cider has been known in Europe only since the Moors brought it from Africa. From Spain it passed into France,

---

[1]Most of this article is taken from Brillat-Savarin.—ED.

and the conquering Normans naturally took it to England. Cider has been the subject of serious controversy. To the Norman, it is the true nectar of the masters of Olympus; to the inhabitants of countries where the vine prospers, it is a barely translucent, insipid beverage. However that may be, the Norman has remained faithful, and cider has penetrated other parts of France, where it is almost as popular as wine.

The first mention of this drink in France is found in the capitularies of Charlemagne, in which there are references to its manufacturers. But the Moors had brought it across the Strait of Gibraltar long since. Here is the story:

In the year 610, Mohammed proclaimed his Koran. Without positively proscribing wine, he presents it as a pernicious liquor to be taken only medicinally. So, in all the Tatar towns I have visited, the wine merchants called their establishments *balzam*, which means pharmacy. As soon as wine is sold in a pharmacy it is no longer wine. In effect, it is a medicine.

Further to obey Mohammed, the Arabs imitated the ancient Hebrews and made cider from apples and pears. St. Jerome, the first to mention cider in writing, found that it was a common drink among the Hebrews.

Pasteur's work on the fermentation of cider has shown us that its fermenting agent is none other than millions of little animalcules, or rather cryptogams, half animal, half vegetable, which perform the singular task of changing sugar into alcohol – which for them is a mere matter of digestion.

COCK. The cock is without doubt the most vigilant, glorious, and courageous of birds. One needs only watch him strut in his harem of hens to realize that he rivals the peacock in pride. He shows his vigilance by never sleeping more than two hours at a time, tearing man from his slumbers with raucous song beginning at one in the morning. Levaillant reports in his memoirs that his cock was the only animal which was undisturbed by the approach or the roar of a lion.

The cock has been mixed up in sorcery from the earliest times, and in Basle, Switzerland, the magistrates condemned a cock to death for having laid an egg.

During the First Empire, there was a question of adopting the ancient Gallic cock as armorial emblem on the French flag. But when the matter came up to the Emperor Napoleon I, he said: "I won't have it. The fox eats the cock." He chose the eagle.

In cookery, the cock is used mainly to make a consommé to which the ancient formularies attribute heroic virtues under the name of *cock jelly*.

Nevertheless, the virgin cock, celibate of the barnyard, owes to his continence and to his virtue a flavour and an aroma that highly distinguish him from his uncle the capon. He is eaten roasted on the spit, simply, barded with bacon, for it would be outrageous to lard him, and dishonourable to put him into a stew.

COD. The cod's fecundity is equal to its voracity. In a very large cod, weighing sixty to eighty pounds, up to nine million eggs have been found. It has been calculated that if nothing happened to prevent the hatching and growth of its progeny, within three years one could walk over the Atlantic Ocean on solid codfish.

The cod breeds in December off the coast of Spain and in spring off the coast of America. At this time the voracity of these fish knows no bounds. They form themselves into tight ranks and pursue their prey, especially mackerel, until millions of these are pushed right up on shore. The habitat of the cod is the banks of Newfoundland, Cape Breton, Nova Scotia, New England, Iceland, Norway, and the Dogger Bank. The cod fisheries were the first to be established by the European people. We have proof that such fisheries were organized at the beginning of the ninth century, for towards the end of it we find them well established on the coasts of Norway and Iceland. In 1368 Amsterdam had a fishery established off the coast of Sweden. According to Anderson, France sent its first fishing fleet to the banks of Newfoundland in 1536. As a matter of fact, a hundred years before Christopher Columbus' expedition, Basque fishermen hunting whale observed the abundance of cod off Newfoundland and caught them in great numbers. In 1578, France sent a fleet of 1050 fishing vessels to Newfoundland, Spain 110, Portugal fifty, and England thirty.

Boiled Fresh Cod. Prepare a court bouillon with water, salt, whole scallions, parsley sprigs, carrot scrapings, 1 clove of garlic,

2 or 3 sliced onions, thyme, bay leaf, basil, and 2 cloves. Boil these ingredients 45 minutes, skim, take off the fire, cover with a cloth, and set aside 30 to 45 minutes. Pass through a fine sieve. This bouillon can be used for anything that must be cooked in salted water.

Clean your fresh, fat cod, removing the gills and washing in fresh water. Tie up the head. Simmer in the court bouillon, never letting it quite come to a boil. Drain and serve with boiled, peeled potatoes with melted butter on the side. Cod may also be served with an oyster sauce, a white sauce with capers, or a sauce *à la bonne morue.* (Beauvilliers' recipe.)

Sauce à la Bonne Morue. Put 4 ounces of butter into a pan with 1 tablespoonful of flour, a good pinch of chopped parsley, a chopped scallion, salt, pepper, nutmeg, and 1 glass of cream or milk. Stir and boil fifteen minutes. Pour over your fish.

Fresh Cod Hamburg. Prepare a fresh, fat cod. Steam 72 oysters. Drain, reserving the juice. Make a béchamel sauce, using half this juice and half cream for liquid. Reduce the sauce until it clings to the spoon. Season with a little salt, pepper, nutmeg. Mix the oysters with it and put the mixture inside the cod. Make shallow, even cuts on the fish. Beat together 6 raw egg yolks, 5 ounces of melted butter, salt, and nutmeg. Brush the whole surface of the cod with this mixture. Sprinkle completely with bread crumbs. Baste these with melted butter. Pour 1 glass of wine on to a platter of the proper size, put your fish on and bake in a hot oven 1 hour. (From the German via the *Dictionnaire de Cuisine.*)

Lobster Sauce for Cod Hamburg. Take a large cooked lobster. Remove the meat. Crush the shells and intestines in a mortar. Add 6 ounces of butter. Put mixture into a pot on the stove and stir with a wooden spoon until all the butter is melted. Add a ladleful of good bouillon. Bring to a boil. Remove. Force through a very fine sieve into a bowl. Let the butter rise and remove it with a spoon. Add to this sauce an equal quantity of heavy cream. You will have diced the lobster meat, which you will add to the sauce, with the red butter, just before serving.

This makes a highly effective dish when carefully prepared.

Fresh Cod Italian Style. Stuff with chopped, pounded whiting and anchovies. Put into a shallow dish with butter and parsley under it. Add a bottle of white wine. Sprinkle with bread crumbs mixed with grated Parmesan cheese. Pour melted butter over. Bake. If necessary, brown under the broiler to a golden colour. Use any sauce you think fit.

Fresh Cod Norwegian Style. Cut a small fresh cod into 4 or 5 pieces. Bone it. Marinate in hot butter, lemon juice, chopped parsley, shallots, and *fines herbes*. Turn over. Bread. Pour hot butter over it. Serve with a white-wine sauce, to which add raw egg yolks and nutmeg.

Brandade.[1] Among the Provençal and Languedoc stews that have gained great favour in Paris, we must single out the salt-cod *brandade*. A restaurantkeeper at the Palais Royal made his fortune on it, and people sent down for his *brandade* constantly. Since many of our readers would no doubt be happy to make this Southern dish at home (I have not found the recipe printed anywhere, not even in the *Cuisinier Gascon*, which is strange), we shall give directions for making it, which we learned in a city of Languedoc that enjoys a well-earned reputation for good food.

Let me say first that the peculiar name *brandade* is not found or defined in any dictionary, but must derive from the old verb *brandir*, which means to stir, agitate, shake forcibly and for a long time. It is this almost continuous action which is indispensable for properly preparing this stew. This fact may prevent the general introduction of the dish into our cookery, for things that take much patience are not popular with all cooks.

Take a fine piece of salt cod and soak it 24 hours to freshen and soften it. Then bring it to a boil in fresh water and remove at once.

Put butter, oil, parsley, and garlic into a casserole and melt on a gentle fire. Meanwhile, flake the codfish into small pieces, which you put into the casserole, and stir constantly for a long time, adding oil, butter, or milk as you see it thicken. Keep on stirring until the codfish is reduced to a sort of cream. If you want to make it green, crush spinach and pour the juice into your *brandade*.

As you can see, this is a very simple recipe. But we cannot repeat too often that the perfection of a *brandade* depends above all on the long and patient stirring of the casserole, which produces the

[1] This entire article is credited by Dumas to Grimod de la Reynière.—ED.

metamorphosis of cod from a naturally coarse ingredient to a sort of cream. You must never stop stirring for a moment. If you do, you will have a béchamel, not a *brandade*.

A properly made *brandade* is a delicious dish, and although salt cod is naturally indigestible, thus transformed it becomes as easy to digest as vanilla-flavoured bread and milk.

COFFEE. Coffee grows on a low bush with scented flowers. It originated in Yemen, in Arabia Felix. Today it is grown in several countries. The Arabian historian Ahmed Effendi believes that coffee was discovered by a dervish in the thirteenth century, or the year 650 of the Hegira. The first European to speak of it is Prospero Alpino of Padua, who went to Egypt in 1580 with a consul of the Venetian Republic.

Coffee was unknown in France before 1657. But Posée-Oblé says in his *History of the Plants of Guiana*, a decoction of coffee known as *cahuet* was sold in Paris in the time of Louis XIII. The Venetians were the first to bring it to Europe, and it was introduced to France through Marseille. Its use became universal. The doctors were alarmed, but their sinister predictions were treated as fantasies. Despite their arguments, the cafés were not deserted. In 1669, when the ambassador of Mohammed V of Turkey brought a large quantity to Paris, we are told that it sold for up to forty écus (two hundred francs) a pound.

In 1676, an Armenian named Pascal opened a café at the Saint-Germain fair, later moving it to the Quai de l'École. He made a fortune for himself. At the beginning of the following century, a Sicilian named Procope re-established the café at the fair. The best company in Paris came there because he sold good merchandise. Later, he set himself up in a hall opposite the Comédie Française, which became the rendezvous of theatregoers and a battlefield for literature. Voltaire spent two hours in this café every day. In this period, more than three thousand coffeehouses were established in London. Mme de Sévigné fought against this fad with all her strength, and predicted that coffee and Racine would both be forgotten together.

Coffee had become universally accepted in France when Napoleon published his decree on the Continental system. This deprived

France, at the same time, of coffee and sugar. Beet sugar was substituted for cane sugar. Coffee was made to go further by the addition of chicory, which was fine for the grocers and cooks, who became fanatical over chicory. They claimed it made coffee taste better and was healthier besides. The unhappy part of it is that now that the decrees are no longer in effect the cooks still keep chicory on their list of staples, and still continue to mix it with ground coffee — supposedly for their employers' benefit. The employers ordered coffee purchased in the bean. But moulds were made expressly to squeeze chicory into the form of coffee beans.

Voltaire and Delisle abused coffee. But it is not a poison, as originally claimed. On the contrary, it is an antidote for the stupefying poisons. It acts rapidly on opium, belladonna, etc. It must be taken very strong, and a spoonful every five minutes.

We can give the reader excellent advice by informing him of the coffee essence sold by Trablit, the pharmacist on the Rue Jean-Jacques-Rousseau. A few drops of Trablit's essence is enough to give milk a colour and aroma that could never be obtained with ordinary coffee.

COOT. Called *lenten game* because, like teal and flamingo, it may be eaten on meatless days.

The coot is like a fish. It looks like a duck and lives out its life on the sea, plunging to the bottom for the little shellfish on which it feeds. It also eats insects, marine plants, and small fish, which contribute mightily to its flavour and aroma. The male is better eating. The female has a wild marine flavour that no seasoning can overcome. The finest cooks have been defeated in the attempt. Their best try, coot with chocolate, though a masterpiece of the art, has few admirers.

Roast Coot. Pluck and clean. Parboil. Broil on the spit, basting with butter, salt, pepper, and vinegar. Serve with *sauce Robert*, or with a mixture of the coot's liver chopped fine with mushrooms, salt, pepper, nutmeg, the whole cooked together, and the juice of an orange added before serving.

Coot with Chocolate. Clean, pluck, and parboil. Put into a pot with salt, pepper, bay leaf, a bouquet of *fines herbes*. Pour over it 1 cup of chocolate prepared as for a beverage. Cook. Prepare a mixture of the liver, mushrooms, truffles, morels, chestnuts – or some other similar mixture, if you prefer. Serve this over the coot on a platter.

CORN or FIELD SALAD. An herb eaten in salads with beets, celery, white chicory, and endive. This tender and tasty salad is the first to appear in spring.

COURT BOUILLON. A lenten bouillon for use in fish sauces. Cook together white wine, red wine, butter, fine spices, bay leaf, and *fines herbes*. Use this to cook fish in. Serve the fish with an oil-and-vinegar sauce.

Court bouillon *au bleu* is simply boiling wine in which fish is cooked to give it a fine bluish colour.

CRABS. There are many varieties of crab, but only the big Brittany crabs and the little Channel crab are fit to serve at table – and even their flesh is difficult to digest. Their eggs are better, and the Negroes in Africa find them very nourishing. The Caribs live almost exclusively on crabs.

Crabs are cooked in salted water like lobsters and crayfish, with fresh butter, parsley, and a bunch of leeks. Let them cool in their cooking liquid. Take the white meat out of the shell and mix it with the milt or roe. Add cress, coarse pepper, a little virgin oil, and a little verjuice. Garnish the dish with the big claws. This is an elegant dish, especially during Lent.

CRANE. Cranes are great destroyers of reptiles, worms, and insects, which they eat along with frogs and small fish. When they migrate from the north and east with the coming of cold weather, they gather in great flocks and choose a chieftain to lead the way. They fly in triangular formation to cleave the air more easily and, if the wind is too violent, form into circles. On the ground, they have sentinels to watch over the flock while it sleeps. Each of the sentinels, to avoid falling asleep, holds one foot in the air clutching a stone, so that the shock of its dropping would awaken them should they be overcome by fatigue.

Varro says that the Romans raised and fed cranes very carefully, and ate them because of the delicacy of their flesh. I believe, however, the reference must have been to very young cranes, because the flesh of older ones is tough, insipid, and hard to digest.

CUCUMBER. Stuffed. Peel and trim 3 or 4 cucumbers. Cut off the stem end. With a larding needle remove all the seeds. Rinse well in water with a dash of vinegar. Blanch in boiling water. Dip in cold water. Drain. Stuff with chopped white chicken meat, bread, herbs, spices, whole eggs to bind. Line the bottom of a pot with bacon and put your cucumbers on it. Season with salt, pepper, bouquet of parsley, scallions, 2 cloves. Add 1 tablespoonful of rich broth. Cover with paper. Bring to a boil. Simmer. Drain. Sauce with a sharpened, reduced espagnole.

Cucumbers à la Poulette. Blanch. Slice. Sauté in butter with a pinch of flour. Add water, salt, pepper. Cook to reduce water. Add chopped parsley and a bit of nutmeg. Thicken with egg yolks and cream. Continue to cook, but do not boil, until thickened.

CULLIS. Is prepared in advance and kept on hand to finish certain dishes whose liquids must be thickened.

First of all, your cullis should be neither too thick nor too thin. It should have a fine cinnamon colour.

Put veal fillet and diced bacon into a skillet, the proportions depending on how much cullis you want to make. Add 3 or 4 carrots and put on a low fire. When the juices have oozed out of the meat, place on a hot fire. When it is done, remove meat and vegetables, and make a *roux* in the skillet with flour and butter. Let it colour nicely. Add hot bouillon, return the meat, and simmer for 2 hours. Strain and reserve for use as needed.

Fish Cullis. Melt a piece of butter in a casserole. Slice onions and carrots and fry to a nice colour. Add water and fish with salt, pepper, nutmeg, and *bouquet garni*. When the fish is well cooked, strain and use as needed.

CURASSOW. A bird about the size of a small turkey, wild in the South American forests. These birds have a sweet nature. They congregate in great flocks in the vast forest, living on fruits and buds. The curassow is monogamous. When a female is not paired, she seeks the caresses of the first male she comes across, and lays her eggs wherever she may be, without preparing a nest. As often as not, she drops them during the evening, after she has perched for the night. But when she comes under the protection of a male, she always lays her eggs in one nest, which he prepares for her in advance.

"I must add," says M. Pomme in a letter to M. Geoffroy Saint-Hilaire, "that it is rare, at least in France, for a female to incubate. Only one of those I have been able to acquire was broody. Only five laid eggs. The sixth sought the male, and coupled frequently, but never laid. All the females I acquired were frigid during the first year after their arrival. In the second year they all coupled, but rarely laid eggs, and when they did the eggs had no shells. It was not until the fourth year that this disability disappeared completely. In the third year, there is a shell, but it is fragile and imperfect. Each female lays three times a year if it does not incubate. If it does incubate, it lays only once, generally two eggs, sometimes three. Incubation takes thirty-one or thirty-two days."

Curassows are readily domesticated. They are found in the streets of Cayenne, and knock on the door of their master's house with their beaks to be let in. They hold their master back by the coattails and follow him. If they are prevented, they wait for him and give cries of joy on his return. Their manner is proud and solemn, their flight heavy and noisy. They have a sharp cry, and when they walk along quietly they make a sort of dull, constant murmur, very deep and concentrated. This is no doubt produced by the hardness of their tracheal rings and the fact that their neck has a fold between the head and chest.

General Lafayette imported two of these birds, which became perfectly acclimatised to the environs of Paris. They were housed in a great closed-in henyard, with many chickens, and they quickly acquired the customs of the place. They ran for food whenever the ducks, turkeys, chickens, and guinea fowl were fed. They mingled with their messmates, went to pasture with them, pecked their nearest neighbours or were themselves attacked by some male bird jealous of his ancient privileges and his odalisques, furious to see these intruders not merely penetrating his seraglio but sharing his food. None of this prevented the young curassows from growing and developing wonderfully in the summer days.

The meat of the curassow is white, tender, and flavoursome. When the bird is young and has been properly fed and well prepared, our fine gourmets prefer him to young turkey, young peacock, or young guinea fowl. They are roasted like the last-mentioned, after cleaning, trussing, and larding. They take about 1 hour on the spit and should be basted with butter or lard. They are served with the juices from the dripping pan mixed with a little glaze and strained.

CURLEW. Called the sea crow because of its resemblance to the common crow. About three feet long, it is dark, almost black, with green and purple lights. It lives along the shores of lakes and feeds entirely on fish.

The curlew is a sad and sombre bird, said to bring misfortune. Its flesh has a bitter, swampy odour, which makes it very disagreeable to the taste. Be that as it may, the Mexicans who sometimes eat it find it pretty good.

DINNER. A major daily activity, which can be accomplished in worthy fashion only by intelligent people. It is not enough to eat. To dine, there must be diversified, calm conversation. It should sparkle with the rubies of the wine between courses, be deliciously suave with the sweetness of dessert, and acquire true profundity with the coffee.

DONKEY. Tastes change. We have recently seen the horse almost dethrone the steer. It would have been simple justice, for the steer had dethroned the donkey. Maecenas was the first among the

Romans to use the flesh of the domestic donkey. In Persia and Numidia there are wild asses which were once called onagers, but are now called zebras. The Persians prefer their flesh to that of the gazelle. So did their ancestors. When Shah Abbas gave a great feast for the ambassadors, thirty-two wild asses were slaughtered and served. Their meat, ordinarily reserved for the royal table, was said to be exquisite.

In the sixteenth century in France, Chancellor Duprat raised and fattened young donkeys for his table, and if the writers of the time are reliable, all his guests found them delicious. They must have been, for this meat was commonly used for a long time.

In the country of the Kalmucks I have eaten the meat of a young donkey, which seemed to me to be halfway between beef and veal, and excellent.

DUCKS AND DUCKLINGS. There are forty-two varieties of duck. One of the best is the musk duck, whose flesh is very delicate. But its rump must be cut off before cooking, or the odour of musk will be so strong the bird will be next to inedible. Barbary ducks are the biggest. They are less delicate, and prone to smell musky. But when crossed with other varieties they produce a hybrid that does not have this disadvantage. Rouen ducklings, highly esteemed for their size and other qualities, are produced in this manner. The wild duck is nearly always grilled on a spit.

The young wild duck shot at the end of August is called an *albran*. In September he becomes a duckling and is definitely a duck in October. *Albrans*, which are to an ordinary duck as a partridge is to a hen, are broiled on the spit and served on toast soaked in their own juices, to which are added the juice of bitter oranges, a little soy sauce, and some grains of fine pepper. This is a delicate, distinguished dish. It has been honoured by this gloss from the author of the *Memoirs of the Marquise de Créqui:*

"When the hunters or the purveyors furnish them in large numbers in the country, and one wants to make an entree of them, they may be made into salmis, served over an olive ragout or on mushroom caps in béchamel sauce. We cannot agree that they may be cooked with turnips, as the *Almanach des Gourmands* advises. This is too vulgar an accompaniment for *albrans*, wild ducklings, or even wild ducks. It is suitable only for farmyard ducks and ducklings. We follow rather the precept and decision of M. Brillat-Savarin:

" 'Preparation of this noble game with such a vegetable would be an unsuitable and even an insulting procedure, a monstrous alliance, degradation, and dishonour.' "

Wild Duck on the Spit. Before buying a duck, examine it carefully. The webs of the feet should have a good colour and not be dried out. To tell whether it is freshly killed, open the beak and make sure there is no bad odour. Feel the rump and the belly. They should be firm. The duck should feel heavy in the hand. If it has all these qualities, buy it. I have noticed that the females are more delicate than the males, though the latter generally cost more.

Pluck and singe your duck. Cut off the neck. Cut off the wings close to the body. Eviscerate. Truss up the feet close to the body and rub them with the duck's liver. Put the ducks on the spit and broil them rare. Serve with two whole lemons.

Ducks with Sauerkraut. Boil sauerkraut in bouillon with little fresh sausages, dry sausage, and lightly salted bacon, cubed. When your sauerkraut is half cooked, remove this garnish and substitute your trussed duck. To serve, surround the duck with sauerkraut and decorate this with the sausages and bacon.

Duckling Sticks. Split a duckling in half and bone each half. Spread on each a dressing made of cooked poultry, suet, blanched bacon, parsley, scallions, mushrooms, a clove of garlic, salt, and pepper, the whole chopped and mixed with 4 egg yolks. Roll each piece and wrap in several thicknesses of cheesecloth, tying each end so it will retain its shape. Braise with vegetables. Serve with lemon juice.

Duckling with Fines Herbes. Blanch a duckling and flatten the breast with the side of a cleaver. Sauté in fat. Into a pot put veal, ham, parsley, chopped mushrooms, and melted lard. On this lay your duckling, breast down. Cover with bacon slices and braise. Add cullis to the gravy, strain, season, and add the juice of an orange.

Wild Duck with Cardoons. Clean, truss, put on the spit, wrap in buttered paper. Two minutes before they are ready to take off the spit, remove the paper. Put into a pot, with 4 tablespoonfuls of white wine and a similar amount of liquid glaze. Reduce the liquid by half. Untruss the birds and arrange on a platter with a garnish of cardoon stalks and leaf ribs with espagnole sauce. Pour sauce made as above over all and serve.

Wild Duck with Orange Sauce. Clean and truss 4 wild ducks. Skewer and roast over a lively fire 12 to 14 minutes, brushing them with oil in the process. Salt, slice off the breasts, and lay them in a flat pan with a little glaze on the bottom. Heat for 1 minute to dry the moisture from the breasts. Arrange on a platter and pour over them the following sauce:

Orange Sauce. Take the zest of an unripe orange. Cut it into julienne strips, cook in water, and drain in a sieve. Then put them into a little pot and pour over them 1 glass of clear, reduced aspic. Heat. Just before serving, thin the sauce with the juices of 1 lemon and 1 orange.

Wild Duck Régence. Truss, lard with thick bacon strips, brown in lard with a little flour to thicken, or half roast on the spit. Put in a pot with good bouillon, salt, pepper, fine spices, *fines herbes* in a cloth. Simmer. When half done, add sliced turnips heated in a *roux* and about 1 glass of good wine. When the ragout is done and the sauce thickened sufficiently, serve hot.

Another Method. Make a forcemeat of veal sweetbreads, mushrooms, wild duck meat, scallions, parsley, salt, and pepper, and cook. Stuff your ducks with this forcemeat, roast on the spit, and serve with a cullis containing mushrooms. Or with the following sauce:

Boil 2 glasses of wine, 2 or 3 slices of onion, clove, and a little pepper. When it is reduced to half, strain, add beef gravy, heat, pour over the duck.

Wild Duck with Cauliflower. Roast your ducks on the spit. Cook cauliflower florets in flour, water, salt, and a bit of butter. Drain. Take a good game essence, add butter and coarse pepper, heat, and stir well on the stove. Arrange the ducks on a platter with the cauliflower around them, pour the sauce over the cauliflower, and serve hot.

Wild Duck with Turnips. Roast as above, or else lard the ducks with seasoned strips of bacon and braise in a pot with bacon, sliced beef, onions, carrots, parsley, sliced lemon, *fines herbes*, pepper, salt, and clove over and under the ducks.

Peel turnips and carve them in olive shape; brown lightly in lard. Drain. Simmer with good gravy; stir in a good cullis. Arrange your ducks on a platter and pour the turnip ragout over them. Serve hot.

Wild Duck with Olives. Roast or braise the ducks as above. Cook 2 or 3 little mushrooms in good meat broth, then add a good clear veal-and-ham cullis. Pit some olives, plunge into boiling water, drain. Add to the mushrooms. Let them come to a boil. Pour over the ducks on a platter. Serve hot.

Wild ducks are sometimes erroneously associated with lentils in cookery. This is an unpardonable profanation.

EAGLE. The size, nobility, and pride of the king of birds do not give it a tender and delicate flesh. Everyone knows it is tough, fibrous, and evil-tasting and that the Jews are forbidden to eat it.

Let us leave it to soar and defy the sun, but eat it not.

EEL. The Egyptians set eels among the gods and worshipped them. They raised them in ponds, and special priests were charged with feeding them daily on cheese and entrails. They decorated them with jewelled collars.

Athenaeus calls the eel the daughter of Jupiter. One seeks in vain to discover how an animal that lives in the mire, where it breathes noisome gases that sometimes make it poisonous, could acquire such a genealogy.

Everyone knows that these animals have such an affinity for the mire that when ponds are emptied they bury themselves in it and are persuaded to leave it only by firing guns to frighten them. Those which are extracted from this domicile reek of it. This inconvenience can be overcome by putting them, alive, for three days and nights in a basin with running water or simply in a bucket filled with spring water into which you throw salt and barley soaked in red wine. The same can be done with carp when they have a swamplike odour.

Generally, our cooks make an incision around the eels' necks and pull their skins off. It is better first to lay them on a brazier of live coals, so that the skin swells and folds. The charred skin can then be removed with a cloth, pulling from head to tail. This eliminates the skin oil and improves the eel as to both flavour and digestibility.

Eel on the Spit. Skin as above. Cut off the head and the tip of the tail. Clean by making two incisions, one at the throat, the other under the tail, and poking the thick end of a wooden skewer through, from the throat down. Make sure nothing is left inside. Cut off the head, the end of the tail, and the fins. Skewer and tie it in the shape of a ring with string. Put into a pot and pour mirepoix sauce over it. Cook until half done. Drain. Wrap and put it on the spit. Roast. Unwrap, remove string and skewers. Glaze. Put on a round platter and serve with a brown italienne or a ravigote sauce.

Matelote of Eel Marinière. Take a Seine carp, an eel, a tench, a perch, and cut them in pieces. Slice 2 large onions. Put the onions on the bottom of a copper pot, then all the heads, then the body pieces, so the pieces from nearest the tail are on top. Season with salt, pepper, a *bouquet garni*, and a few cloves of garlic. Pour over all 2 bottles of white wine. Bring to a quick boil. Add 1 glass of cognac and flame. Add 20 or 30 little onions fried in butter. Make little balls of flour and butter and sprinkle into your matelote. Shake to mix well. Serve hot, garnished with croutons and crayfish cooked in Rhine wine. (Vuillemot's recipe.)

Matelote of Eel with Eggs and Carp Roe. I have often observed gastronomes deeply preoccupied while eating a matelote made with carp, tench, and other fish. This preoccupation arises from fear of strangling. One can't even dip one's bread in the sauce, good as it is, for fear a hidden fishbone will reveal itself in one's oesophagus. I'm going to make a simple suggestion. Make your matelote out of ingredients that don't have bones – that is, out of eels, whose bones are negligible, out of eggs, and out of milt or roe. The preparations are the same. The 20 or 30 little onions fried in butter are just as important. The seasoning is the same. But you will fry 4 or 5 eggs in a pan that lets them spread out as widely as possible. These you will place in the bottom of your serving dish. On top of that, with a fork, place the pieces of eel, the roe and the milt. Pour the sauce over. Float a small glass of rum or brandy over the whole, flame, and serve hot.

EGGS. Hen's eggs are those most commonly used for human consumption.

"It is obvious," says M. Payen, "that this alimentary substance contains all the principles indispensable to the formation of animal tissue, since it is sufficient, without addition of other food, for the germination and growth of a little animal composed of muscle, tendons, bones, skin, etc."

When eggs are fresh, we won't say the only way, but certainly the best way, to eat them is boiled in their shells. They lose nothing of their delicacy. The yellow is tasty, the white is milky, and if you have been sufficiently sybaritic to cook them in bouillon, and if they are neither overdone nor underdone, you are eating egg at the height of its perfection.

To some people an egg is an egg. This is an error. Two eggs laid at the same moment, one by a hen that runs loose in the garden, the other by one that feeds in the henyard, can be utterly different in flavour.

I am one of those who insist that my egg be put in cold water and slowly brought to a boil. In this manner, the whole egg is uniformly cooked. Otherwise, if an egg is dropped into boiling water it is likely to break, and the white might be hard and the yolk uncooked.

Poached Eggs. Here is the recipe from the *Cuisinier Imperial de 1808*, repeated in the *Cuisinier Royal de 1839*. You are free to adopt for your own:

Have 15 poached eggs drained and placed on a platter. At the same time have 12 ducks, almost done, roasted on the spit. Take the ducks off the spit, cut them to the bone, drain off their juices, season juice with salt and coarse pepper. Reheat but do not boil, and pour over the poached eggs.

Poached Eggs without Duck Juice. Bring salted and vinegared water to a boil in a shallow pan. Break your eggs into it gently without breaking the yolks. When they have reached the desired consistency, remove them and trim off any portion of the white that may have spread too wide and thin. Only the freshest eggs poach well. Poached eggs are served, in a platter, over hot gravy.

Scrambled Eggs. Melt butter in a shallow pan; break your eggs into it; add salt, pepper, nutmeg; stir. Just before serving, add a drop of lemon juice or verjuice.

Scrambled eggs with asparagus are made the same way. Add cooked asparagus tips after mixing the eggs with the butter.

Gravy or bouillon may be added to eggs while scrambling.

If by good fortune you have sautéed kidneys with champagne sauce at the same meal, take 4 or 5 tablespoonfuls of the sauce and mix into your eggs while scrambling.

If by extra good fortune you also have chicken broth, add half of this and half of the kidney sauce. You will then have eggs prepared in the most delicate and delicious fashion possible.

Fried Eggs. To fry eggs you can use butter, lard, or oil. Butter is best. Fried oil always has an unpleasant flavour.

Heat butter until it starts to brown. Break 5, 6, or 8 eggs into a plate. When the butter begins to sputter, slip the eggs into the pan, taking care not to break the yolks. Sprinkle with salt, pepper, and a few chopped chives. Fry the eggs to a good colour, slip from the pan on to a platter. Pour a little tarragon vinegar into your buttered pan, heat, add a handful of chopped parsley, and pour over the eggs.

Eggs au Gratin. Mix white bread crumbs, butter, a chopped anchovy, parsley, shallots, 3 egg yolks, salt, coarse pepper, and nutmeg. Sprinkle nutmeg on a platter that can be used for cooking and spread the mixture evenly on it. Heat over a slow fire. Break a chosen number of eggs over this. Cook gently. Pass under the grill to set the egg whites. When they are done, sprinkle with salt, pepper, and nutmeg.

Mirrored Eggs. Cover the bottom of a platter with salted butter, break your eggs into it side by side, taking care not to break the yolks. Sprinkle with 4 or 5 tablespoonfuls of cream. Dot with butter. Sprinkle with salt, coarse pepper, grated nutmeg. Put over heat but finish quickly under the broiler to set the whites without hardening the yolks.

Eggs à la Pauvre Femme. Break 12 eggs into melted butter in a shallow pan. Dice crustless bread and fry in butter to a light golden colour. Drain. Sprinkle over the eggs. Bake. Before serving, pour over them a reduced espagnole sauce. Serve with tender ham or with kidneys.

Eggs with Basil. Hard-boil 12 eggs. Peel. Cut in halves lengthwise. Remove the yolks and mash with chopped parsley, garlic, scallions, basil, cooked mushrooms. Mix thoroughly with bread soaked in cream and then squeezed out, a good piece of butter, salt, pepper, and 6 raw egg yolks. Cover the bottom of an oven platter with this mixture. Fill the eggs and pile the mixture on to make each half egg as large as a whole egg. Lay these on the platter, sprinkle with soft bread crumbs, and bake to a nice colour. When done, drain off the butter, wipe off the edges of the platter, and serve.

The proportion of butter, bread, and hard-boiled yolks in the mixture above should be equal. Other flavourings may be used for the stuffing. White veal sauce mixed with extra-heavy cream may be poured over before serving.

Eggs Béchamel. Heat 4 or 5 tablespoonfuls of béchamel sauce. Slice 15 hard-boiled eggs into it. Do not let boil, but heat thoroughly. Finish with butter and nutmeg. Arrange on a platter and surround with croutons.

Eggs with Mushrooms. Poach 8 fresh eggs in water. Take a quantity of mushrooms, dice, cook in water with a piece of butter mixed with flour, a bouquet of parsley and scallions, and a little salt. When they are cooked and the sauce reduced sufficiently, thicken with cream and 4 egg yolks. Add the juice of 1 lemon. Serve around the poached eggs.

Eggs with Crayfish. Make a ragout of crayfish, truffles, mushrooms, and a few cut-up artichoke bottoms, cooking them in fish bouillon and butter. Season with salt, pepper, and a bouquet of *fines herbes*. Skim off the extra butter, mix with a crayfish cullis. Poach your eggs in boiling water and trim well. Arrange on a platter.

Check your ragout for seasoning and pour it over the eggs. Serve very hot.

Eggs Tarragon. Blanch tarragon and chop very fine; add to eggs in a bowl with salt, pepper, and 1 glass of cream. From this make 3 small omelets, which arrange on a platter. Sauce with a *roux* of flour and butter, a little bouillon, 1 glass of wine, seasoning, simmered and passed through a sieve.

Eggs Parmesan. Beat your eggs with grated Parmesan cheese, salt, pepper. Make 5 little omelets, which sprinkle with Parmesan, roll, and arrange on a platter. Sprinkle with Parmesan, wipe off the clear part of the platter, and put in the oven to glaze the cheese. This should not take more than 15 minutes. It is important that this dish be served very hot.

Eggs à la Philippsburg. Make forcemeat with finely chopped and mashed cooked fish or meat, and line the bottom of the platter you will use for serving. Break your eggs over this as for mirrored eggs (above). No salt is necessary. Sprinkle with grated Parmesan. Cook on the stove. Pass under the grill at the last moment to glaze the Parmesan, but not long enough to harden the egg yolks.

Eggs en Filets. Take 2 onions and 2 mushrooms. Cut into strips. Put into a skillet with butter and toss. Add a pinch of flour, stir. Add 1 glass of champagne, broth, and cullis. Simmer. Hard-boil 12 eggs. Keep the yolks intact. Cut the whites into strips and heat in the mixture, seasoning with salt and coarse pepper. When ready to serve, add the whole yolks to heat through. The sauce should not be too thin.

Eggs Père Douillet. Break 7 eggs into a bowl, mix with 1 tablespoonful of veal gravy, 1 tablespoonful of reduced cullis, 1 tablespoonful of consommé, salt, and pepper. Pass through a sieve ¼ hour before you are ready to serve. Heat your serving platter moderately, pour your eggs on it, cook under the broiler at a sufficient distance. Do not overcook; serve still trembling.

Eggs over Eggs. Take 4 eggs. Separate and set the whites aside. Chop a few capers, 2 anchovies, parsley, and scallions and mix with the yolks. Brush your serving platter well with melted butter. Break 6 other eggs on it. Beat the 4 egg whites. Add the egg yolks mixed with capers and anchovies and beat again, adding salt, coarse pepper, and nutmeg. Pour this over the eggs in the platter. Put in a very hot oven. The eggs should not harden. It takes only a few moments to cook them.

Eggs à la Paysanne. Bring ½ pint of heavy cream to a boil in a platter, break 8 eggs into it, and season with salt and coarse pepper. As they begin to cook, put under the broiler. Take care the yolks do not harden, and serve immediately.

Eggs with Liver. Take chicken, goose, duck, or game-fowl livers. Chop. Sauté lightly in butter with parsley, scallions, mushrooms, and garlic, all finely chopped. Let cool. Mix thoroughly and beat with 12 eggs seasoned with salt, fine spices, and 1 tablespoonful of cream. Make an omelet from this mixture.

Omelet with Fines Herbes. Beat your eggs thoroughly with chopped parsley, tarragon, and chives. Add ½ glass of cream and beat again. Pour into hot butter in a skillet. Constantly bring the egg to the centre allowing the liquid to flow to the sides to cook, but take care the omelet is of even thickness, and on the semiliquid side. Remove to a buttered platter sprinkled with fresh *fines herbes*. Serve drooling. (Excuse the expression. Each art has its own language, which is essential to communication among its practitioners.)

Omelet with Mushrooms and Cream. Make a ragout by cooking diced mushrooms in butter. Cool. Beat your eggs with salt and chopped parsley. Mix a few cooked mushrooms with the eggs and make an omelet. Thicken the mushroom ragout over heat with egg yolks and cream and serve over the omelet.

Similar omelets can be made using creamed morels, creamed green peas, creamed asparagus tips, artichoke bottoms, creamed white truffles, black truffles, spinach or sorrel.

Arabian Omelet. I have been concerned in this book to give recipes of peoples who have no true cuisine. Here, for example, is a recipe the Bey's cook was good enough to give me.

Thanks to import houses, which are so numerous even in secondary cities, ostrich eggs are available almost everywhere now. They sell at one franc each today, and each ostrich egg is good for ten hen's eggs.

Here is how to make an Arabian omelet:

Chop 1 onion and 1 sweet pepper (previously put on the grill and the skin removed) and sauté gently in ½ glass of olive oil, but not sufficiently to colour the onion. Add 2 big tomatoes (peeled, seeded, and cut into little pieces), salt, and a touch of cayenne. Reduce the juice of the tomatoes, set aside, and add 8 anchovy fillets.

Rub the bottom of a bowl with garlic. Pierce both ends of an ostrich egg and blow the contents into the bowl. Season and beat well. Put ½ glass of olive oil into an omelet pan, heat, and pour in the egg. When the omelet has thickened, add the sauce described above, turn over the omelet, and 2 seconds later slide out on to a round platter.

Kirsch Omelet. Beat 6 eggs in a bowl with a pinch of salt, 3 tablespoonfuls of sugar and 1 of kirsch. Make an omelet of this. Roll. Set on a long platter. Sprinkle with powdered sugar. Make whatever pattern your fancy dictates on the omelet with a hot poker. Heat ¼ glass of kirsch, mix with 3 tablespoonfuls of apricot jam, and pour into the platter around the omelet.

Rum Omelet. As above, using rum instead of kirsch.

Oyster Omelet. Steam open oysters. Fry two thirds of them in butter. Add a little of their juice, pepper, and a little cullis. The oysters must not be too well done, for this dish must have a delicate flavour.

Break your eggs and season with salt and chopped parsley. Add a few croutons. Hit the remaining oysters 3 or 4 times with a knife and add to the eggs with a little cream. Beat together. Fry as an omelet. Turn over into a round platter big enough to surround the omelet with the separately prepared oysters. Pour the juice over the omelet. Serve hot.

Omelet with Apples. Put into a bowl 2 tablespoonfuls of flour, mix in a bit of salt and 1 tablespoonful of sugar, 2 whole eggs, 2 extra yolks, 3½ ounces of melted butter. Mix this with ¾ glass of tepid milk, and put through a sieve.

Peel and slice 6 russet apples and sauté in 5 ounces of butter. As soon as they are really hot, pour the above mixture over them, spreading both evenly. Keep on the fire, lifting here and there to let the liquid run under and cook. When the omelet becomes detached from sides and bottom when the skillet is shaken, lift it to put fresh butter underneath. Sprinkle the surface with brown sugar. Turn the whole omelet over with the aid of a plate, slip back into the skillet, and put on a hot fire to glaze the sugar. The moment to take it off by turning on to a platter must be nicely judged. If you take it off too soon, slip it under the broiler to perfect the glazing. Serve on a platter with an overturned plate in the middle so the omelet will have a thick, rounded appearance. (Recommended by Urbain-Dubois, cook to His Majesty the King of Prussia, for those who like their dishes very simple.)

EGGPLANT. The white and the purple are the best. They may be eaten either as salad or cooked. Here are the best ways to prepare them:

Eggplant à la Languedocienne. Split your eggplant lengthwise. Remove the seeds. Cut up the flesh into small pieces and sprinkle with salt, pepper, and nutmeg. Grill over moderate heat and sprinkle with fine oil.

Eggplant Salad à la Provençale. Peel and slice, macerate for 2 hours in vinegar flavoured with salt, pickled-walnut brine, black pepper, and a little garlic. Press the slices and use in a salad with water cress, radishes, stuffed olives, hard-boiled eggs, and a few slices of tuna.

Eggplant Parisienne. Cut in half and remove the flesh from 2 purple eggplants, leaving the skin of each half intact. Chop the flesh with white chicken meat or roast lamb, or lean suckling pig, or any other well-cooked white meat. Add 5 ounces of marrow, or, if you prefer, season with a pinch of nutmeg, 5 ounces of bacon, and a little salt. Add white bread, crumbed, mixed with the yolks of 5 eggs. Chop and mix all well together. Fill the eggplant skins and bake in an open dish, basting with marrow or bacon fat.

ELEPHANT. Let the reader be unafraid. He is not condemned to eat a whole elephant. But next time he finds himself in possession of the trunk or feet of an elephant, we ask him to prepare them as we shall indicate, and let us know how he likes them.

Today, Cochin China is probably the only country where elephants are eaten, and their flesh is considered a great delicacy there. When the king has one killed for his table, he sends pieces to his grandees as a mark of special favour. But the parts that are most esteemed are the trunk and feet. Levaillant says they make an exquisite dish. "The broiled feet," he adds, "are a dish for a king. I could not have imagined that so heavy an animal could provide so delicate a dish. I gobbled my elephant's foot without bread."

We are indebted for the following recipe to M. Duglerez of the House of Rothschild:

Take 1 or more feet of young elephant, skin them, and bone them after soaking in warm water for 4 hours. Cut them into 4 pieces lengthwise and once across. Parboil for 15 minutes. Dip in fresh water and dry with a cloth.

On the bottom of a heavy pot with a tight lid put 2 slices of Bayonne ham, then your pieces of elephant foot, then 4 onions, a head of garlic, some Indian aromatic spices, $\frac{1}{2}$ bottle of Madeira and 3 ladlefuls of bouillon. Cover tightly and simmer for 10 hours. Remove the fat. Add 1 glass of port and 50 little green pimentos blanched in boiling water to preserve their colour.

The sauce should be well flavoured and very sharp.

The Indians don't go to all this bother. They are not so well initiated into the mysteries of high-class cooking as we are. They simply wrap the feet in leaves and cook them in the hot coals.

ÉMINCÉ. Slices of roast meat prepared as a ragout. *Émincé* of mutton should be served on creamed endive: *émincé* of roebuck on mushroom purée; *émincé* of roast beef on a *sauce piquante; émincé* of boiled beef is called *miroton*.

ENTREES. Hot dishes served with or after the soup.

ENTREMETS. (Side dishes) Preparations such as vegetables, cooked creams, and certain pastries, served with the roast.

ESSENCE. Game. Take 1 pound of beef, 2 partridges, 2 wild rabbits, and 1 veal shank. Put into a heavy pot with 1 pint of wine and boil until the wine is completely reduced. Add another pint of white wine, onions, carrots, wild thyme, cloves, basil. Boil. Skim. Strain.

Vegetable Essence. Put 4 pounds of beef, 1 old hen, and 1 veal knuckle into a big pot with 24 to 36 carrots, onions, and turnips, 2 or 3 heads of lettuce, chervil, bunch of celery, cloves. Fill with bouillon and treat like consommé. When the meats are cooked, strain the essence and reduce if necessary.

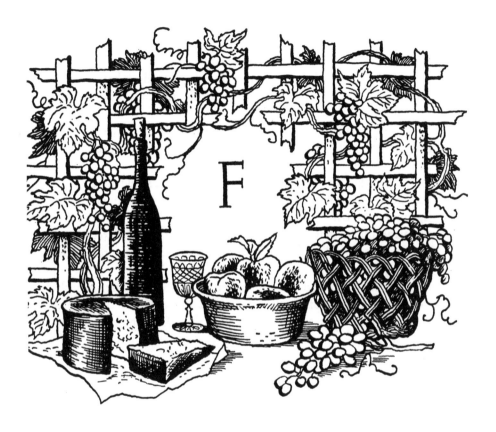

FALCON. A bird of prey, trained and used for hunting before the invention of firearms. I have eaten roasted falcon. It had a strong flavour, but not bad.

FENNEL. A very aromatic umbelliferous plant, whose seeds have an odour of anise. Fennel is eaten like celery, especially in central Italy. It is not unusual to come across people with a head of fennel under one arm, munching it with bread for lunch or dinner. The odour, at first agreeable, becomes disagreeable when fennel is used too freely, as it is, for example, by the Neapolitans, who put it into everything.

FIG. In spite of the reputation of Argenteuil for its figs, there are really no good figs grown in France except in the South. The figs of Marseille are second only to those of Capodimonte and of Sicily, which are second to none. They are eaten fresh or dried.

Everyone who has travelled in Italy knows that the worst insult to a Milanese is to show him your thumb protruding between two fingers — to "fig" him. This aversion for the fig dates back to events reported by Rabelais as follows:

"The Milanese, having revolted against Frederick, chased the empress, his wife, from the city, making her ride on an old mule, facing the tail.

"Frederick, having reconquered the city and made all the rebels prisoners, thought up the idea of having his executioner insert a fig under the tail of the same mule, and demanding from each of the vanquished that he remove it, present it to the executioner, saying '*Ecco il fico!*' and then replace it. The penalty for refusal was hanging.

"Several preferred to hang rather than submit to such humiliation, but the fear of death determined the action of the greater number. From this comes the fury of the Milanese when anyone 'figs' them."

FIGPECKER. "For flavour, the figpecker, like the quail and the ortolan, wrapped in buttered paper and roasted in the ashes, leaves nothing to be desired" (Vuillemot).

"Among small birds, the first, par excellence and without contradiction, is the figpecker. It fattens at least as well as the robin and the ortolan. In addition, nature has endowed it with a slight bitterness and a unique aroma so exquisite that it mingles with and beatifies all the digestive powers. If a figpecker were the size of a pheasant, it would sell for the price of at least two acres of land" (Brillat-Savarin).

"Few people," Brillat-Savarin continues, "know how to eat small birds like figpeckers, ortolans, warblers, and robins. Here is the method given to me by Canon Charcot, a born gourmand, being a canon, who by strenuous study raised himself to the status of a gastronome.

"First remove the gizzard. Then take a very fat little bird by the beak, sprinkle it with salt and pepper. Drop it into your mouth without touching it with teeth or lips, bite off close to your fingers, and chew vigorously. An abundance of juice will flow and envelop your mouth, and you will taste a pleasure unknown to the herd."

King Ferdinand of Naples, a great hunter and gourmand, built a château that cost him five million on the hill of Capodimonte, because migrating figpeckers killed themselves by striking the cliff in their flight. There were standing orders that, whenever this happened, the King was to be notified, no matter where he might be, even in council.

The day the council was debating the question of war with France, which the Queen wanted and the King did not, he attended, fully determined to set a vigorous veto to this unfortunate bluster. But no sooner had the discussion been opened than word was brought that the figpeckers had been beating themselves against the cliff at Capodimonte. The King tried to keep himself firmly in hand, but he was unsuccessful.

"Do what you want," he said, rising and leaving the council room, "and go to the devil."

War was declared, and the figpeckers, which had already cost him five million, came close to costing the King his throne.

[**FINE SPICES.** *A mixture of finely ground spices and herbs. A typical combination might be* 10 *parts of white pepper,* 6 *of pimento,* 2 *of mace, and* 1 *each of nutmeg, cinnamon, clove, bay leaf, sage, rosemary, and marjoram. Often mixed with salt. –* ED.]

[**FINES HERBES.** *Parsley, chives, chervil, tarragon, or any* 2 *or* 3*, or sometimes just the parsley, chopped fine. A bouquet of* fines herbes *would be the same herbs tied in a bundle. –* ED.]

FOOD. What is food?

Any substance that, being put into the stomach, is assimilable through digestion and renews the losses of the human body.

So the first quality of food is ease of digestion. From this the epigraph of our book:

"Man does not live on what he eats but on what he digests."

The three kingdoms of nature contribute to feeding man, the vegetable and animal kingdoms more abundantly than the mineral, which provides only seasoning and remedies. Even the air has a more or less nourishing principle, according to whether it is cold or hot.

It is generally believed that humanity originated in India, so charged with nutritive principles is the Indian air. The fitness and vigour of butchers are attributed to the emanations of fresh meat that continually envelop them.

Democritus lived three days without eating and without feeling hunger, just by breathing in the smell of warm bread.

Viterby, a Corsican condemned to death by a jury at Bastia, decided to die of hunger. But, sustained by the nourishing air of his country, he did not die until the forty-eighth day. It is true that on the forty-third, unable to resist the tortures of thirst, he drank half a glass of water.

[**FOUR ROOTS.** *Beets, carrots, parsnips, turnips.* — ED.]

[**FOUR SPICES.** *A mixture of four spices ground together. A typical mixture might be:* 10 *parts of cinnamon,* 10 *parts of nutmeg,* 10 *parts of black pepper,* 3 *parts of cloves. Another common formula calls for* 4 *ounces of white pepper,* ½ *ounce of cloves,* 1 *ounce of ginger, and* 1¼ *ounces of nutmeg.* — ED.]

FRANGIPANE. A sort of cream frequently used to garnish pastries. It is named after its inventor, Don Cesare Frangipani, descendant of the famous Frangipanis who were always ready to break their bread (*frangere panem*) for charity.

FRICANDEAU. Larded and glazed fillets or slices, especially of veal.

Old-fashioned Fricandeau. An old recipe that is better than any current one. Most cooks put too much bouillon in their fricandeau, with the result that it has no flavour — which prompted Beaumarchais to say:

> *Dans vos restaurants nouveaux,*
> *Tous vos plats sont suprêmes,*
> *Et pourtant les fricandeaux*
> *Sont toujours les mêmes.*

[In your new restaurants, all your dishes are supreme, but just the same the fricandeaux remain the same as ever.]

There are fricandeaux and there are fricandeaux, as the following method of preparation will show.

Take the eye from a very white leg of veal. Trim it and lard it. Butter the bottom of your casserole, line it with a good mirepoix — carrots, large onions in rings, a *bouquet garni* — and add the veal. Stew to evaporate all moisture from the meat, then add consommé — just enough to reach but not cover your larding. Cook gently in the oven, basting frequently. Strain the liquid and reduce it, using it to glaze the veal; what is left over, use to flavour the sorrel or chicory you will use for garnish. (Vuillemot.)

Fricandeau of Sturgeon, Pike, or Salmon. Cut your fish into slices a little over 1¼ inches thick. Trim and lard. Dip into flour, then put them into a pot, the larded side down, over melted bacon. Brown lightly and remove from the fire. Chop up truffles and arrange them on a platter around your fricandeaux. Baste with ham stock, cover with another platter, and cook gently for 1 hour.

FROG. There are many varieties of frogs, differing in size, colour, and habitat. Sea frogs are monstrous and are not used for food. Neither are land frogs. Only aquatic frogs are good to eat. They must be caught in very clear, fresh water, and should be fat, fleshy, green with black spots.

In the Middle Ages many physicians were against using this meat for food, though it is white and delicate and contains a gelatinous ingredient that is less nourishing than that of other meats. Bernard Palissy, in his treatise on stones in 1580, put it this way: "And in my time, I have seen very few men who would eat either turtles or frogs."

Nevertheless, frogs were served on the best tables in the sixteenth century, and Champier complained of what he called a bizarre taste. A hundred years ago, an Auvergnat named Simon made quite a fortune in Paris fattening frogs sent from his countryside and selling them to the finest houses, where they were very much the mode.

In Italy and Germany, great quantities of these batrachians are eaten. The markets are full of them. Englishmen, who hold them in abhorrence, and sixty years ago caricatured the French as frog-eaters, should read a passage in the *History of Dominica*, by an Englishman named Thomas Atwood.

"The frogs, called by the French *crapaux*," he says, "are very numerous in Dominica, and are an article of food to both the French and the English, many of whom prefer the *crapaux* to chickens. They make fricassees and soup of them, and the latter is recommended to sick people, especially in consumptive cases."

Frog Soup. Take the number of frogs required and bone the legs. Choose the largest and marinate with verjuice, salt, and *fines herbes*. Dip into batter and fry in butter to a good colour. They will serve as garnish all around your soup. With the rest of the boned legs make a ragout, with milt, mushrooms, and other garnishings, in water and flour. After cooking, cover with good bouillon, and serve garnished with the fried legs.

Frog legs may also be skinned, leaving the backbone to attach them, and prepared like chicken fricassee.

FRYING. Action of cooking meats, fish, or vegetables in butter, oil, or lard. Oil heats to at least twice the degree of water. Such heat would quickly desiccate most substances, were not the precaution taken to bread them, dip them into batter, or similarly protect them from the caloric action.

Brillat-Savarin might have said of the frying cook what he said of the roasting cook: "One becomes a cook, but one is born a roasting cook." His frying cook received special instructions from him. He himself tells, with his usual wit, about the lecture he gave Master Laplanche, his cook, one day. The professor sat in the great armchair he devoted to meditation before calling before him those to whom he needed to give counsel or reproaches.

This day the gastronomic judge prepared himself with suitable solemnity for his recital. His right leg was vertical to the floor, his left forming an irreproachable diagonal. His back was straight, and his hands rested on the lion heads terminating the arms of the venerable chair from which he held court. His high forehead indicated his love of serious study, his mouth his taste for pleasant distractions. His air was composed, his pose sculptural.

Master Laplanche [said the professor in a grave tone that went to the very heart of his audience of one], all who sit at my table acclaim you a first-class soup cook. This is very good, because soup is the first consolation of the needy stomach. But I note with distress that you are still only an indifferent frying cook.

Yesterday, I heard you sigh over that sole triomphale which you served limp, pale, and discoloured. My friend Récamier glanced at you with disapproval. M. Richerand turned his pointed nose westerly. And President Séguier deplored this accident as he would a public disaster.

This misfortune has befallen us from our neglect of theory, the full importance of which you do not realize. You are a bit opinionated, Master Laplanche, and I find it difficult to convey to you that the phenomena that occur in your laboratory are nothing else than the laws of nature in action; that certain things that you do without thinking, and simply because you have seen others do them, none the less derive from the highest scientific thought. Listen carefully now, and absorb what you hear, so you will never again have to blush for your work.

The liquids you expose to the action of fire cannot all absorb equal amounts of heat, nature having arranged them differently. This is an order of nature whose secrets we do not know, but which we call caloric capacity.

For example. You could dip your finger into boiling spirits of wine with impunity. If it were brandy, you would pull it out quickly, and with even greater alacrity if it were water. And an immersion of the shortest duration in boiling oil would wound you cruelly, for oil will reach a temperature at least three times that of water. It is for this reason that different liquids act differently on foods plunged into them. Those which are treated with boiling water soften, dissolve, and are reduced to porridge. Bouillons are extracts thus produced. Those which are treated with oil, on the contrary, harden, darken in colour, and end by carbonizing. In the first case, the water dissolves and extracts the juices of the foods plunged into it. In the second, the juices are preserved because they are not soluble in oil, and if the food becomes dry it is because the continued application of heat vaporizes its liquid portions.

The two methods have different names. The action of boiling food in oil or fat is called frying. I believe I have told you already that for kitchen purposes oil and fat are almost synonymous, fat being a solidified oil, and oil a liquid fat.

Fried foods are well received at banquets. They introduce a piquant variation, are pleasant to look at, retain their original flavour, and may be eaten by hand, which always pleases the ladies.

Frying gives the cook, if need be, plenty of means to disguise what has appeared on the table the previous day. It also provides means to meet emergencies, since it takes no longer to fry a carp than to boil an egg.

The major element in good frying is surprise. That is what we call the sudden immersion in the boiling fat or oil, which at the moment of contact carbonizes or scorches the exterior of the body plunged into it.

Surprise creates a sort of vault to contain the object, prevent the fat from penetrating it, and concentrate the juices, which consequently are submitted to an interior cooking that retains the full flavour of the food.

For surprise to be effective, the boiling liquid must be hot enough so that its action will be sudden and instantaneous. But to reach this point it must be heated a long time over a very hot fire.

The following method is used to ascertain whether your oil or fat has reached the correct temperature. Cut a piece of bread the size and shape used for dipping into soft-boiled eggs, and dip it into your pot for five or six seconds. If it comes out firm and well coloured, use the fat for frying immediately. Otherwise, stoke your fire and try again.

Once you have effected your surprise, damp your fire so that the cooking will not be too hasty, to give the juices that you have enclosed within the food opportunity to cook long enough to suffer those changes which unite them and heighten the flavour.

You will no doubt have observed that the surface of well-fried objects cannot dissolve either sugar or salt, which, however, they will need according to their nature. Therefore, you must reduce these substances to their finest powdered form so they will adhere most easily, and when you sprinkle them on fried food it will be seasoned by juxtaposition.

I shall not speak to you of the choice of oils and fats. The various dispensaries I have provided for your library give sufficient light on that subject.

However, when you have trout weighing less than a quarter of a pound, whose provenance is one of those live-water brooks which murmur far from the capital, do not forget to fry them in the finest olive oil you have. This simple dish, sprinkled with salt and accompanied with lemon slices, is worthy of being offered to a cardinal.

Treat the smelt, of which the adepts make so much, in the same manner.

The smelt is the figpecker of the sea. Same small size, same fineness of aroma, same superiority.

These two prescriptions are based on the nature of things. Experience has taught us that olive oil should be used only for operations that can be performed in a minimum of time and do not demand very high temperatures. This is because prolonged heating develops a disagreeable empyreumatic flavour in olive oil, deriving from particles of parenchyma, very difficult to eliminate, which become carbonized.

You have tried out my great frying kettle, and you were the first to have the glory of offering to a startled world an enormous whole fried turbot. There was great jubilation among the elect on that day.

Now go. Continue to take the greatest care with everything you do, and never forget that once guests have set foot in my parlour, it is our duty to care for their happiness.

FUMET OF PARTRIDGE. Take 1 bottle of old white wine, 2 wild rabbits, and 2 old partridges cut in quarters. Add onions, carrots, parsnips, celery, mushrooms, and a *bouquet garni* in a bag with the four spices. Cook together. Skim, add 1 quart of reduced consommé, simmer for 2 hours. Strain. Return to the stove and reduce to a glaze. Add a little espagnole sauce. Hold in reserve for seasoning, especially for scrambled and poached eggs.

GARLIC. An edible plant whose bulbs are used for seasoning. It has an acrid, volatile juice that makes the eyes water. Applied to the skin, it reddens and even burns it.

Everybody knows the odour of garlic except the one who has eaten it and wonders why everybody turns away from him. Athenaeas says that no one who had eaten garlic could enter the sacred temple of Cybele. Virgil refers to it as useful to restore the strength of reapers, against the heat, and the poet Macer says that it was used to prevent people who feared being attacked by snakes from falling asleep. The Egyptians worshipped it. The Greeks detested it. The Romans ate it with delight. Horace, who suffered indigestion on the very day of his arrival at Rome, from a sheep's head prepared with garlic, had a horror of it.

Alfonso XI, King of Castile, held it in such aversion that in

1330 he founded a knightly order the statutes of which provided that knights who ate garlic might not appear at court or communicate with the other members for at least a month.

Provençal cooking is based on garlic. The air of Provence is saturated with garlic, which makes it very healthful. Garlic is a major condiment in bouillabaisse and in the most important sauces. A sort of mayonnaise used with fish and snails is prepared by crushing garlic in oil. For the lower classes of Provence, breakfast often consists of a crust of bread dipped in oil and rubbed with garlic.

GIBLETS (ABATIS). The comb and kidneys of the rooster, the wing tips of hens, the spinal marrow, gizzard, and neck of the turkey, calves' sweetbreads and brains, are called giblets (*abatis*).

Cockscombs and cock kidneys are used to embellish all the great ragouts and for the fillings of hot pastry and *vol-au-vents*. But to make a separate dish of them, they must be cooked in a pot with bouillon containing beef marrow, mushrooms, slices of artichoke bottoms, or truffles and cross-cut slices of celery, according to the season. At the moment of seasoning they are mixed with a thickening composed of 4 egg yolks and the juice of ½ lemon. Do not let this sauce thicken too much. The consistency of the stew is already mucilaginous enough. It is customary to serve this in a casserole with rice or in a *vol-au-vent*. It is a family dish not generally served at an important dinner. The true popular giblet dish is made from turkey, and it is one of the finest dishes in the middle-class cuisine.

Turkey Giblets with Turnips. Singe and pluck 12 turkey wing tips. Add the necks, the feet, and the gizzards. Cut thick strips of ham into a pot and brown them to a nice colour. Take them out and brown the wing tips lightly in the ham fat. Season with salt, pepper, and nutmeg. Slice and add, with the giblets, a few large onions. When the whole is partly cooked, add a few tablespoonfuls of flour and let it brown lightly. At this point, skim off the fat, add a *bouquet garni* and consommé to the level of the giblets, cover with a piece of buttered paper, and put into the oven. Let simmer until three quarters done. Meanwhile, you will have peeled some very tender white turnips and cut them in the shape of garlic cloves, frying them to a nice colour. Add salt and pepper, letting the pepper dominate, a bunch of parsley, a bit of sugar. When they are well

glazed and partly cooked, drain off the butter in which they were
fried. Strain the giblet liquid. Return it. Add the turnips to the
giblets, skim off the fat well, put the wing tips on top, and leave on
a low fire until cooked. (Recipe from Verdier, Maison d'Or.)

Turkey Giblets with Turnips (Another recipe). Take the
giblets of 2 turkeys and 4 ounces of bacon cut into little cubes and
parboiled to eliminate the salt. Make a light *roux* and add the bacon
pieces; brown them; add your cut-up giblets and a bouquet of
thyme, bay leaf, and parsley. Cook lightly. Add hot water and ½
bottle of white wine. Let simmer.

Fry onions and white turnips in a little butter with salt and
powdered sugar. When they are golden in colour, put them into
your ragout, add a few cooked potatoes, mix, skim off the fat well,
and serve hot. (Vuillemot's recipe.)

GLAZE. Veal. Cut a veal rump into 4 pieces. Put it into a
pot with 3 hens and a good quantity of whole vegetables. During
the cooking add some desalted bacon rind. Skim from time to time.
The gelatin in pork adds greatly to the clarification and consistency
of the jelly. Fill the pot with consommé. Simmer 3 or 4 hours, then
strain through a napkin to clarify.

To make an ordinary glaze, reduce the gravy from a stew, and
just before using it add a piece of fresh butter.

GODIVEAU. This is the name of a certain type of forcemeat from which little balls are formed to fill tarts and *vol-au-vent*.

Godiveau à la Bourgeoise. Remove the tendons and cartilage
from a rump of veal and chop with 1 pound of beef suet. Mix well,
adding chopped parsley and scallions, salt, and the four spices. Chop
and pound well together, adding eggs until the paste has the proper
consistency. Add a little water to soften it, and make into balls for
hot pastries.

Godiveau à la Richelieu. Trim 1 pound of veal rump and 1½
pounds of flocculent beef suet. Chop the veal fine, add the suet,
chop again. Mix in 1 ounce of spiced salt, a bit of nutmeg, and 4
eggs. Chop fine once more. Pound in a mortar until the veal and
suet are indistinguishable. Put on ice for a couple of hours. Divide
into two parts. Pound each part again, this time adding pieces of

ice, which makes the *godiveau* smooth and well mixed. Be careful to add just enough ice to give it the right pasty consistency. Add 2 tablespoonfuls of *velouté* and fine-chopped chives and use as above.

"When I say macerate or pound ice into the meat," says the Marshal de Richelieu's cook, "it is because the ice is of great assistance in giving the *godiveau* that perfect smoothness which is so desirable. In summer it is impossible otherwise to blend the fat thoroughly with the veal. In winter ice is not so important."

Godiveau of Game with Mushrooms. Proceed as above, using partridge or wild-rabbit meat, and 4 tablespoonfuls of white mushrooms chopped and sautéed with garlic in butter.

Lenten Godiveau. As above, but use river carp macerated and passed through a sieve, with 4 ounces of bread soaked in milk and 4 tablespoonfuls of *fines herbes* (chopped shallots, parsley, mushrooms, and truffles).

GOOSE. Geese were long held sacred by the Romans because while the dogs slept a goose which had remained awake – history does not tell us why – heard the noise made by the Gauls in scaling the Capitol. She awakened her friends, who took up her terrified cries and awakened Manlius. Lafosse, who wrote a tragedy on the saving of the Capitol, had the ingratitude not to say one word about the geese in his two thousand lines of Alexandrine verse.

But when Julius Caesar conquered Gaul, the Roman army took to eating geese like the Gauls, who had no reason to hold Manlius' allies in veneration. Soon word got as far as Rome that the Picardy geese made wonderful eating, and the people of Picardy, natural traders, began to drive their flocks of geese, devouring everything along the roads, all the way to Rome.

According to Pliny, a Roman consul named Metellus Scipio invented the art of fattening geese and making their livers delicate.

The famous and erudite physician, Julius Caesar Scaliger, has a special soft spot for geese, which he admires not only physically, but morally.

"The goose," he says, "is the finest emblem of prudence. Geese lower their heads when flying under a bridge, no matter how high its arches may be. They are sensible to the point where, when they are ill, they purge themselves without seeking the advice of a physician.

"They are so foresighted that when they pass by Mt. Taurus, the home of eagles, they take care to forestall their natural garrulousness by each carrying a stone in his mouth, to make sure their cries will not discover them."

Geese may be educated up to a certain point. Lémery the chemist saw a goose turning a spit on which a turkey was broiling. She held the end of the spit in her mouth and used her long neck, pushing and pulling, as a handle. Every once in a while she was given a drink.

Goose à la Chipolata. Clean, pluck, and truss with string a fine, fat, white gosling, feet tucked in. Cover the bottom of an iron pot with bacon, a mirepoix of vegetables, scraps of butcher meat, 2 slices of ham, the giblets from your goose, a bouquet of parsley and scallions, 3 carrots, 2 or 3 onions (1 with cloves in it), a clove of garlic, thyme, bay leaf, a little basil, and some salt. Put your goose on this base, add a good glass of Madeira, a bottle of white wine, some cognac, a ladleful of good poultry consommé. Cook on this braising base about 1 hour. Drain. Arrange the gosling on a platter and pour a chipolata (which see) over it.

Roast Goose Saint-Martin. Bone a fine, fat Normandy goose and stuff with onion purée cooked in drippings from your broiling pan, chopped goose liver, 12 chipolata sausages, and 40 or 50 grilled or roasted chestnuts peeled and seasoned with salt and the four spices. Roast. Serve, on a long, wide piece of toasted bread soaked in the goose drippings, season with coarse pepper and lemon juice.

Broiled Gosling. Take a tender gosling with good white fat. Pluck, eviscerate, clean. Cut off the feet. Remove the wings. Truss and tie with the legs stretched out. Spit and broil. Do not overcook. When the juices spurt when you prick the bird, it is done. Brush with lemon juice after broiling.

Vuillemot judiciously observes that all hollow meats should be lemoned when they are taken off the spit.

Goose with Sauerkraut. Having broiled your goose on the spit, take a quantity of sauerkraut, wash repeatedly, cook with slices of salt pork, cervelat, and sausages, bouillon, and some of the fat from the goose. Simmer 2 hours. Arrange the sauerkraut around the bird, top it with the sausages and cervelat (skinned and sliced), and pour meat glaze over all.

Preserved Goose Wings and Legs à la Façon de Bayonne.
Take the wings and legs of as many geese as you have or wish, and
rub them well with salt into which you will have mixed saltpetre.
Arrange in a crock with bay leaf, thyme, and basil. Cover with a
cloth and let stand 24 hours. Remove and clean off the wings and
legs. Broil over a moderate fire. Let them cool, then arrange as
tightly as possible in jars. Cover them with cool but liquid lard. Let
stand 1 day, then seal hermetically with paper or parchment. Keep
in a cool place and use as needed.

GRAPES AND RAISINS. Innumerable varieties of grapes
have been developed since the time of Noah, who first cultivated
the vine. The grape is the earliest of the autumn fruits to appear
upon our tables, the most nourishing of the fruits that do not over-
winter, and the one whose juices are least harmful — when fully ripe,
that is. Tissot reports that soldiers suffering from chronic dysentery
were moved into a vineyard and soon recovered after eating great
quantities of grapes.

When Richard the Lionhearted was still only Duke of Guyenne,
he issued a memorable edict to the people of his duchy. "Anyone
who takes a grape from another's vine," said he, "shall be fined five
sous, or suffer the loss of an ear."

From this we gather that a Gascon's ear was not worth much
in 1175. They have become dearer since. Not even the littlest Gascon
today would sell his ear for all the vines in the world, though they
all love grapes.

The little foxes, the hare, and some small birds fatten a good
deal in autumn. Their flesh becomes delicate and makes very fine
eating. But as soon as the grape harvest is over, they become thin
and their flesh loses the fine flavour imparted to it by the grapes.

Grapes are made more nourishing by the process of drying them
into raisins. They are then excellent to sweeten the stomach. People
with weak stomachs find it helpful to chew two or three raisins,
with the seeds, after a meal. They contribute to good digestion.

GUINEA HEN. When raised in the open, the guinea hen is
as delicate eating as a pheasant. It should be prepared in exactly the
same manner.

HALCYONE. Few people know that this bird with the sweet name recalling the unhappy loves of Alcyone and Ceyx, is none other than the swallow from the shores of Cochin China, called salangane, whose nests the Chinese eat with such delight. The finest varieties are found in the Moluccas and Philippine Islands. They produce little gelatinous nests shaped like a holy-water font. These are composed of a semi-transparent white substance, hard as a horn, with light cottony layers inside. On the outside, this substance has the appearance of very white gelatin, dried out and carefully applied in filaments.

This bird, called halkyon in Greek, is known as *chim* in Tonkin and *salangan* in the Philippines, which have become rich just from selling the nests. The resin of which they are composed is called calambac, and is unknown in Europe. The Indians call it *timbach*.

It crunches under the teeth and has a delicious flavour. In China it is worth its weight in gold. There they call the nests *sacaïpouka*.

Following a recipe sent to me from Java: after cleaning the nest we soak it to soften and separate the filaments, place it under a roasting bird, whose juices it will absorb. Or simmer it twenty-four hours with a capon in a hermetically sealed earthen vessel. We also make very tasty and nourishing bouillons, soups, and ragouts from it.

HARE. Civet of Hare. Skin, clean, and cut into pieces, being careful to keep the blood, which set aside in a cool place. Make a *roux* with flour and butter and heat a few small pieces of bacon or salt pork in it. Mix your hare into this *roux*, and, when it is hot, cover with half bouillon, half red wine. Add salt, pepper, *bouquet garni*, 1 clove of garlic, 1 onion with 2 cloves stuck into it, and a bit of grated nutmeg. When the hare is half cooked, add the liver and lungs. Cook over a hot fire until the liquid is reduced by three quarters.

Have 12 little white onions, glazed to a nice colour in butter, and $\frac{1}{2}$ glass of white wine. Add cut-up mushrooms and artichoke bottoms. At the same time fry little bread croutons in oil.

When all these garnishings are ready, mix the hare's blood into your ragout. Arrange the pieces on a platter, crown with the little onions, pour the sauce over it, add the bits of artichoke bottom, the salt pork, and the mushrooms. Put the croutons on top of all. Serve very hot.

Hare Chops à la Melville. This recipe was borrowed from A. Gogué, formerly chef of the kitchens of Lord Melville, first lord of the admiralty.

"If I give you this recipe," writes that excellent cook, "it is not because I invented it, nor because these chops bear the honourable name of the lord to whom I was privileged to serve them on several occasions. Pride aside, hare chops, as I shall describe them are worthy of appearing on a good table, and therefore appear naturally in this book. And let us not imagine it is going to take 5 or 6 hares to prepare this dish — like the one I have seen in a book on *haute cuisine* in which the fillets of 10 leverets are required for a *blanquette*. No, we shall need only the front halves of 2 hares. This division is unavoidable, but the hind parts need not be wasted.

"Clean 2 hares, saving and setting aside the blood. Remove the fillets from the front quarters smoothly, without spoiling their shape. Divide these into 3 pieces each, cutting them on the bias so that each has a pointed end and a blunted end. Flatten them gently, giving them a chop shape, which is easy when you have cut them as I said.

"Now take 12 little bones from chicken wing tips, sharpen one end of each, and insert one into each cutlet. Lacking these chicken bones in sufficient number, use the hare's own ribs, the purpose being to imitate the shape of a lamb chop.

"The chops thus prepared, season with salt and pepper, brush lightly with beaten egg yolk, bread with very fine white bread crumbs. Dip in hot melted butter and bread again. Smooth with the blade of a knife. Sauté in butter like ordinary chops.

"The sauce for these chops is prepared as follows:

"Put into your pot slices of onion and sticks of carrot, add the debris from the hare from which you have taken the fillets, cut into suitable pieces, with 1 clove of garlic, 2 cloves, a *bouquet garni*, and 1 glass of white wine. Simmer until about dry, then add a ladleful of bouillon to take up the essence that has formed on the bottom. Simmer for $\frac{1}{2}$ hour. Strain, then work into an espagnole sauce, if you have it; otherwise, into a light *roux*. Just before serving, mix this sauce with the blood you have reserved.

"As for the hare's haunches that remain, they will not be wasted. From them we shall make a civet, or some other dish. So you see this dish of 12 chops *à la Melville* can be made without too great expense. What we desire in cooking is that it be the best possible, using the simplest and most inexpensive means."

HASH. When veal, beef, chicken, game, or other meats are left over from the previous night's dinner, chop them all together finely until completely mixed. Then go out and buy some sausage meat, about one fifth by weight, and half cook it. Mix your hash into it, add a piece of fresh butter, and stir until the meats are completely blended. Salt and pepper. As your hash dries in cooking, keep adding a tablespoonful at a time of good bouillon. Add a pinch of cayenne pepper. Taste to determine when to stop cooking.

HERRING. Everyone knows herring. I shall even say that

few don't like it. Alive, it has a green back, white sides and belly. Dead, the back turns blue. It is the child of the North Pole. From its place of birth to the forty-fifth latitude it is found in every sea. Beginning on June 25, when, in Holland, one begins to see what is called *herring lightning*, it forms in banks several leagues in every dimension, and so thick the fish stifle each other by the millions. Sometimes the nets are torn by the great weight of the catch. Like the pillars of fire and smoke of the ancient Israelites, their migration may be followed day and night – at night by their brilliant phosphorescence, by day by the flocks of fish-eating birds that follow them, dipping every now and then and rising with a streak of silver in their beaks. Whales, sharks, porpoises, and dolphins follow them, biting into the bank and eating the herring in enormous quantities.

Bloch, says Victor Meunier, has stated that from a single Swedish port, more than seven million are taken annually. But the fecundity of this fish conpensates for all the destruction of its progeny: 66,606 eggs have been counted in a single female. There are seven females for every male.

Herring fisheries are becoming more important, while cod fisheries are losing ground. Le Havre, which once sent out up to forty boats for cod, this year sent out only one.

The art of smoking herring was invented by a Dutch fisherman named Beukels or Bruckalz, who died in 1449. The finest herring one can eat fresh in Paris come from the Normandy coast. Freshly salted herring must always come from Rotterdam or Enkhuizen, in Holland. It is cut into slices and eaten raw without any more preparation than a salad. The finest smoked herring, the biggest, fleshiest, most golden, the best juniper-smoked, come from Ireland. Salted herring scarcely appear on rich men's tables, but everywhere they abound they are of utmost utility to the workers and the poor.

A very pleasant and appetizing fricassee is made of herring cut into small pieces and fried without desalting, then mixed with flaky boiled potatoes, chopped raw leek, and a few leaves of rosemary.

Fresh herring is an excellent fish that would have a great fuss made over it if it were expensive and hard to find. It should be chosen with red gills, brilliant scales, and well-rounded belly, for then it is fat. But it rarely appears in full, savoury form until the end of August or mid-September.

In the sixteenth century, the canons of the Cathedral of Rheims still persisted in a somewhat bizarre practice. On Maundy Thursday, after Tenebrae, they went in two processional files to the church of Saint-Remi, each one dragging a herring behind him on a string, each trying to step on the herring of the one in front and to prevent the one behind stepping on his. This extravagant custom was suppressed only by discontinuing the procession itself.

As everyone knows, herring fisheries are one of England's most productive industries, and great quantities of the fish are exported to Italy for Holy Week. When Pope Pius VI was driven from Rome, conquered by the revolutionary French, the matter was brought to the attention of the parliamentary committee in London that occupied itself with the herring industry. One of the members observed that Italy would now turn Protestant. "God preserve us from it!" cried another member. "Why," said the first, "would you be annoyed to see the number of Protestants growing?" "Why, no," was the answer. "But when there are no more Catholics, what shall we do with our herring?"

Fresh Herring with Mustard Sauce. Clean, scale, and wipe 12 herring. Marinate in oil with salt and parsley. Fifteen minutes before serving, grill on both sides. Return to the platter in which they marinated, and sauce with a white butter sauce into which you have blended 1 tablespoonful of fresh mustard. If you serve them cold, use any oil dressing you consider appropriate.

Fresh Herring with Fennel. Split your herring down the back, brush with melted butter and salt, wrap in fennel, and grill. Serve with a brown sauce into which you have blended fennel leaves and stalks blanched in white wine and chopped fine.

Fresh Herring Matelote. Put your herring into a pot with butter, parsley, mushrooms, scallions, 1 clove of garlic, 2 good glasses of Burgundy or Bordeaux, salt and pepper. Cook on a hot fire, serve with its own sauce, reduced, and garnish with fried croutons.

Smoked Herring à la Sainte-Menehould. Soak in cream to desalt. Cook for 20 minutes in a Sainte-Menehould made as follows. Into a saucepan put 1 ounce of butter mixed with flour and milk, parsley, scallions, garlic, thyme, bay leaf, basil, a little pepper. Bring to a boil and keep stirring. Add your herring and cook. Dip them in melted butter and cook under the grill until they have a good colour. Serve on a remoulade.

Preparation of Smoked Herring for Good Use Later. Desalt and grill good Irish herring. Let them cool. Remove the fillets, which you will use later to make sandwiches with fresh butter; to garnish an hors d'oeuvre, dressing them with fine oil and the juice of bitter oranges; to put on top of dishes of buttered noodles or lasagne, or of mashed potatoes, chestnuts, sweet potatoes, or creamed white beans; to make a coarse hash with which to season an omelet or scrambled eggs, adding chopped olives, cream cheese, and a little walnut cordial.

HORSE. "To eat horse" is a proverbial way of saying to eat something hypertough. Horse meat is, in fact, tougher than beef. It is red and oily. Though it is very nourishing, it is doubtful that it will ever enter into the common daily diet. It is unlikely that this noble animal, which man associates with military glory, will ever serve generally as food, except in times of siege or famine. Until the horse is bred, fed, and fattened solely for food purposes, like beef, it will be seen on the table only in hard times. Then, and only then, treat it and prepare it like beef.

HOT CANAPÉS (RÔTIES). These are served as garnishes or entremets.

Veal-Kidney Rôties. Take the kidneys from a roast loin of veal. Chop and pound them very fine with their own fat, a little parsley, the peel of a lime, a little sugar. Spread on little slices of bread. Butter a pie dish and arrange your *rôties* on it. Put them into the oven until they have a nice colour. Sprinkle with sugar and pass under the broiler to glaze.

Rôties à la Richelieu. Make a salpicon of diced veal sweet-breads, cockscombs, and artichoke bottoms. Dice mushrooms and heat in butter, moisten with gravy, add the salpicon, cook with white veal stock, season, thicken with raw egg yolks. Let cool. Spread on bread slices, brush with beaten egg, fry, serve with a reduced white veal stock.

Capon Rôties. Make a forcemeat of roast capon with sugar and lime rind. Prepare like either of the above.

Cucumber Rôties. Cube, marinate, and press your cucumbers. Heat in butter with scallions and parsley, add gravy and bouillon, reduce. Thicken with 3 raw egg yolks. Let cool. Add 2 more raw egg yolks. Spread on slices of bread. Smooth with whole beaten egg. Bread. Fry. Serve with gravy.

Bacon Rôties. Dice a pound of bacon and a slice of ham. Dry out and drain. Mix with parsley, scallions, 4 egg yolks, coarse pepper. Spread on slices of bread. Fry. Pour a cullis, which must be very lightly salted, into your platter, adding a dash of vinegar. Put your *rôties* into this sauce and serve.

Similar *rôties* can be prepared with spinach, with green beans, with poultry livers, with ham, with anchovies, and with fish, by adapting the above recipes.

HUNTER. A pleasant, jovial, healthy man; a good eater and a better drinker; early sleeper and early riser, and sleeping soundly in between. Generally speaking, ladies do not care for hunters. That is the portrait of a hunter as sketched by Elzéar Blaze, one of the mightiest hunters before the Lord since Nimrod, in his book *Le Chien d'arrêt* (*The Pointer*).

I shall examine the hunter from another point of view. You see, far across the fields, a man with a gun and a dog. If he avoids you, it is because he doesn't have a hunting licence or permission to hunt on this land, or because he has no game in his bag.

There are hunters and there are poachers.

There are hunters for pleasure and hunters for the pleasure of eating.

I remember, when I was very young, hunting with a farmer named Moquet. When he missed a partridge, he seldom failed to exclaim:

"Sapristi! He would have tasted good with cabbage!"

If it was a hare:

"Sapristi! He would have been so good with little onions!"

To this hunter, who hunts for pleasure and for gastronomy, we shall give a bit of advice; not on how to hold his gun, nor on how to aim, to handle his dog, to walk upwind, nor even on how to hum a little tune when he sees a hare, but on how to put the game into his bag.

As every hunter knows, a game bag has two parts, one of leather and one of net. The former has special little pockets for licences, ammunition, and hares. But only for hares. Not for other game.

If the hunter's bag overflows, he should fasten his small game such as quail, partridge, and young pheasant to the outside of it, tied to the meshes with string. The net itself should be reserved for partridges, pheasants, and other large birds that won't be damaged by being crushed together. If it is very hot, he should never put a hare into the leather pouch without first making him piss. He should never put a partridge into the net without first removing his large intestine with a twig. Any hunter who does not know how to perform these operations should learn from a hunter who does.

The most important recommendation is never to fire on a quail from closer than twenty-five paces. Quail flesh, essentially delicate, will never, in hot weather, arrive home fit to eat if it is torn up with shot. It is better to let a bird go, to be taken another day, than to render it inedible.

In this respect, the Italians are better equipped than we. The net of their game bags is barrelled out with osier so that the air circulates through it and the game will not be crushed by its own weight. The hunter loses no kudos from this arrangement. The osier permits a full display of fur and feather as the net itself.

HYDROMEL. Pliny attributes its invention to Aristaeus of Cyrene, son of the sun. Simple hydromel is a mixture of honey with a much larger quantity of water. It is good for coughs, but not everybody likes it.

Vinous hydromel, or mead, is composed of one part honey and three parts water. Very little warmth is necessary to start the fermentation. It becomes as strong as Spanish wine, and keeps very well. The ancient Egyptians esteemed it highly. It has a very pleasant taste and strengthens the stomach when taken in small doses.

ICE. Has been used in Southern countries from the remotest antiquity. Seneca reproached the Romans for the pains they took to have their drinks iced. Hippocrates speaks of the difficulty of obtaining ice and snow. The inhabitants of hot countries have at all times prized cold drinks, and ice-cold water is one of the great delicacies of the Orientals, the Italians, and the Spanish, who use porous earthen vessels to obtain it.

In the sixteenth century, the use of ice was unknown in France. When Francis I went to Nice for conferences with Pope Paul III and the Emperor Charles V, his physician was astonished by the wine cooled with ice from the mountains around the city.

But *ices* as such were unknown in France until 1660, when a Florentine named Procope for the first time introduced the subjects of Louis XIV to the attractive sweetness of these delicacies. The café he established in the Rue de l'Ancienne Comédie is still in existence today. Now ices are well known and are seen in summer on all good tables.

JULIENNE. This name is given to a soup made from all sorts of herbs and vegetables, notably carrots, cut very small. Now these chopped vegetables are preserved through dehydration, which allows us to make julienne at any time.

The recipes of Marc Heliot show that julienne was not always made exclusively of vegetables. It had for base, in fact, a shoulder of mutton that was half roasted, then put into a pot with a slice of beef, a piece of veal, 1 capon, and 4 pigeons. This was cooked for 5 or 6 hours to make a rich broth. Three carrots, 6 white turnips, 2 parsnips, 3 onions, 2 parsley roots, 2 bunches of celery, 3 bunches of asparagus, 4 handfuls of sorrel, 4 white lettuce heads, a good pinch of chervil, were chopped fine. In season 1½ pints of little green peas were added. The meat was removed, and the vegetables were cooked in the broth, in which slices of bread that formed a part of this ancient pottage were also simmered.

JUNIPER. The berries of the juniper, a low-growing, ever-green, spiny shrub. Many fine properties are attributed to juniper. It preserves the brain, strengthens the sight, cleans the lungs, banishes wind, and facilitates digestion. It is also frequently employed in medicine.

Juniper Ratafia. A healthful cordial that aids digestion. Infuse fat, ripe juniper berries in brandy. Add a proper amount of sugar, and bottle.

KANGAROO. The kangaroo is a native of New Holland (Australia) and its surrounding islands. Essentially a fruit eater in the wild state, when acclimatised it becomes easy to feed and eats anything one gives it. It is said that the kangaroo will even drink wine and brandy if they are offered.

There is no doubt that the kangaroo could be most usefully and easily multiplied in Europe, either wild or domesticated. The kangaroo's flesh is excellent, especially when it has grown up in a wild state. Its rapid growth and its height contribute to produce a large quantity of meat in a short time. In addition, its singular shape favours the production of much good quality meat in the hind-quarters, tenderer than beef and more nutritive and in larger quantity than mutton.

The strong and muscular tail of the kangaroo makes the best and tastiest of soups. Kangaroo meat is prepared like wild rabbit, with which it bears a close affinity, except that it is more aromatic, the result, no doubt, of the nature of its diet.

Sautéed Kangaroo Fillet. Take 2 fillets, trim, season, and arrange in a pot with melted butter. In another pot, prepare a broth from the bones and scraps of meat from the animal, strain, remove the fat. Pour into a pot with 4 tablespoonfuls of vinegar, add a *bouquet garni*, reduce to a light sauce, add 2 tablespoonfuls of currant jelly and a piece of lemon zest. Ten minutes later, add a handful of raisins soaked in warm water. Let the whole simmer about 1 hour. Poach the fillets, drain, set them on a platter, and pour the sauce over them.

KID. At three or four months, kid is still free of all goaty flavour and odour.

The royal kid is thus described by Jean Leclercq:

"After it is skinned and cleaned very well, I roast it whole, basting with good fat and spiced wine. Also, I salt it twice, once when I put it on the fire and once when I take it off the spit. In making sauce for kid, do not omit or be sparing with strong-flavoured old wine of Spain, sour saxifrage, and royal mustard. Everyone shouted at me, and the king first of all, when they saw me in the courtyard: 'Hola! Master Jehan, Master Cook, you want to make us burst with good living, with your Epiphany kids, you sauce us and roast us alive, good man!' And I would laugh at these pleasantries that the good prince and great French king every day told me in the Louvre, may God grant him grace and receive him in celestial glory."

Although it would be difficult to prepare a kid as Jean Leclercq indicates, something has remained of this recipe. Today on the Day of Kings, following tradition, in certain provinces, kid is seasoned with sage and sugared wine to which are added the four spices.

KIDNEYS. The characteristic of kidneys is that their meat never becomes tender from cooking. They are usually soft and compact in texture, which makes them difficult to digest. There are some young animals, however, whose kidneys are sufficiently tender and well flavoured — lamb, veal, suckling pig, and a few others. Beef kidneys are always a little stony and too highly flavoured. We advise the reader not to use them too freely.

Lamb Kidneys Mousquetaire. Remove the fat, split, skewer, season with salt, pepper, finely chopped shallots. Rub a pot with butter, bacon, or any culinary fat. Arrange your kidneys in it. Put on the fire or on hot ashes. Cover. Put hot coals on the lid. Cook only a moment or two, which is all they require. Arrange on a platter. For sauce, add a little water, white of bread, salt, pepper, and a dash of vinegar to the pot in which they were cooked.

Skewered Lamb Kidneys. Split the kidneys partway through. Skin them. Do not separate the halves completely. Pass a wooden skewer through each on a diagonal, so it cannot close. Dip in melted butter, bread, grill, turning as necessary. Remove from the skewers, arrange on a hot platter, put a little cold maître d'hôtel sauce in each, squeeze lemon juice over them, and serve.

Grilled Lamb Kidneys. Cut the kidneys nearly through, skewer, season with salt and pepper. Grill. Serve with shallot sauce.

Lamb kidneys are good with any sauce, provided they are served rare.

Marinated Kidneys. Prepare as above. Marinate in oil with parsley, scallions, and garlic, all chopped fine. Add powdered thyme, bay leaf, and basil, salt, fine spices. When they have absorbed the flavour of the marinade, skewer, roll in the marinade, then in white of bread. Grill, basting with the marinade, and serve with shallot sauce under them.

Ragout of Lamb Kidneys. Parboil the kidneys. Skin. Lard. Heat in a pot with butter, parsley, scallions. Add good bouillon, salt, pepper, cloves, mushrooms, morels, beef palate, chestnuts, a bouquet of *fines herbes*, a little beef cullis, and stew.

Lamb Kidneys with Cucumbers. Wrap the kidneys in bacon slices and braise. Slice very thin and mix into a cucumber ragout (see under RAGOUTS).

Sautéed Lamb Kidneys. Peel and split 12 kidneys. Eat them raw. We are obliged to our friend Nadar for this primitive recipe.

However, if you prefer, put them into a skillet with melted butter, salt, and pepper. Put on a hot fire. When they are browned on one side, turn over. Arrange on a platter with as many croutons fried in butter. Put a little fat and 2 tablespoonfuls of reduced espagnole sauce into the skillet, bring to a boil, add a little butter and the juice of 1 lemon. Pour this sauce over the kidneys and serve.

Beef Kidneys with Onions. Fry slices of onion in butter. When half done, add thinly sliced beef kidney, salt, and pepper. Add no liquid; the juices of the onion and kidney as they cook are sufficient. When done, add a little mustard and a dash of vinegar. Serve as a side dish.

Fried Beef Kidneys. Slice very thin. Fry in butter with chopped parsley, scallions, and shallots, salt and pepper. Remove when done. Stir 1 glass of wine and a little water into the pan. Thicken with 3 egg yolks. Pour over the kidney slices and serve as a side dish.

Sautéed Veal Kidneys. Skin, slice thin, put into a hot skillet with butter, salt, pepper, nutmeg, chopped shallots and parsley, and cooked, sliced mushrooms. Add a little flour, white wine, a few tablespoonfuls of reduced espagnole sauce. Just before serving, add a little butter and the juice of 1 lemon.

Grilled Veal Kidneys. Do not remove the fat from veal kidneys grilled on the spit or roasted in the oven.

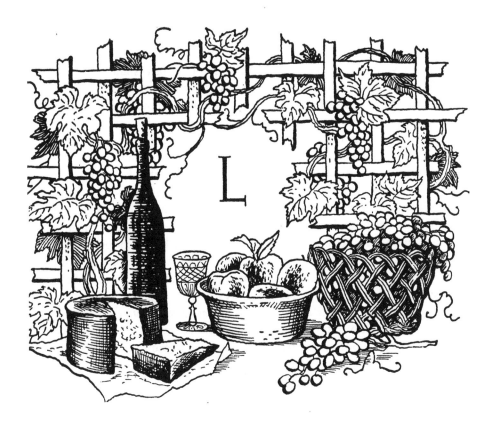

LAMB. The name of this nice little animal [*agneau* in French] is given a truly poetic derivation. According to the bucolic etymologists, it comes from the word *agnoscere*, to recognize, because it recognizes its mother as soon as it is born.

Lamb is at its best from December to April. It must be at least five months old and must be milk-fed.

From remotest antiquity to the present time, lamb has been the favourite dish of the Eastern peoples. The Greeks gave few feasts at which lamb did not constitute the most important dish. One of the prophets rebuked the Samaritans for eating too much of it. At one time its use was forbidden to the Athenians.

Lamb Hungarian Style. Cut 12 large Spanish onions in rings and put into a skillet. Add butter and flour and stir over the fire into a *roux*, being careful to brown but not to burn the onions. Add salt, pepper, a bouquet of herbs, a good pinch of Hungarian paprika or, if you don't have it, a few grains of cayenne. Meanwhile, you will have cut your breast of lamb into 2-inch pieces and browned them in fresh butter. Pour the contents of your skillet over the lamb, add ¼ cup of good consommé, and simmer 1¼ hours, adding new consommé every 15 minutes.

This is one of the best dishes I ate in Hungary.

Saddle of Lamb English Style. The saddle is the best part of the lamb. It is roasted and accompanied to the table by an English sauce well liked by those Parisian gourmets who have not been instilled with unconquerable horror of everything from beyond the Channel by our two hundred and seventeen years of war with England.

Put ½ pint of consommé into a pot with a bit of chopped fresh sage. Boil 5 minutes. Add 2 crushed shallots, 2 or 3 tablespoonfuls of good vinegar, 2 ounces of sugar, and a bit of black pepper. Salt, strain, and serve on the side in a gravy boat.

The author of the *Memoirs of the Marquise de Créqui*, from whom we have borrowed this recipe, takes occasion to attack those exclusive gourmands whose patriotism makes them oppose the introduction of foreign dishes into French cooking.

"We still find," he says indignantly, "people who claim to be gourmands who protest against the use of sugar mixed with acids or with salted meats – a combination often extremely good. We constantly encounter these obstinate reactionaries on the march of culinary progress, which after all can only be developed if all peoples forswear national prejudices in a true cosmopolitan spirit."

Whole Lamb. Truss your lamb, tie it up, put it on a spit, and wrap in buttered paper. Just before serving, take off the paper to let it brown. Take it off the spit and arrange on a platter with paper sleeves on the ends of the hind legs. Serve with poivrade sauce.

Lamb Kromeskis Polish (Croquettes). Dice cold, partly cooked lamb. Similarly dice cooked mushrooms and calf's udder. Put into a pot a piece of meat glaze the size of a pigeon's egg, a little consommé, ginger, and coarse pepper. Heat, thicken with egg yolks, then add the lamb, mushrooms, and udder. Cool. Shape into croquettes and wrap in slices of calf's udder. Dip into croquette batter and fry in the skillet to a good colour. Serve with *sauce piquante* or with fried parsley.

Sliced Lamb à la Landgrave. Slice a lamb fillet, salt, and season with the four spices and a little paprika. Fry and keep hot. Put into a pot ½ cup of bouillon to ½ tablespoonful of rye flour, add a little pickled walnut juice, a little ketchup and mushroom essence, 1 ounce of butter. Bring to a boil, stirring constantly. Pour this over your sliced lamb, make sure the whole is hot, and serve.

[*See also recipes under the heading* SHEEP AND MUTTON, *and the Index. –* ED.]

LARDING. A culinary term for the insertion of strips of bacon or other meat through a piece of flesh with a larding needle. For proper larding, the strips should be half as thick as one's little finger, and well seasoned with salt and pepper. Surface larding, commonly called barding, is done with very thin strips of bacon, symmetrically disposed, sometimes in deliberate designs.

LARKS. They have the double distinction of being loved by both poets and gourmets. They were much sought after for the tables of the Athenians. On the island of Lemnos they were held sacred because they had saved it from the grasshoppers.

The lark is very delicate and highly esteemed for its flavour. It is only really good from November until February. It fattens with surprising rapidity in foggy weather.

Larded and roasted, it is very good to eat, but only after a solid dinner. Grimod de la Reynière is of the opinion that the biggest lark, like the finest robin, is at best no more than a package of toothpicks, better, in the hands of a man with a good appetite, for cleaning the mouth than filling it. The illustrious gourmet adds: "The lark pies of Pithiviers are as fine eating as the palate of a gallant man can find. The crust is excellent and the seasoning inimitable."

Lister, the gourmand physician of a gourmand queen, established as a matter of principle that if a dozen larks ready for the spit average less than 1.05 ounces each, they are inedible. If they weigh that much, they are passable. If they total 14 ounces, they are excellent. So take care you weigh your larks before roasting them.

Larks in a Casserole. Take 12 to 24 larks, depending on the number of your guests, pluck them (the larks, not the guests), singe them. Put them into a pot and cook them with butter until half done. Take them off the fire, drain them, and draw them, discarding the gizzards. Crush the rest of the innards in a mortar with chicken or goose livers and truffles. Season with salt, pepper, nutmeg, etc. Fill your birds with this stuffing. Put the stuffing left over on the bottom of a shallow casserole and bury the stuffed larks in it so they can scarcely be seen. Cover with a slice of bacon and a piece of buttered paper. Bake for ½ hour. Just before serving, remove the bacon and paper, drain the platter, sprinkle the dish with fresh bread crumbs, and rest easy over the results.

This divine dish may be eaten with any sauce you desire. I have often feasted on it with currant jelly, taking a half mouthful of each to a bit. (Elzéar Blaze's method.)

LEEK. Originally from Spain, the leek is now cultivated in all the temperate regions of Europe. The poor eat it raw with bread, and in every household it is used to flavour soup. It has a diuretic quality that may be utilized in dietetic cooking. It is rarely used in French soups except for flavouring. There are places, however, where it is made into a ragout, and a leek soup with meat is worthy of consideration. In Lorraine, tarts are made with leeks.

LEGUMES. These are seeds that come in pods and are picked by hand. This word has been used incorrectly [in French] to describe all sorts of vegetables used for the nourishment of man and beast. It has been applied not only to the fruits, but to the roots, stems, leaves, etc.

Nevertheless, this name may be correctly applied only to the leguminous family of plants, such as peas, lentils, beans, etc. Among the legumes that are eaten by man, some are healthful and readily digested. Others, on the contrary, are very difficult to digest. It is incorrect, therefore, to eat these legumes exclusively, for they are heavy, and good only for the most vigorous stomachs, for workmen and country people accustomed to painful and laborious living.

[*Dumas throughout his cookery book follows the example of fifty million other Frenchmen, and in the original never refers to any vegetable at all except as a "légume".* — Ed.]

LENT. Lent is the annual fast established in the Roman Catholic Church. It begins on Ash Wednesday and ends with Easter. There is disagreement on the origin of Lent. Some attribute it to Moses. Others say it was observed in Egypt, and was one of the customs brought back from that country by the Israelites. All nations that have laws have some sort of Lent. One is forced to the conclusion that the custom was not established solely to please God, but for reasons of health, a preparation by proper dieting for the dangerous change of season. Since during the infancy of nations the peoples would not have followed a hygienic counsel, it was made into a religious precept and accepted as a superstition.

The severity of Lent, and its duration, have varied from country to country. In the Western Church, one evening meal of fruits and vegetables was permitted. Dairy dishes, eggs, meat, and wine were forbidden. Fish was permitted, but most of the faithful abstained from eating it. The diet appears to have been even more rigorous in the East, where most Christians lived on bread and water and a few vegetables. The Greeks have four fasts besides Lent, for Christmas, the Apostles, the Transfiguration, and the Assumption. But they are only seven days long.

Lent is probably less observed in France today than in any other country. This was not always the case. When the clergy became rich and powerful, they used the influence of the Church for the enactment of the most rigorous laws of abstinence. While they satisfied their sensuality by breaking the monotony of meat eating with the most exquisite fish, while their insatiable cupidity piled up gold by selling dispensations to the rich, the poor man who had no gold to ransom his miserable sin was hanged for tasting meat just once during Lent. The butcher who sold it was whipped and chained to a post with an iron collar. We read in the capitularies (A.D. 780) that Charlemagne, to force the Saxons to adopt Christianity, decreed that any Saxon who refused to be baptized or who ate meat during Lent should suffer death.

In 1522, one Passeigne, by sentence of the provost of Sens, was whipped before the door of the cathedral for having eaten pork and beans during Lent. Under Henry III the death penalty was abolished, but whipping continued. Voltaire reports that on July 28, 1729, near Saint-Claude, one Claude Guillon had his head cut off because, being famished, on March 31 he took, cooked, and ate the flesh of a horse that had been killed and abandoned in a field.

Another incident, much more recent, is reported by Saint-Edme in his *Treatise on the History of Legislation Regarding Sacrilege*. In 1823, during Lent, four individuals from the department of the Pyrenees went on business to Céret. They went into an inn, ordered chops, and were served. They informed. The king's prosecutor cited the innkeeper, and he was condemned for outrage of religious morals to a year's imprisonment and a fine of three hundred francs. He appealed, however, and the tribunal at Perpignan reversed the verdict. About the same time, however, in Rome, a butcher was arrested, taken to the Fontana di Trevi Square, and branded by the executioner. A placard related his crime, which was to have eaten meat on a Friday, at an inn, with friends.

LEPORIDE. For the past six thousand years, more or less, scientists have been reproached with struggling against God, though unable ever to create even the smallest animal. Weary of reproaches, they set to work and, in the year of grace 1866, finally created the leporide. In doing this they defied not merely God, but even Buffon.

Observing the antipathy between rabbits and hares, despite their generally similar appearance, Buffon pronounced: "Never do the individuals approach each other."

Buffon was mistaken.

The antipathy between the two was not racial. It had to do with the characters of the animals. If no two animals are more alike physically than the rabbit and the hare, neither are any two more different morally. The hare is a dreamer. His dwelling is the surface of the earth. He leaves his form only after the most elaborate precaution of turning the mobile organs of his hearing in every direction. He wanders about mostly by day, and does not return to his form after being chased from it two or three times.

The rabbit, on the other hand, seeks his repose in long, subterranean tunnels, which he himself digs and of which no one else knows the turnings. He emerges imprudently, generally at sundown, paying no attention to the noise he makes. Then, since he is very fond of clover, young shoots of grain, and wild thyme, he goes forth to seek these elegant hors d'oeuvres that are lacking in his forest. There he is ambushed by the huntsman and made to pay for his imprudence.

It has been said that the antipathy between the hare and the rabbit is such that a warren invaded by rabbits is immediately evacuated by hares, and vice versa. This is true. But this is because the noisy, freedom-loving rabbit sleeps by day and wakes by night, while the hare does the opposite. It is obvious that such a difference in living habits must make it impossible for two such creatures to share a habitation.

But it was precisely on this fact that the scientists counted. They took a litter of rabbits and a litter of hares whose eyes had not yet opened and fed them on cow's milk, which, having no relation to either, could not inculcate preconceived prejudices through their nourishment. The two litters were kept in a dark room where, when their eyes opened, they were unable to observe the slight differences between their two species.

The animals believed themselves to belong to the same family. They were well nourished and had no reason to quarrel. They lived in brotherly friendship until they felt the early onset of love needs.

Then one day the scientists, who watched in relays so as to miss nothing of the conjugation adjudged impossible by Buffon, saw a rabbit doe and a buck hare approach each other with a more than fraternal tenderness. Then the little colony began to promise growth in such proportions as to leave no doubt of the crossing of these two races which supposedly could not even approach each other.

Twenty little ones resulted from this mysterious work of science. But nature held its own. The doe rabbits always littered eight or ten little ones, the doe hares never more than two. All that remained was to continue the experiment and give the lie completely to Buffon, who had said: "If, through an error, or weakness, or violence, the two races should make a *rapprochement*, the hybrids would not be capable of reproduction."

These abnormal litters were isolated from all others of their kind. To the great satisfaction of the scientists, they followed their parents' example and cross-bred among themselves. The crossing and reproduction continued.

Now we have completely new animals, the joy of their creators, who have named them leporides. They take after both the rabbit and the hare, but are bigger than either, weighing up to thirteen and fourteen pounds each.

Their meat is whiter than the hare's and darker than the rabbit's. They may be served with sauces invented for either. Within the next two or three years they should be sufficiently abundant to take an honourable place in our forests and our markets. I have been told they have already appeared in the markets at Mans and in Anjou.

The Société d'Acclimatation sent me one of these animals, on condition that I eat it. I can affirm that they have in no way degenerated from either of their ancestors.

LIVER. There are truly only three ways to prepare calf's liver: on the spit, *à la bourgeoise*, and *à l'italienne*.

Roasted Calf's Liver. It should be large, fat, and light in colour. Lard with thick strips of bacon seasoned with spices, *fines herbes*, and garlic.

It is easy to roast a calf's liver in the oven, of course, but a spit is a different matter. It's like putting a pound of butter on the spit. The big problem is to hold the liver so it will turn. Heat the centre of the spit, but not until it reddens. Your liver being wrapped in slices of bacon and tied up, slip it over the hot spot. The heat will sear it and hold it firmly until it is cooked. (Vuillemot.)

Roast over a slow fire. Serve in its own juice with the fat removed, adding the juice of a bitter orange or a dash of muscat verjuice.

Calf's Liver à la Bourgeoise. Lard with thick strips of seasoned bacon. On the bottom of a heavy pot put slices of bacon. Add the liver, with carrots, a *bouquet garni*, onions (one of them stuck with cloves), grated nutmeg, salt, and coarse pepper. Cover with slices of bacon. Add bouillon and 2 glasses of red wine, slices of lemon pitted and with the skin removed, or, if you have no lemon, some verjuice, and simmer. When cooked, remove the fat, reduce the gravy, and use it to make a *roux*, separately. But, for God's sake, never put pickled gherkins in a sauce for calf's liver.

Calf's Liver à l'Italienne. Cut a calf's liver into slices. Put into a casserole fine oil, melted lard, white wine, parsley, scallions, mushrooms, salt, and coarse pepper. Lay your liver slices on this base.

Season. Add more of your bottom mixture and continue, alternating, until you have used all the liver. Cook on a slow fire. Skim off the fat and serve in its own sauce, or an italienne sauce.

LOBSTER. (An article dealing also with trussed poultry and some other matters.)

I love the sea. It is essential not only to our pleasure but to our very basic happiness. When I have not seen it for a long time I am seized with an irresistible longing, and on any convenient pretext I take the train to Trouville, Dieppe, Le Havre. This time I went to Fécamp. I had no sooner arrived than I was invited on a fishing. party.

I know these fishing parties. You don't catch anything, but on the way home you buy a fish for dinner.

This time, contrary to custom, we took two fine mackerel and a cuttlefish. But we bought a lobster, a plaice, and a hundred shrimp. We met a mussel merchant on the road and added a hundred of his shellfish. We discussed at length to whose home we would go to prepare dinner, and finally settled on a big wine dealer who put his cellar at our disposal. He assured us that his cook had a *pot-au-feu* and that we would find the makings of several dishes she had obtained for his dinner.

But his cook, though he claimed she was a *cordon bleu*, was unanimously dethroned, and I was elected in her place. Now, if the housewives will follow me carefully, not losing a single detail or what goes on, they will add two or three new dishes to their repertoire.

As we had been promised, there was a *pot-au-feu* that had simmered since ten in the morning, which made it eight hours. A *pot-au-feu* reaches its peak after eight hours' cooking. France, as I have said elsewhere, is the only country in the world that knows how to make a *pot-au-feu*, and probably my concierge, who has nothing to do but take care of hers, and pull the string to open the doors, eats better soup than any Rothschild. To return to our cook. She had a *pot-au-feu* simmering, two pullets ready for the spit, a beef kidney that had not yet been told with what sauce it would be served. a bunch of asparagus beginning to bolt, tomatoes, and white onions.

I spread everything on the kitchen table, called for pen and ink, and presented the following menu for the approval of my guests:

Tomato and Shrimp Soup
* * *

Lobster à l'Américaine
Plaice à la Sauce Normande
Mackerel Maître d'Hôtel
Sautéed Kidneys with Burgundy
* * *

Pullets à la Ficelle
Fried Cuttlefish
* * *

Tomatoes à la Provençale
Scrambled Eggs with Kidney Gravy
Asparagus Tips
Hearts of Lettuce à l'Espagnole (without oil or vinegar)
* * *

Dessert Fruits
* * *

Wines: Château d'Yquem, Corton, Pommard, Château Latour
* * *

Coffee
* * *

Benedictine Champagne Brandy

This menu was received with enthusiasm, but everyone wanted to know how long it would take to prepare such a dinner. I asked for an hour and a half, and was granted this time – with some astonishment. They had thought it would take three hours. The great talent of the cook who wants to be on time is to prepare in advance and have all the ingredients of his dishes conveniently at hand. This is a matter of fifteen minutes.

Now, since it is impossible to develop all these dishes simultaneously with a pen, permit me to describe them dish by dish.

Tomato and Shrimp Soup. Bring salted water to a boil with 2 slices of lemon and a mixed bouquet. Put your shrimps into the boiling water.

Into another pot put 12 tomatoes from which you have squeezed the water, 4 big white onions (sliced), a piece of butter, 1 clove of garlic, and a mixed bouquet.

Your tomatoes and onions cooked, put them through a fine sieve, add a piece of meat glaze and a pinch of pepper, return to the fire, and let all this thicken to a purée. Then add an equal portion of bouillon and ½ glass of the water in which the shrimps were cooked. Stir to a boil. Add your shrimps, and your soup is done.

Of course, though I am giving each recipe separately, everything must go along at the same time.

Lobster à l'Américaine. Among the various methods of preparing this dish, we choose Vuillemot's. We ask the reader to give us his, and especially her, undivided attention, for this is very complicated.

1. Prepare a pot with 2 large onions cut in quarters, a mixed bouquet, 2 cloves of garlic, 1 bottle of good white wine, ½ glass of ordinary cognac, a ladleful of good consommé, salt, pepper, and a few grains of good Spanish pimento. Bring to a boil. Throw in your lobster. Half an hour is long enough for cooking.

Wait! The rest is not so simple.

2. Let your lobster cool in its liquid, if you are not in a hurry. The less hurry, the better. Remove the flesh and cut it into strips. Sprinkle with a little of its cooking liquor, put into a saucedish with a piece of buttered paper over it, and set aside in the warming oven.

3. Take 8 fine tomatoes, cut them in two, squeeze out the watery part and discard it. Butter a casserole and put your tomatoes in. Season with salt, fine white pepper, a little paprika, and fresh butter. Bake. Keep warm.

4. Dice 2 large onions, squeeze them in a cloth to remove the gluten. Sauté with a little butter until golden, add 1 tablespoonful of flour, moisten with half the liquor from the lobster pot, let it thicken on a corner of the stove, reduce to half, and add 2 large tablespoonfuls of tomato purée. Reduce another third, adding meat glaze. Strain. Add a little lemon juice, butter the size of a walnut, and set aside.

5. Finally take the lobster coral and the roe or milt if any, crush in a mortar with a piece of butter, put through a sieve, add a bit of pimento.

Arrange your lobster meat in the shape of a crown on a platter. Put the tomatoes on top, and between them pour the lobster butter you have just made. Glaze with sauce (step 4, above) and serve.

Since this dish is a trifle complicated, a novice should not attempt it. It takes quite a cook to tackle it.

Plaice à la Sauce Normande. Plaice is a fish with very white, lean flesh, estimably halfway between the sole and the dab; it tries in vain to attain the flavour of the former and the reputation of the latter.

Put your plaice on a buttered platter, season with salt, pepper, 1 glass of white wine, and put into the oven.

Put a piece of butter into a pot and stir until it darkens a little. Add a little flour. Pour the wine and butter from the plaice into the pot, leaving just enough so the fish will not dry out. Reduce the sauce to half.

Steam 30 mussels and 10 or 12 mushrooms. Put the juice into your sauce. Reduce it again to half, thicken with 4 egg yolks and ½ glass of fresh cream. Arrange the mussels and mushrooms around the plaice and pour your sauce over the whole. Dab with bits of butter. Let your fish rest in the oven 2 minutes, then serve.

As for the mackerel maître d'hôtel and the sautéed kidneys with Burgundy, I have nothing to teach anyone on the preparation of these dishes. This is the A B C of cooking.

But for this menu, make the kidney sauce a little thin and when it is completely ready, set ½ glass of it aside. You'll see why in a moment.

Pullets à la Ficelle. Right up to the moment that I put on my pullets *à la ficelle* I had submitted to the observations of the cook, who had become my assistant. But when that decisive moment arrived, observation turned to opposition. Since I had no time to lose,

I threatened a *coup d'état* that would result in her being sacked on the spot. This had its effect, and five minutes later my two pullets were roasting and turning side by side like a pair of spindles.

Today, however, I have the time to give you my reasons, and to explain the superiority of pullet *à la ficelle* to pullet on the spit.

All animals have two orifices, an upper orifice and a lower orifice. In this respect a chicken equals man. Diogenes said it twenty-four hundred years before me, the day he threw down a plucked cock on the agora at Athens and cried: "There is Plato's man."

Well, it is necessary to stop up one of these orifices. The upper one is stopped in the Belgian manner, by stuffing the neck into the chest and sewing up the skin around it.

Now let's go on to the lower, much more important, orifice. Your cook has already removed the intestines and the liver, throwing the first away. The liver has been chopped with *fines herbes*, scallions and parsley, mixed with a piece of butter, and returned to replace the intestines, there to perfume the whole.

Now what is the cook's purpose here? To retain the greatest amount of juices in the animal he intends to cook. If you pass a spit through the chicken to broil him, and a skewer to hold him on the spit, you not only fail to stopper the two openings nature made in him, but you add two more through which the juices can escape.

But if, on the contrary, you tie his feet together with string, and suspend him vertically by this string, with the lower orifice on top and the upper orifice stoppered up; if you take fine, fresh butter, mix it with salt and pepper, and baste this bird taking care to pour some of this butter into the lower, which is now the upper, orifice — then you have fulfilled all the logical conditions for preparing an excellent pullet. All that remains is to watch it cook, and to cut the string when the skin starts to break and send out little puffs of steam. Lay it on the platter and pour over it the juice from your dripping pan.

And never let a drop of bouillon mingle with the butter you use to baste your pullet. I believe I have already said it somewhere else, but it bears repeating, that any cook who puts bouillon into her dripping pan should be mercilessly and ignominiously dismissed.

As for the cuttlefish, that's as simple as any fish.

Fried Cuttlefish. Cut in pieces, roll in flour, dip in boiling oil or fat, remove when done. You will have something resembling fried calf's ear, with a slightly musky flavour.

As for the scrambled eggs with kidney gravy, asparagus tips, and stuffed tomatoes *à la provençale*, this is child's play.

Break 12 eggs into a bowl, discarding 6 whites. Beat them, add ½ glass of (chicken, if you have it) consommé, ½ glass of kidney gravy you have set aside, and leave them to the cook, who has merely to pour them into a pan and stir.

Essential: Serve soft. Scrambled eggs continue to cook in the platter.

Now. the tomatoes. Cut them in two, drain off the juice and seeds, fill with chopped chicken, veal, game from yesterday's dinner if you have it, and mushrooms. Sprinkle with the finest olive oil you can lay hands on, then salt and pepper, and parsley and garlic chopped together. Add a touch of hot pepper. Cook under the broiler, basting with the oil.

Salad Without Oil or Vinegar. This is a memento of Spain. There the vinegar has no bouquet, and in exchange the oil has a rancid odour. It is impossible, therefore, to eat salads, even when the heat and the dryness of the air give you a violent appetite for fresh, raw vegetables.

Well, I took care of this by substituting yolks of eggs for the oil, and lemon juice for the vinegar. This mixture, suitably seasoned with salt and pepper, made an exquisite salad, which we finish preferring to our own French salads.

Exactly an hour and a half after I had started, dinner was on the table. Four hours later we were still eating.

Now here's an article that contains a lot of cooking, I believe, but very little lobster. Let us return to this interesting animal.

Lobster. A crustacean widely used in cooking. The spiny lobster is not so finely flavoured and not so highly prized. Its flesh is chopped up into mayonnaise to make an excellent sauce for large fish, such as turbot.

Buy only live lobsters. Pick the heaviest. Plunge them into boiling salted water with a piece of butter, a sprig of parsley, a red pepper, and 2 or 3 white stalks of leek. After ¼ hour, add 1 glass of Madeira or Marsala and let the lobster cool in the liquid. Then split it down the middle of the back. Serve with a sauce, which must be prepared beforehand, as follows:

Remove all that is edible from a boiled lobster, mix well with oil, 1 tablespoonful of good mustard, 12 drops of Chinese soy sauce, a handful of *fines herbes*, 2 crushed shallots, and a good quantity of finely ground white pepper. Finally, add 1 glass of anisette or even a cordial made with anise flavouring. Beat with a fork like an omelet and add the juice of 2 or 3 lemons, depending on size of the lobster.

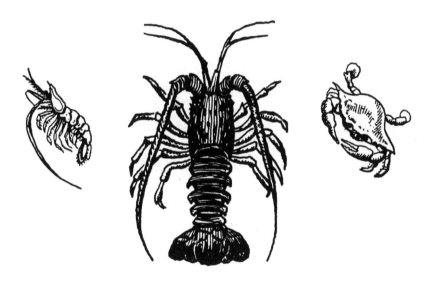

MACARONI. Macaroni was introduced to France by the Florentines, probably about the time Catherine de Médici came to wed Henry II. But it never became very popular, though everyone is familiar with these long tubes of paste like hollow vermicelli.

In preparing macaroni, choose neither the thin nor the fat, but those about the diameter of a wheat straw. Cook in salted water or, even better, in bouillon, until three-quarters done, or until they are fully swollen. Meanwhile, you will have grated Parmesan cheese and prepared beef sauce as follows:

Take 3 pounds of rump of beef, 6 tomatoes, and 6 white Spanish onions, cover with consommé prepared the day before, and boil for 3 hours. Press the broth through a sieve.

On the bottom of a casserole put Mainz ham, which has been cooked, mashed to a pulp, and pressed through a sieve. On top of this a layer of macaroni. Sprinkle with Parmesan. Spread on a layer

162

of beef sauce, to which you will have added tomatoes, white onions, salt, pepper, garlic, and paprika if you have it. This sauce should be fairly thick. Repeat, starting with the macaroni, and continue until the casserole is filled. Pour the last of the sauce over the whole.

Pour a glass of ice water on top and serve as a pottage.

In Naples, the glass of ice water is obligatory. (Mme Ristori's recipe.)

Don't imagine the Italian workers take all this trouble to prepare their macaroni. They are content to boil their tomatoes with water, salt, pepper, and a little paprika if they have it.

Macaroni Home Style. Boil for ¾ hour in salted water with 1 onion with a clove stuck in it and a piece of butter. Drain well. Put into a pan with butter, equal quantities of grated Gruyère and Parmesan cheese, a little nutmeg and coarse pepper, and a few table-spoonfuls of cream. Stir and sauté.

Macaroni au Gratin. Prepare as for Home Style, sprinkle with grated Parmesan cheese and bread crumbs, and brown in the oven.

MACE. The exterior husk of the nutmeg. Frequently used as an aromatic spice in cookery or confectionery.

MACKEREL. One of the most beautiful and courageous of all fish. When it is taken alive from the line into the boat, it seems made of azure, silver, and gold. A Norwegian historian tells of a seaman who suddenly disappeared while swimming in the ocean. When his body was found ten minutes later, it had already been largely devoured by the mackerel.

Mackerel Maître d'Hôtel. Choose very fresh mackerel, all of equal size so that they will be done at the same time. Cut off the tips of their snouts and tails. Put on an earthenware platter, sprinkle lightly with salt, pour oil with parsley and scallions over them. Keep turning them in this marinade at least ½ hour, longer if they are very large. To make sure the milt or roe does not spill out, cover the bellies with a leaf of romaine lettuce and bake belly up. Arrange on a dish when they are done, putting a cold maître d'hôtel sauce inside and a thickened maître d'hôtel sauce over them.

Mackerel Fillets Maître d'Hôtel. Slice 6 fillets from 3 mackerel. Cut each one in two and trim. Melt butter in a skillet, put your fillets in it skin side down, sprinkle lightly with salt, brush with melted butter. Cover with a piece of paper, set aside in a cool place, and prepare the following sauce:

Put 2 tablespoonfuls of reduced *velouté* into a pot with chopped parsley and shallots. Bring to a boil. Add butter and the juice of a large lemon. Soak and then parboil the milts and roes with a bit of salt. Put into your sauce and simmer a little. Just before serving, put your fillets on the fire and brown quickly, turning once. Drain off most of the butter. Arrange on a platter with a border of croutons fried in oil and butter, heat your sauce, and serve.

Mackerel English Style. Clean 3 or 4 very fresh mackerel. Trim the tail. Tie up the head. Split, but not through the back. Put a good handful of fresh fennel into the fish cooker, and the mackerel on top. Cover with lightly salted water and simmer. When done, drain, remove the fennel, and serve with either of the following sauces.

Fennel Sauce. Clean, chop, and blanch a few sprigs of fennel and set aside in a colander. Put equal amounts of *velouté* and butter sauce into a pot, heat, and spoon. Just before serving, add the fennel. Stir well together, add salt and a little nutmeg.

Gooseberry Sauce. Take 2 handfuls of half-ripe gooseberries. Split and remove the seeds. Blanch in hot salted water. Drain. Stir into a sauce like the one above, with or without fennel.

Mackerel Flemish Style. Prepare the fish as above. Mix butter with chopped scallions, parsley, and shallots, salt, and lemon juice. Fill the cavity of the fish with this butter. Wrap them with buttered paper, tie up with string and grill slowly, about ¾ hour. When they are done, remove the paper, arrange on a platter, and serve.

MAIGRE. This is the name given to foods that are permitted on fast days, as against *gras* foods whose use is forbidden on such days.

Various people have contended that abstinence from meat is incompatible with health. This is an error. It has been proved that a meatless diet is in no way contrary to the nature of our bodies, provided some attention is paid to the choice of foods and that these be not perverted by abuse of seasoning, which is so often the cause of harm to the human organism on a meatless diet.

It is equally an error to hold that a meatless diet is better, more digestible, nourishing, fattening, and strengthening than one in which meat is used. All this depends more or less on the strength or weakness of the particular stomach.

There is no relation between a *maigre* (lean) diet and thinness of the body. We see fleshless men devour huge quantities of meat without ever getting fat. And we see soft and languorous women who remain fat in spite of the lightest vegetable diet.

We do not deny that most *maigre* foods, especially fish, are very good. But it does not follow that they are better than meat. The learned Nonius, who wrote a treatise justifying fish, agrees that meat is the healthiest food. Man, he says, only abandoned fruits and herbs because he found by experience that meat sustained him better.

As for which foods are permitted on fast days, there are so many, they change so much, depending on climate and custom, and the Church is so ready to hand out dispensations that we refer our readers to that institution.

In the department of the Seine, the use of butter and dairy products was generally forbidden. In 1815, Louis XVIII ruled: "You shall not serve or permit to be served for Lenten meals either flesh, or fish, or products of flesh or fish, or eggs, or butter, or milk, or soft, cooked, or melted cheese. Aside from that, we shall eat anything we desire."

But today the archbishop of Paris has authorized the use of eggs and dairy products during Lent, and this has been very good for poor people, who cannot afford fish, so dear in Lent, and who consequently risked the wrath of heaven by eating forbidden foods.

[**MIREPOIX.** *A mixture of diced raw vegetables, ham, bacon, put under the meat for braising. A typical mirepoix might be composed of onions, carrots, ham, with a bay leaf and a sprig of thyme.* — ED.]

MOREL. A sort of spring mushroom, differing from ordinary mushrooms in having a pitted surface instead of gills. We have never heard of any accidents arising from the use of morels. They stimulate the appetite, fortify and restore the stomach, and are very useful in sauces. Christians, frightened by the example of Claudius, ate morels long before they could bring themselves to try mushrooms.

An anecdote whose authenticity we cannot guarantee, although we have read it in the *Life of St. Pardoux*, supports the above assertion about the edibility of morels. It seems that a peasant, having found some morels, wished to show his respect for the saint by making him a present of them. On the road a great lord named Raynacaire met him, seized the morels, and had them served for his dinner. But the legend says that *by divine intervention* they gave him a frightful colic, of which he was only cured by swallowing oil that had been blessed by St. Pardoux.

MUSHROOMS. A name that is applied to a great variety of fungi. Many are poisonous. Even the edible ones can prove toxic to people who, like the Emperor Claudius or Petronius' Trimalchio, are tempted to overindulge in them.

Mushrooms à la Bordelaise. Take the biggest cèpes you can find. They should be dry, fleshy, firm, and must be fresh-picked. Wash and drain them. Cut the skin lightly with lines to make diamond shapes on the top. Brush with fine oil, sprinkle with salt and coarse pepper, and let them marinate 2 hours. Grill them on one side. When they are done – which you can tell by feeling whether they are flexible under the fingers – arrange on a platter and serve with the following sauce:

Heat sufficient oil to sauce your mushrooms, having added to it while still cold finely chopped parsley, scallions, and a clove of garlic. When it gets really hot, pour it over the mushrooms and sprinkle with lemon juice or, what would really be better, verjuice.

Mushrooms à la Bordelaise (Another Recipe). Prepare and marinate your mushrooms as above, adding garlic to the marinade. Chop up the stems and trimmings of the mushrooms, press in a cloth to remove the moisture. Heat these a moment on the fire in oil with salt, pepper, chopped parsley, chopped scallions, and garlic. Put the mushrooms upside down in a baking pan and distribute the oil, herb, and chopped-stem mixture on each. Bake. Baste with the juices in the pan. Sprinkle with lemon juice and a dash of verjuice, and serve.

Crust with Mushrooms. Peel mushrooms and sauté in butter with a bouquet of parsley and scallions. Sprinkle with flour. Stir. Add bouillon consommé, bring to a boil, simmer. Season with salt, coarse pepper, a little nutmeg. Take the upper crust, hollowed out, of a round loaf of bread. Butter it. Dry it out over a grill. Stir raw egg yolks mixed with cream into your mushrooms. Put the crust on a platter and fill it with the mushroom sauce.

Special Note. I confess that nothing frightens me more than the appearance of mushrooms on the table, especially in a small provincial town. There always comes into my mind this notice in the paper:

"Yesterday M. X——, his wife and eldest daughter went for a walk in the forest of ——. They brought back a dish of mushrooms, which they had for dinner. This morning husband and wife were dead of poisoning, and no hope was held out for the daughter."

The worst thing about mushroom poisoning is that when the first symptoms appear it is already too late to do anything about it. Properly speaking, there is no antidote to mushroom poisoning. The first thing to do while waiting for the doctor is to administer an emetic.

MUSTARD. [*In the original, this article appears at the back of the book as an advertisement for the House of Alexandre Bornibus, 60 Boulevard de la Villette, Paris. It is signed at head and tail by Alexandre Dumas. Other, more formal advertisements — for caterers, gold and silversmiths, food purveyors, wines, patent medicines, etc. — do not have this distinction. — ED.*]

The Greeks and Romans did not have pot mustard such as is sold nowadays, but they used mustard in ragouts, and powdered mustard on their roasts, as we do. The name was the same in both tongues, indicating clearly that it passed from Greece to Italy. They called it, whether whole or ground, *sinapis.* Aristophanes and Menander, in their satiric pieces, have preserved a number of recipes for ragouts in which ground mustard was used. The Old and New Testaments both frequently refer to mustard seed.

The Romans at the end of the Republic and the Empire had too corrupt a taste merely to use mustard in its primitive simplicity. They used it with tuna brine to make a sauce they called *muria.*

Then they used one-tenth mustard to make up the horrible mixture they called *garum.* Besides mustard, this was composed of the intestines, heads, and gills of anchovies, mackerel, and dolphins. All this was ground up with mushrooms, bay leaf, thyme – and what else? No one knows. Nothing, perhaps. That could be the joke. And this concoction was sold at five hundred francs for a quart and a half.

Plautus, who lived in the third century B.C., seems to have detested mustard as much as Horace, two hundred years later, detested garlic. In his *Pseudolus* the cook calls mustard a frightful poison that makes the eyes water when it is pounded in a mortar. In *Truculentus*, harping on the same subject, he had Astrophius say: "If this man fed on mustard he could not be more sour and insensate."

Pliny the Elder, the same whose curiosity caused him to perish when Pompeii was destroyed by the eruption of Vesuvius, advises that mustard mixed with vinegar should be used as a condiment.

But here is Columella, who, in his *De re rustica*, written in A.D. 42, gives us something very close to the modern recipe for mustard: "Clean the mustard seed very carefully. Sift it well and wash in cold water. After it is clean, soak it in cold water two hours. Stir it, squeeze it, and put into a new, or very clean, mortar. Crush it with a pestle. When it is well ground, put the resulting paste in the centre of the mortar, press and flatten it with the hand. Make furrows in the surface and put hot coals in them. Pour water with saltpetre over these. This will take the bitterness out of the seed and prevent it from moulding. Pour off the moisture completely. Pour strong white vinegar over the mustard, mix it thoroughly with the pestle, and force through a sieve."

You see, except for the advice of the celebrated gastronome Courchamps, who, while he does not absolutely proscribe vinegar, prefers hot water or white wine, here we are in A.D. 42 devilishly close to modern mustard.

You want an improved recipe? Here is one from Palladius, in his own book, also called *De re rustica*, in the fourth century: "Reduce twelve pints of mustard to powder. Add a pound of honey, a pound of Spanish oil, a pint of strong vinegar. Blend thoroughly and use."

But the barbarians swarmed over Europe. Charlemagne, that magnificent emperor who in his day was served at table by kings, the kings by dukes, the dukes by marquises, the marquises by counts, the counts by barons, the barons by chevaliers, and the chevaliers by equerries, so that while the kings ate at nine in the morning the equerries were not fed until nine at night — this great emperor, in his capitularies, refers to mustard merely as an edible plant whose leaves may be eaten either cooked or in a salad. But not a word of mustard ground up and mixed with wine or vinegar.

Dijon alone preserved Palladius' recipe, and if mustard was not invented there, at least Dijon restored it. When did the Dijonnais restore the indispensable condiment to the table? It is impossible to say. But under St. Louis the vinegarmakers were accorded the right to make mustard.

In the thirteenth-century *Cries of Paris*, we find:

Fine, good vinegar!
Mustard vinegar!

The sauce peddlers ran through the Paris streets at dinnertime, crying, "Mustard sauce! . . . Garlic sauce! . . . Scallion sauce! . . . Verjuice sauce! . . . Ravigote sauce! . . ."

Anyone who wanted sauce for his meat opened his window, called the sauce seller, and was served immediately with the sauce of his choice.

Understandably, imitators appropriated and exploited the name of Dijon mustard. But Dijon maintained its supremacy. A manuscript of the thirteenth century refers to Dijon mustard. In the fourteenth century, Jean Millot included in his book of *Proverbs*:

There is no town, if not Dijon.
There is no mustard but in Dijon.

It was useless for the South to make its own mustard, substituting grape juice for vinegar. A new slogan answered: "Saint-Mexant mustard is good. But Dijon mustard is better."

When the Duke of Burgundy entertained King Philip of Valois with public celebrations, one hundred gallons of mustard were consumed at a single dinner.

According to Froissart, when Edward III of England invaded France he ordered his captains to burn everything along their route.

The magistrates of Saint-Didier threw themselves at his feet, begging him not to put the plains to the torch because, as they said, the destruction of food and food production would produce a famine.

"Bah!" said the ferocious Plantagenet, "war without burning is sausage without mustard!"

The earliest cookery book to appear in France, *Le Viandier*, by Taillevent, who was cook to Charles VII, praises mustard highly. His ancient French is difficult to read, but I have done it for you, and here is what he says:

"One evening after a great battle with the English, Charles VII, with his three inseparable companions, Dunois, La Hire, and Xain-trailles, came to lodge in the little town of Sainte-Menehould, of which only five or six houses remained standing, it having been put to the torch.

"The King and his suite were dying of hunger. There was nothing left in the ravaged countryside. Finally, four pig's feet and three chickens were procured. The King had no cook with him, and the wife of a poor toolmaker was entrusted with the preparation of the chickens. As for the pig's feet, they were simply laid on the grill.

"The good woman roasted the chickens, dipped them in beaten eggs, rolled them in bread crumbs with *fines herbes*, and covered them with a mustard sauce. The King and his companions left only bones.

"King Charles VII often afterwards asked for chicken *à la Sainte-Menehould*. Taillevent understood perfectly what he meant, and prepared it exactly as the toolmaker's wife had done."

Louis XI, who loved to drop in unexpectedly for dinner on his companions, the bourgeois of Paris, nearly always carried his own pot of mustard with him. In the accounts of J. Riboteau, receiver-general of Burgundy, we find an order placed by him with an apothecary at Dijon for twenty pounds of mustard for the King's personal use.

Among the popes who held brilliant court at Abignon was John XXII, who did not disdain the pleasures of the table. He loved mustard, and when he cast about for an appointment for a good-for-nothing nephew finally made him "chief mustardmaker". This is the origin of the expression "chief mustardmaker to the Pope", applied to a stupid and vain person.

When they returned to Rome, the popes took their predilection for mustard with them. But the mustard they used had little in common with the modern preparation. It was composed of bread crumbs and mustard seed macerated in water and vinegar, then passed through a sieve.

Louis XIV granted a coat of arms to mustard: funnel argent on azure.

Following the discovery of America, the Portuguese developed an immense trade in Eastern and Western spices, an irruption against which mustard struggled bravely. Dijon prepared regulations to reassure the public as to the methods and ingredients used in the manufacture of its mustard. But in spite of everything the vogue for mustard waned.

Then along came Jean Naigeon, who made a single change in the preparation of mustard that brought a recrudescence in sales and public favour. It was the inspiration of genius. Naigeon was the first to substitute verjuice – that is, the juice of unripened grapes – for vinegar. In consequence, no more sugar, no more acetic acid, in the mustard; only tartaric, citric, and malic acids.

Let us mention in passing that this Jean Naigeon was the father of the Naigeon, an atheistic publisher, who published an edition of Diderot's works.

In 1742 Paris began to compete seriously with Dijon. One Capitaine, a vinegarmaker of Paris, began to employ white instead of red vinegar for his mustard, and to produce fine mustards with capers and anchovy essence. These innovations gained wide favour.

Ten years later, another vinegarmaker, named Maille, made himself a European reputation in his specialty. Named purveyor to Mme de Pompadour, he took the not-too-ambitious title of vinegar distiller to the king of France and the emperors of Germany and Russia. An intelligent man, understanding the sensuality of his period, he began by making different vinegars for the use of men and women. His clientele soon included all the elegants, the petty aristocrats, duchesses, marquises, countesses, young coxcombs, and gallant abbés. The boudoir was a sure path to the kitchen. Before Maille, there were only nine varieties of vinegar. He added ninety-two toilet vinegars and likewise multiplied his table vinegars. He made twenty-four varieties of mustard:

Red mustard; fine mustard with capers; with anchovies; powdered mustard; garlic mustard; tarragon mustard; nasturtium mus-
tard; lemon mustard; *à la Choiseul*; *à la Choisy*; with pickles; with
fines herbes; Greek mustard; *à la maréchale*; *à la marquise*; *à la reine*;
à la romaine; with truffles. All these, except those with capers and
anchovies, were his own invention.

Good things bear their own longevity. Maille's mustard has
come down to us, and is still the preferred mustard of many honourable gourmands.

Bordin flourished as a contemporary of Maille. In 1762 he invented a so-called health mustard. He composed the recipes for forty
different varieties of mustard, including imperial mustard; with
champagne; with rocambole; with mushrooms; with roses; *à
l'italienne*; with vanilla.

In 1812, counting the twenty-nine new varieties of mustard invented by Acloque, pupil and successor to Maille, and not counting
Capitaine's mustard or Dijon mustard, there were eighty-four varieties available in France, when Grimod de la Reynière announced the
discovery of three more, respectively from Chalon-sur-Saône,
Besançon, and Saint-Brieuc. He noted in the *Almanach des gourmands*:
"An apothecary-chemist of Saint-Brieuc has just set up a mustard
factory, the product of which is not without merit. It is especially
strong and highly flavoured. This manufacturer, Maout by name,
proposes to establish himself in Paris also."

This brief mention was sufficient to turn attention to M. Maout's
product. Dr. Gatald, Portalis, and Cambacérès, the triumvirate who
reigned over the French table for half a century, declared themselves
in its favour. And as long as supper was eaten in France – that is to
say, as long as a certain delicacy in eating was observed – the Celtic
mustard of M. Maout appeared on the best tables, alongside those
of Maille and Bordin.

I have been asked which mustard I prefer above all. Until I
tasted and appreciated the mustard made by Alexandre Bornibus, I
preferred the aromatic mustards of Maille and Bordin to all others.
But when, by chance, I tasted Bornibus' mustard, I knew at once it
was the best of all.

I said by chance, because this is how it came about:
I was writing a novel the scene of which was mainly Bourg-en-

Bresse. When I inquired the best route to visit this place I was told to go to Mâcon and from there take the branch line to Bourg. I was asleep when we arrived at Dijon, and when I heard the name of the station announced I was all confused. Was the branch line to Bourg from Dijon or from Mâcon? I couldn't remember. Since I had no luggage except my valise, I jumped down from the train and went through the station, asking where the line to Bourg was.

Finally I came on a coachman who told me my mistake. I ran back to the train. The ticket man asked for my ticket. I told him to look through those I had just given him on leaving the train.

While he was looking, the locomotive coughed, spit, sneezed, and went off.

The gateman laughed. "You'll be the first in line for the train to Mâcon in the morning," he said, and gave me back my ticket.

"I'll stay the night," I decided, "and take this opportunity to see the cathedral and visit my friend Louis Boulanger."

Boulanger, a painter whose earliest canvases had shown great promise, was director of the museum at Dijon, and I was delighted at the opportunity to see him. But since I could not drop in on him at eleven o'clock at night, I went meanwhile to the Hôtel du Parc.

I asked for supper, and was served two chops in mustard and half a cold fowl.

'What mustard do you want?" the waiter asked.

"Why, Dijon mustard, of course," said I.

"I know that," said the waiter, looking as though he had discovered a complete idiot. "But what I'm asking is whether you want men's mustard or ladies' mustard."

"Oh," said I, "so there's a difference between mustard for men and mustard for women?"

"For ladies."

"All right. For ladies."

"Yes, sir. Since a lady's palate is more delicate than a man's, ordinary Dijon mustard is too strong and sharp for them. So, M. Bornibus has invented a special mustard."

"And who is this Bornibus?"

"Why, he's the most fashionable mustardmaker. Everybody is talking about his mustard."

"Now I remember. I know him by reputation, but I don't know his mustard. Give me some."

"Which one?"

"Both."

"Sir, you will eat ladies' mustard?"

"If I can eat the strong, I can eat the weak," said I.

So he brought me both kinds of mustards with my chops.

I am no great expert on the subject of mustard. I have always had a fine stomach, and never made great use of this "preface to appetite," as Grimod de la Reynière calls it. But on this occasion, at sight of the fine canary-yellow colour, I plunged in the wooden spoon and made two pyramids, one of men's mustard, one of ladies', on my plate.

I must say that from that moment I made a turnabout and developed an enthusiasm for Bornibus' mustard.

When I returned to Paris, I visited Bornibus' establishment at 60 Boulevard de la Villette. He very kindly showed me around and explained that the superiority of his product was due to the machinery he had invented for the preparation of his mustard, and above all the combination and choice of his basic ingredients.

MUTTON. See SHEEP.

OLIVES. As they are picked from the tree, olives are bitter and have a disagreeable flavour even when ripe. It is necessary to pickle them in oil and brine to remove this natural bitterness and make them into an agreeable food, leaving only slight bitterness sweetened by their own natural oil and the effects of the brine.

The Greeks, who attributed a divine origin to the olive, venerated it so that for long only virgin men and women were permitted to take part in its culture, and a vow of chastity was required from those who gathered in the harvest.

Olives added to ragouts, being more or less cooked in the process, are always better and more digestible than the raw.

Olive Ragout. Lightly sauté chopped parsley and chives, add 2 tablespoonfuls of gravy, or bouillon reduced to half, 1 glass of white wine, capers, an anchovy, and pitted olives. Add a little olive oil and a bouquet of *fines herbes*. Bring to a boil and thicken with chestnut purée.

[*Since olive ragout is used only for underdone meats — ducks, for example — all you really need do is pit a few olives, parboil them, put them into a reduced espagnole sauce with the duck drippings, stir in* 1 *tablespoonful of good olive oil and the juice of 1 lemon, and serve. This simple method, trust my experience, is better than any condiment that a false science might invent. — VUILLEMOT.]*

ONIONS. If it is necessary to have something in sight when writing about it, then it is providential that I came to Roscoff just as I was about to set down the word.

In fact, nowhere else in France, and not even in ancient Egypt, can there ever have been greater quantities of this bulb, the boast of antiquity, sung by the poets, and to which the Egyptians accorded divine honours, than in this corner of Armorica. There are years when Roscoff exports thirty to forty boatloads to England.

Onion Ragout. Cook onions in hot ashes under the coals. Peel. Simmer in a clear cullis of veal and ham. Thicken with a little cullis. If you wish, add a little mustard.

Onion Soup Vuillemot. Cut 4 peeled white onions down the middle, discarding both ends, and slice to make half rings. Separate the rings and sauté lightly in butter. Add a sprinkle of flour, and sauté the whole to a golden yellow. Add water in which string beans have cooked, consommé, or plain water. Season with salt and fine ground pepper and simmer, but *do not boil*. Pour into a soup tureen, over buttered bread. Serve with grated Gruyère cheese on the side.

Onion Soup à la Stanislaus. On his journeys from Lunéville to Paris each year to visit his daughter the Queen, ex-King Stanislaus of Poland stopped at an inn in Châlons, where he was served such a fine, delicate onion soup that he refused to continue on his way without learning how to make it. His Majesty, wrapped in his dressing gown, went down to the kitchen and insisted that the chef perform before his eyes. Neither the smoke nor the onion fumes that made his eyes tear distracted his attention. He observed carefully, took notes, and went on his way only when he was certain he had mastered the art of making excellent onion soup. This is the recipe:

Take the top crust of a loaf of bread, break it into pieces. Heat each piece on both sides before the fire. Rub the hot bread with butter and toast lightly over the coals. Put aside on a plate. Fry 3 large onions, diced, in butter until they are golden brown, which cannot be achieved without constant stirring. Add the crusts of bread. Keep stirring. When the onions are thoroughly browned, add boiling water, stir to detach everything from the pot. Season. Simmer at least 15 minutes before serving.

It is incorrect to imagine that this soup will be improved by using bouillon. On the contrary, such an addition will make it more nourishing, less delicate.

Milk Onion Soup. Let me say first of all that the most important thing to remember is that cream must be added to the boiling soup.

Chop fine 12 or 15 onions. Parboil to remove the first bitterness. After a few minutes, drain, put into a skillet with a big piece of fresh butter. Let them colour. Add milk. Boil for 15 minutes, press through a sieve. Boil another 15 minutes to thicken. Taste, salt, pepper, or sugar if you prefer. Add cream and pour over toasted croutons.

ORTOLAN. [*A bunting.* – ED.]

In Toulouse they know how to fatten ortolans better than anywhere else. To kill them they asphyxiate them by plunging their heads into very strong vinegar. It is a violent death that improves their flesh.

For the best methods of eating ortolans, see the article on figpeckers.

Ortolans à la Toulousaine. Clean and dress. Rub with half a lemon. Put them on a spit. Cover with butter mixed with lemon juice. Bread. Broil at a fairly high temperature 7 or 8 minutes, basting from the dripping pan. At the last moment salt, take off the spit, arrange on a platter. Pour the contents of the dripping pan over them and serve immediately with lemon quarters. Add a few crusts of bread to the platter.

Ortolans in Terrine. Chop up equal amounts of partridge flesh and fat pork. Don't be content with chopping, but season and crush in a mortar until smooth in texture. Cover the bottom of an earthenware casserole with this mixture. Sprinkle with chopped truffles. Cut off the feet and heads of your ortolans. Sprinkle with seasoned salt. Arrange them in the casserole. Repeat the process. Finally, put a layer of your mixture on top and sprinkle with truffles. Cover with slices of bacon. Put a bay leaf on top. Cover the casserole and bake.

Ortolans in Ramekins. Prepare 12 ortolans, put into oiled ramekins with 1 tablespoonful of reduced Périgueux sauce under them. Bake. Put more Périgueux over them and serve.

OSTRICH. The biggest, most famous, and most anciently known of so-called edible birds. In Deuteronomy Moses forbids the Jews to eat its flesh. Later it became popular with the Romans. It is said that Heliogabalus had six hundred ostrich brains served at a single meal.

Ostrich flesh is not very good. It is tough and tasteless. But the wing, which is the tenderest part, and the breast, can be eaten.

Ostrich eggs are very big. Some have been observed that weighed as much as thirty hen's eggs, and travellers have reported that they are fine eating. [See *Arabian Omelet*, under EGGS.]

The Arabs today, like the Hebrews of old, abstain from eating ostrich flesh, but they use its fat to prepare various dishes, and to rub on their bodies for rheumatism and other ailments.

OYSTERS. The oyster is the most disinherited of molluscs. Being acephalous – that is to say, having no head – it has no organ of sight, no organ of hearing, no organ of smell. Its blood is colourless. Its body adheres to the two sides of its shell by a powerful muscle that it uses to open and close it. Neither has it any organ of locomotion. Its only exercise is sleep; its only pleasure, eating. Since the oyster has no way to go after food, food comes to it, or is brought to it by the movement of the water. Its food is composed of animal matter suspended in water. In 1816, Bedan proved that oysters could gradually be acclimatised to fresh water. The Greeks were especially fond of Sestos oysters. I tasted them while passing through the Bosporus. They were nothing special.

Someone once cried: "The gods are departing!" and this eloquent phrase aroused the greatest admiration. But lately another cry has been heard: "The oysters are disappearing!" Certainly there is no connection between the hermaphroditic mollusc, attached to its rock for all eternity, and the inhabitants of Olympus. Well, Bossuet's famous, eloquent cry: "Madame is dying! Madame is dead!" did not make so great an impression as the cry of gastronomic distress: "The oysters are disappearing!" From sixty centimes a dozen their price immediately rose to one franc thirty centimes.

The sensation was enormous. The oyster, treasure of the gourmand, was about to escape from him! The oyster, which, according to Dr. Réveille-Paris, is the only alimentary substance that does not cause indigestion!

The Romans, much more gourmand than the Greeks, rendered almost divine honours to the oyster. No fine dinner was served that did not include raw oysters on ice and oysters seasoned with garum, a sort of brine whose recipe has been handed down to us by Pliny.

Apicius, that celebrated gourmand who cut his throat because he had only six or eight million sesterces (which is about two million in our money) left, had found a method to preserve oysters. In our day he would have patented it and lived on his royalties.

Oysters are taken by dragging, and the oystermen divide the oyster banks into zones so that while one is being exploited the oysters may grow and multiply in the others. Oysters are not taken in May, June, July, or August. To compensate, these are the months when mussels are at their best.

Oysters should not be eaten as they come out of the sea. At least no disciple of Lucullus nor any of Brillat-Savarin's apostles would commit such heresy. Oysters must first be buried a yard deep in sand or gravel. A Roman named Sergius Orata was the first, around 200 B.C., to have the idea of putting oysters to fatten in Lake Lucrinus. He became rich from the sale of them.

Mirabeau's uncle, speaking of the sea, said: "That field which ploughs itself." But he did not say: "That field which sows itself." For long the sea was believed to be inexhaustible. But now we see that it is becoming depopulated. The whales are disappearing. The mackerel weaken. Oysters are getting scarce.

"The ocean can be turned into an immense food factory," says Eugène Noël. "It can be made into a more fruitful laboratory than the earth. Fertilize it! Seas, rivers, ponds! Only the earth is cultivated. Here is the art of cultivating the waters. Hear, ye nations!"

And in fact fish, especially the edible varieties, are capable of

growing more on less nourishment than any other creatures. Pisci-
culture has been practised in China from time immemorial. There
everyone has a fishpond into which are thrown the household leav-
ings, on which the submarine herds live and fatten. The Romans in
this respect did even better than the Chinese. They fattened salt-
water fish in fresh water.

Jacobi, in Germany, discovered the artificial fertilization of
oysters, practised in England first, then in France by a Bresse fisherman named Rémy. Coste and Pouchet made a science of it.

These experiments determined M. de Chaillé and Mme Sarah-
Félix to establish oyster beds at Regnéville. They asked for and
obtained ten hectares of shore. Now, ten hectares is a lot of land in
Paris, on the Place de la Concorde or the Rue de Richelieu. Facing
the ocean, it is a point in an immensity.

The concessionaires first surrounded their farm with a dyke,
higher than the tide, on three sides. The shore was the fourth. Sea
water came in through a great sluice. Then thousands of oysters
were introduced, and tiles were gently deposited for them to attach
themselves to. The idea was to protect the oyster fry from the
dangers of the open sea.

To understand this enterprise it is necessary to know how
oysters reproduce. They are hermaphroditic. At the moment of love
both sexes open like flowers. At this time the oyster is filled with a
white water, and then the oysters are said to be milky and are
inedible.

Davaine has counted up to 1,200,000 eggs in an oyster the size
of a horse's hoof. And since they spawn two or even three times, at
least two million eggs are delivered to the sea's caprice each year.
These eggs are almost invisible. Leeuwenhoek calculated that it
would take a million to make up the volume of a child's marble. The
freshly hatched oysters are able to move about. This ability is given
by nature to the larvae of all fixed animals and permits them to
fasten themselves wherever they wish. But they must choose their
spot carefully. Once fastened, they are there for life.

In the farm at Regnéville, at first, they used ordinary tiles and
faggots of wood, giving the oysters a choice between the sea bottom
and suspension. But the oyster farmers soon discovered that the
faggots got covered with slime, and the little oysters could not fasten

themselves. And the tiles, on the contrary, permitted the oysters to fasten themselves too completely. The oyster found it convenient to use the tile as one of its shells, and when it was removed, either the shell had a hole in it, or the oyster stayed behind on its tile.

So our farmers glued old newspapers by each end to the tiles. The oyster stuck to the paper, but the paper stuck to nothing. In our opinion, not every newspaper is suitable. I know some that could poison the oysters for human consumption, as the Venetian oysters that fasten themselves to the copper bottoms of ships are poisoned.

Oysters are generally eaten in the simplest way. They are opened, detached, a drop of lemon juice added, and swallowed.

More refined gourmands prepare a sauce with vinegar, pepper, and shallots, into which they dip the oyster before swallowing it.

The true connoisseur, however, swallows without lemon, vinegar, pepper, or anything else.

Oysters à la Poulette. Open the oysters, blanch in their own juice, but do not boil. Dip in butter, then in chopped parsley, shallots, and mushrooms; then in a spoonful of oil with pepper and grated nutmeg. Bread with soft white crumbs mixed with oil. Brown under the broiler. Just before serving, sprinkle with lemon juice.

Stuffed Oysters. Make a stuffing from eel meat, 12 blanched oysters, a little parsley and scallions, a few mushrooms, seasoned with salt, pepper, *fines herbes*, fine spices, a piece of good fresh butter, white of bread soaked in cream, 2 raw egg yolks. The whole chopped and pounded very fine. Fill the half oyster shells with this mixture and put on top of it a stewed oyster. Cover this up with the stuffing, brush with beaten egg, follow with melted butter, then fine bread crumbs. Bake to a fine golden colour and serve.

Oysters Parmesan. Drain your oysters and put them on a buttered platter, sprinkle with coarse pepper and chopped parsley. Pour over them ½ glass of champagne, cover with grated Parmesan cheese, and bake. When they are a good golden colour, and the cheese glazed, remove, pour off any excess butter, clean the edge of the platter, and serve.

Oysters à la Minute. Into a pot put 1 tablespoonful of cullis, 1 glass of champagne, a *bouquet garni*, and bring to a boil. Open your oysters and drain them, add the juice to the cullis. Reduce this sauce. Add the oysters for just a few minutes and serve garnished with fried croutons.

Oysters à la Daube. Sprinkle very finely chopped parsley, scallion, and basil, salt, and pepper on oysters on the half shell. Use very little of this seasoning on each oyster. Sprinkle with white wine. Put the other half of the shell back on and grill, laying a hot oven-peel on each a few times during the process. Serve open.

PANTHER. We include this animal because there are people in India who eat it.

The panther is tamed rather than domesticated. It never loses its fierceness of character. Hunters who use panthers have to use the most extreme methods of training and control. Those who have eaten its flesh have found it good. But Galen says it is not so good as bear meat and that its liver has a horrible flavour and is even poisonous at times.

PARMESAN. Despite its name, this cheese is not made at Parma, but in and around Lodi. Its real name is *formaggio lodigiano*, or sometimes *formaggio di grana*. Thirty thousand cows are used in and around Lodi to provide milk for the preparation of this cheese.

PARSLEY. Is the obligatory condiment of every sauce.

"Parsley," says the learned author of the *Traité des plantes usuelles*, "makes food more healthful, more agreeable. It stimulates the appetite and helps digestion."

Bosc is even more positive in his opinion. "Take parsley away from the cook," he says, "and you leave him in a situation where it is next to impossible for him to practise his art."

Parsley, I repeat, must be used in every sauce and every ragout, but there are also two culinary seasonings of which it is the principal ingredient. These are *watter-fisch*[1] court bouillon (see PERCH) and parsley hollandaise.

PARSNIP. There are two varieties, the long and the round. This root is used in making bouillon. It is also fried in butter. Not everyone likes its flavour. Ray says that the English believe that when parsnips get too old they produce delirium and even madness. This plant has been credited with aphrodisiac qualities. It should not be confused with water hemlock, the leaves of which have red stains near their base. In Thuringia, a syrup, used in place of sugar, is extracted from parsnips. In Germany, a species of small, sweet, floury parsnips is grown and eaten in a sort of stew with cubed fresh pork and deer meat.

PARTRIDGE. Of the many varieties of partridge, four are most highly esteemed for their delicacy and flavour. These are the grey, the red-legged, the rock, and the Greek partridge or *bartavelle*. This last was unknown in France before 1440, when it was brought to Provence from the island of Chios by René, King of Naples. It is larger than the red partridge, which it greatly resembles. The back is reddish grey, the chest grey, the belly reddish. This bird never descends into the plains. Its flesh is white and, though slightly resinous in flavour, highly esteemed. In France it is found chiefly in the Alps, sometimes in the valleys of Grésivaudan and Vienne and in Valentinois. Father Poire has said that there is the same distance between a *bartavelle* and an ordinary partridge as between a peach and a chestnut. Cyrano de Bergerac [the writer, 1619-1665] considers *bartavelles* to bear the same relation to partridge that cardinals bear

---

[1]Dumas' spelling, from Courchamps.–ED.

to mendicant friars. Finally, Grimod de la Reynière has said that *bartavelles* merit such profound respect they should be eaten kneeling. The author of the *Memoirs of the Marquise de Créqui* advises very fine larding, or, if the birds are very young, barding, with strips of bacon. But M. Vuillemot has laid down the principle that game should never be larded, and we bow to this authority.

Partridge are usually hunted with setters or pointers. Experienced hunters aver that from ten to noon and from two to four are the best times for taking partridge, which are on the move for forage the rest of the day. They are also taken with snares and nets. Hen partridge in cages, or imitations of their cries, are used to attract the cocks. Young partridge are distinguished from the old by the long wing plumes, which are pointed on the young, rounded on the old.

The flesh of young partridge is lightly stimulating, tender, savoury, and easily digested. The flesh of the old needs prolonged cooking but since it is full of osmazome it is very tasty. An old partridge boiled with other meats gives an excellent flavour to the bouillon, makes it more tonic.

Young Partridge à la Parisienne. Turn in butter, but do not colour. Add 1 glass of white wine, 2 large tablespoonfuls of consommé, and some espagnole sauce with meat glaze added, reduced. Simmer about 45 minutes. Take out most of the sauce. Reduce it and skim off the fat. Just before serving, arrange your partridge on a platter, put a piece of butter into the sauce, strain and spoon it, and pour over the birds.

Young Partridge à la Bourguignonne. Roast 3 partridge on a spit. Dismember them. Sauté in a skillet with 3 tablespoonfuls of oil, a little red wine, salt, pepper, the juice of 1 lemon and a little of the zest. Arrange on a platter, sauce, and serve.

Partridge with Cabbage Home Style. Braise a brace of partridge and put them on a platter. Have cabbage steamed with a little salt pork or bacon. Squeeze it dry in a cloth. Cut it up and arrange in quarters around the partridge. Garnish with slices of cervelat, lightly salted pork and chipolata sausages. Sauce with the reduced gravy from your braising.

Sautéed Breast of Young Partridge. Remove the tendons and fell from the breasts of 4 partridge. Melt 2 ounces of clarified butter in a skillet. Moisten the breasts with butter and arrange them in the skillet. Salt. Cover with a piece of paper and sauté. Prepare a fumet with the "oysters" of the birds, reduce, add 4 large table-spoonfuls of espagnole sauce. Reduce again and skim off any fat before serving. After turning your breasts, drain them. Arrange on a platter with pieces of bread cut heart-shaped, and fried in butter, between them. Finish the sauce with butter, lemon juice, and 1 tablespoonful of olive oil. Cover the breasts with this sauce. If you wish, add slices of truffle in the depressions between the breasts, and serve.

Partridge à la d'Artois. Broil 2 or 3 partridges on the spit, without larding. Remove the legs and wings and arrange in a casserole with a little bouillon to keep warm, but do not boil. Meanwhile, remove all the rest of the meat from the carcass and crush it well in a mortar. Put into a pot a good glass of Madeira, 3 cut-up shallots, 3 sprigs of parsley, a little zest of bitter orange. Bring to a boil. Add 5 large tablespoonfuls of reduced espagnole or white veal sauce. Bring to a good boil. Add the crushed meat, mix, pass the whole through a sieve. Heat this purée in a double boiler. Now drain the legs and wings, arrange on a platter, mixing in croutons fried in butter. To the sauce add the juice of a bitter orange, a bit of white pepper, a piece of butter, heat well and pour over the whole. Garnish the edges of the platter with croutons fried in oil.

PÂTÉ DE FOIE GRAS. The *foie gras* of Strasbourg furnishes the king's table. The operation by which these livers are obtained consists principally in fattening the geese in such a manner as to enlarge this organ. Such a liver, fattened in Strasbourg, will be ten to twelve times bigger than nature intended.

To achieve this, these animals are submitted to unheard-of tortures, worse than those suffered by the early Christians. Their feet are nailed to the floor so that their obesity will not be delayed by movement. Their eyes are put out so that they will not be distracted by any view of the outside world. They are stuffed with nuts and never given anything to drink, no matter what cries of anguish thirst may cause them to produce.

PEACH. Originally from Persia. It has been famous in China from the remotest times. The Chinese poets represent it at times as bestowing the gift of immortality, at others the gift of death. Actual peaches, or porcelain replicas, are given as tokens of friendship and good will. Chinese artists use them very freely in decorating rooms. In Persia it was believed, for many centuries, that they were poisonous, and they were never touched, much less eaten. However, they were exported to Egypt, where the climate improved and sweetened them. Re-imported into Persia, they are now eaten in enormous quantities.

The best peaches come from the environs of Paris. Montreuil especially is famous for the beauty, goodness, and prodigious quantity of its peaches. After them come the peaches from Dauphiné, Angoumois, Touraine, etc.

The Montreuil peach was developed by an ex-musketeer named Girardot. After being seriously wounded, he retired to his little estate called Malassis, between the villages of Montreuil and Bagnolet. Here, with the assistance of La Quintinie, director of the Royal Gardens at Versailles, he devoted himself to the culture and development of fruit trees.

Girardot had a favour to ask of Louis XIV, and La Quintinie arranged that he should present a basket of his peaches to the King, who admired them greatly and went to see the espaliers on which they were grown. There he found Girardot, attired in his old uniform. The old musketeer's favours were granted, among them being a pension and the privilege of presenting the King with a basket of his peaches every year. This custom was kept up by his descendants until 1789.

PEAR. More than three hundred varieties of this, one of our finest fruits, are grown in our orchards.

Pears with Bacon. Cut bacon into little cubes and fry. Peel and cut up cooking pears and steam in a little veal broth. Drain the bacon and the pears and mix them in a pot, adding a pinch of nutmeg, coarse pepper, and a few tansy leaves. Cook together ½ hour and serve this fine German dish with fried croutons, as it is served every Wednesday at the court of Württemberg.

PEAS. We shall deal here only with little green peas, picked before maturity while they are still tender, juicy, and full of sugar. They are without contradiction our finest legume. When they are fresh, tender, and cooked immediately after shelling, they are always proper to serve as a side dish.

Old-fashioned Green Peas. (Recipe from the Abbey of Fontevrault.) Shell 2 quarts of green peas just before cooking, keeping them wrapped in a wet napkin until actually ready to cook. Take a head of lettuce and spread the centre leaves to insert a fresh sprig of savory. Tie up the lettuce and put it into a pot with the peas, a pinch of salt, ½ glass of water, and ½ pound of butter. After 15 minutes' cooking, remove the lettuce. At the moment of serving, mix in 3 tablespoonfuls of extra-heavy cream, mixed with the yolk of a fresh-laid egg, a pinch of pepper, and 1 tablespoonful of powdered sugar.

Green Peas French Style. Put 2 pounds of very fine peas in a pot with water and butter. Stir with the fingers. Drain off the water. Add a bouquet of parsley, a little onion, a heart of lettuce, a little salt, 1 teaspoonful of powdered sugar. Cover tightly and cook on low heat for ½ hour. Take out the bouquet and the onion. Put the lettuce on a platter. Put a piece of butter mixed with flour into the peas and stir over heat until well mixed. Pour over the lettuce. Do not try to thicken. Fresh green peas thicken of themselves.

Creamed Green Peas. Warm a piece of butter mixed with flour in a pot. Add the peas, a bouquet of parsley and scallions, salt, and pepper. Let them stew without adding liquid. Pour off the juice, mix it with cream and a little powdered sugar, pour over the peas, and heat again before serving.

PERCH. An excellent river fish, with flesh as light as it is nutritious. It derives its name from the Latin word *perca* because it has black spots. Seine perch are especially fine. The gourmands of the sixteenth century called them fresh-water partridge. The perch is extremely voracious and will practically destroy any other fish in an aquarium into which it may be put. Its roe is very tasty, and is served in pastry shells after sautéing in fresh butter with a few leaves of parsley. It can also be prepared with champagne, in a matelote, *à la Sainte-Menehould*, or even fried. But the best way of preparing perch is *à la Watter-Fisch*, in a Dutch court bouillon made as follows:

Take 6 big bunches of parsley with their roots. Clean them well, but leave the roots attached. Boil them for 3 hours in salted water with 1 stalk of white leek, 1 parsnip cut in quarters, and 1 medium-sized Jamaica or Cayenne pepper. When the *watter-fisch* is properly seasoned and reduced, take out everything except the parsley roots. Cook your perch in this court bouillon, and serve it in a deep dish with the bouillon and the cooked parsley. With this serve a platter of buttered slices of rye bread.

PHEASANT. Croesus, seated on his diamond-encrusted throne, crowned with his diadem and clothed in purple and gold, asked Solon whether he had ever seen anything so fine.

"Yes," the philosopher answered. "I have seen pheasants and peacocks."

The flesh of the pheasant is perhaps the most delicate and savoury there is. It is served roasted, braised, scalloped, in a salmis, and the breast sautéed. Braised, it may be served with a truffle sauce, on a bed of olive ragout. The author of the *Henriade* [Voltaire] has written a poem far superior to his epic on the Béarnais king. It has only one line:

The bird from the Phasis is a dish for the gods.

One of Brillat-Savarin's finest meditations is on the subject of this magnificent bird.

The pheasant [he says] is an enigma the solution of which is revealed only to the adept. Only they can savour it in all its goodness.

Each substance has its apogee of succulence. Some reach it before maturity — for example, capers, asparagus, grey partridge, and squab. For others it is reached at the moment they attain the full perfection of their destiny, like mutton, beef, roe deer, and red partridges. Others, finally, when they begin to decompose — the medlar, the woodcock, and above all the pheasant.

This bird, eaten within three days of his death, is undistinguished. It is neither so delicate as a fatted chicken nor so flavourful as a quail.

But taken at its point of perfection, its flesh is tender, sublime, and wonderfully savoury, for it partakes of the virtues of both poultry and venison.

That so desirable point is reached when the pheasant begins to decompose. Then its aroma develops and mingles with an oil that requires a little fermentation for its distillation, just as coffee requires roasting for its full development.

To the ordinary person, this moment is discovered through a faint odour and a change in the colour of the bird's belly. But those truly inspired divine it by a sort of instinct that manifests itself in various ways, similar, for example, to that which tells a cook glancing at a bird on the spit whether it must be removed immediately or left for a few more turns.

When the pheasant reaches this point, and not before, it is plucked, and carefully larded with the freshest, finest bacon.

It is not a matter of unimportance that a pheasant should not be plucked too soon. Very careful experiments have established that those which are kept unplucked are better flavoured than those which have hung naked, either because contact with the air neutralizes some of the aroma, or because a portion of the juices destined to nourish the feathers is reabsorbed, and serves to heighten the savour of the flesh.

The bird thus prepared, it must be stuffed, which is done in the following manner:

Take two woodcocks and draw them, reserving both parts, one composed of flesh, the other of the liver and entrails.

You take the flesh and make a stuffing by chopping it with steamed beef marrow, a little grated bacon, salt, pepper, fines herbes, and enough good truffles to fill the interior of the pheasant.

This stuffing must be so arranged that it will not spill out of the cavity, which is sometimes difficult with a bird in an advanced condition. There are various ways to do this — among others, carve a piece of bread to fit and attach it to the opening with tape.

Prepare a slice of bread two inches wider and longer than the pheasant *will be when laid down for roasting. Take the woodcock liver and entrails and crush them with two large truffles, an anchovy, and a piece of good fresh butter. Spread this evenly on the bread and place the pheasant over it so that every drop of juice that runs from it during roasting will be caught.*

When the pheasant is done, arrange it gracefully on the bread; surround it with bitter oranges, and have confidence.

This highly flavoured dish should, preferably, be accompanied with vintage wine of Upper Burgundy. I have established this truth through a series of observations entailing more labour than a table of logarithms.

Spitted Pheasant. Pluck a young, tender, fat pheasant, all except the head and tail, taking care not to tear the skin. Clean, singe, truss, lard it or wrap it in bacon. Wrap the head and tail in paper. Bring the tail back along the body. Put on the spit. Wrap entirely in buttered paper. Roast. Take off all the paper and serve.

Braised Pheasant. Clean and pluck. Cut off the feet. Truss the legs into the belly and lard with thick bacon strips. Put into a heavy pot with slices of bacon and of beaten beef, salt, pepper, fine spices, *fines herbes*, and sliced onions, carrots, and parsnips under it and over it. Put beaten slices of beef and strips of bacon on top and roast in a medium oven. While it is roasting, make a ragout of *foie gras*, veal sweetbreads, mushrooms, truffles, artichoke bottoms, asparagus tips. Start it in lard, add gravy, and let it simmer until cooked. Skim off the fat, mix in a good veal and ham cullis. When the pheasant is done, take it out of the pot, drain, put on a platter, pour the ragout over it, and serve hot.

Braised Pheasant à l'Angoumoise. Peel some truffles and cut them into cloves, which stick into all the fleshy parts of the pheasant. Put into a pot 4 ounces of grated bacon and a similar amount of butter. In it heat some truffles cut into pieces and the chopped skins and scraps of those you used for larding. Season with a little salt and pepper. Let it simmer a few minutes, then add 25 to 30 roasted chestnuts. Stuff the pheasant with this mixture. Wrap it in thin slices of beef, veal, and bacon. Tie it up with string and put into a heavy pot lined with sliced bacon. Add 1 glass of Malaga or white wine and 2 tablespoonfuls of caramel. Cook over a very slow fire.

When it is cooked, remove the bird, take off the string. Skim the fat off the liquid, add some chopped truffles, let it boil a few moments. Thicken the sauce with chestnut purée. Pour it into the platter and place the pheasant on top.

Spitted Pheasant with Pistachios. Broil your pheasant wrapped in bacon and buttered paper and stuffed with its own liver, grated bacon, parsley, scallions, mushrooms, all chopped together and mixed with 3 egg yolks. When it is well cooked, serve on a pistachio ragout made by scalding ¼ pound of the nuts and putting them into a good meat essence.

Salmis of Pheasant. Cook 2 pheasants on the spit and let them cool. Cut into pieces, skin, trim. Warm up with consommé. Put a good glass of red or white wine into a pot, add 3 or 4 chopped shallots, the zest of a bitter orange, and three skimming-spoonfuls of reduced espagnole sauce and a piece of glaze the size of a nutmeg. Reduce the whole. Chop the skins and trimmings very fine, stir into the sauce. Heat without letting it boil, strain through a sieve as you would a purée, and keep hot in a *bain-marie*. Just before serving, drain your pieces of pheasant and arrange on a platter with the thighs and wings on the outside, with croutons shaped like hearts and fried in butter mixed in. Squeeze the juice of 1 or 2 bitter oranges into your salmis, pour over the pheasant pieces, and serve.

PIGEON. Young pigeons are called squabs. They are generally roasted on a spit, but they may be used in other dishes as well.

Pigeons with Green Peas. Pluck, draw, and clean 3 or 4 pigeons. Put their livers back into the cavity. Truss their feet into the cavity. Put a piece of butter into a pot, brown your pigeons in it, and put them aside. Meanwhile you will have cut bacon into large cubes and set it aside in water to desalt for almost ½ hour. Fry these in the butter to a good golden colour. Take them out. Make a *roux* with the butter and flour and bring that to a golden colour also. Return the bacon and the pigeons. Turn them about in the *roux* so they are completely covered. Add hot bouillon little by little until you have the consistency of a sauce. Season with parsley, scallions, ½ bay leaf, ½ garlic clove, and 1 clove. Set aside to simmer. When a little more than half done, add 1 pound of fresh little green peas. Let them cook, stirring frequently. When cooked, taste and add salt if necessary. Take the seasoning out of the sauce, skim all excess fat from it, and reduce it if it is too thin. Arrange your pigeons on a platter, pouring the sauce with the peas and bacon over them, and serve.

Broiled Pigeons à la Nîmoise. Make the following remoulade:

Chop parsley, 2 shallots, and a little onion together and press in a cloth to remove the moisture. Chop gherkins, capers, and an anchovy. Put all into a mortar and crush well with 4 yolks of hard-boiled eggs and some blanched parsley. *Never any garlic.* When thoroughly mashed, add 1 raw egg yolk, and stir in, drop by drop, 1 glass of oil. Season with salt, pepper, mustard, a good tablespoonful of tarragon vinegar, the juice of 1 lemon. Mix thoroughly.

Use this remoulade to serve with your pigeons after preparing them properly, trussing, and broiling on the spit. Remove the strings used in trussing before serving.

Squabs à la Gautier. Take 6 or 7 squabs, all of the same size, none more than 8 days old. Singe lightly, making sure you do not scorch the skin. Pluck, cut off the claws. Warm ¾ pound of butter, add the juice of 2 or 3 lemons and a little salt. Brown your squabs lightly in this butter, taking care not to harden the skin. Take off the fire. Completely cover the bottom of another pot with slices of bacon. Arrange your squabs with their feet towards the centre. Pour the butter over them, add 1 glass of white wine, 1 ladleful of con-sommé, ¼ pound of grated bacon, and a seasoned bouquet. Cover the squabs with slices of bacon and a piece of paper. A quarter of an hour before serving, bring to a boil on the top of the stove, then put into a very hot oven. Drain, arrange on a platter, garnished with a fine crayfish and a fine truffle between each. Sauce with green sauce or crayfish butter, or an aspic.

Pigeons à la Toulousaine. Make a stuffing with liver, bacon, *fines herbes*, a little piece of veal, 1 egg yolk, and some truffles, all chopped together. Stuff your pigeons and broil on the spit. Serve with tarragon sauce or a remoulade over them.

Broiled Pigeons. Bard with bacon. If it is summer, put a grape leaf under the bacon, but make sure it is completely covered with bacon. Skewer, attach to the spit, and broil. Take note that pigeons should be broiled rare.

Pigeons au Blanc. Take 5 or 6 pigeons and prepare for cooking. Soak in cold water ½ hour. Blanch. Dry them. Put into a pot with a piece of butter and heat without letting the butter brown. Sprinkle with flour. Add bouillon and white wine, season with a *bouquet garni*, salt, and pepper. Simmer 15 minutes. Add 2 handfuls of fluted mushrooms and 20 little white onions of even size. Cook. Skim off the fat. Put the sauce into another pot. If too thin, reduce. Mix 3 raw egg yolks with cream or milk and add to the sauce, with a little nutmeg. Add the mushrooms and onions. Thicken but do not let boil. If you will, add a little chopped, blanched parsley. Adjust your seasoning. Arrange the pigeons on a platter and pour the mixture over them.

PIKE. The pike is the shark of fresh waters. Whole ducks have been found in the stomachs of pikes. If allowed to live, they will attain virtually any size and any age. In 1749 one was caught that was nearly 18 feet long, and weighed 350 pounds. The eggs should not be eaten. If cooked with it, they make the flesh itself capable of inducing nausea and vomiting.

Pike à la Chambord. Clean thoroughly so that no trace of milt or roe remains. Clip off the gills and fins. Skin without breaking the flesh. Lard both sides with thin strips of eel flesh, or one side with eel and the other with truffles and carrots cut into cloves; or you may use bacon instead of eel. Cook with a meatless braise.

Put 3 ladlesful of meatless espagnole sauce in a pot with ½ bottle of champagne, reduce, and skim. Add fluted mushrooms, artichoke bottoms, truffles, carp milt, pieces of eel, and simmer 15 minutes. Finish with anchovy butter. Unless you want to keep this dish meatless, add larded veal sweetbreads, pigeons or quail in season, cockscombs and cock's kidneys.

Drain your pike and press it. Arrange your garnish around it on a platter, adding crayfish. Decorate it. Sauce it. Glaze, and serve.

Pike en Dauphin. Scale and clean a large pike. Put a skewer through its eyes and a string around its tail, and tie one to the other in a ring. Place belly down on a meatless braise or a good mirepoix. Bake, basting frequently. Sauce with a brown italienne sauce.

Spitted Pike. Scale. Make light incisions in the sides. Lard with eel flesh salted and peppered. Put on the spit. Baste while cooking with white wine, good oil, and the juice of a lime. When it is done, crush anchovies in the contents of the dripping pan, add oysters (don't let them boil), capers, salt, and pepper. Thicken the sauce with a little gravy or a *roux*, and serve.

Pike à la Tartare. Scale. Cut your pike into several pieces. Marinate with oil, salt, coarse pepper, parsley, scallions, shallots, and mushrooms, chopped very fine. Bread. Grill. Baste with the marinade. Serve plain, with a remoulade in a sauceboat.

PLOVER. There are two varieties, the golden and the grey. Plover stimulates the appetite and is easily digested. But since it does not provide really solid food, persons accustomed to exercise will not find it very satisfying.

"And they told Gargantua that the plover is meat for drunken people already filled with solid flesh."

Plover with Truffles. Prepare 3 or 4 plovers and put into a pot with 2 fine, peeled truffles, a seasoned bouquet, a little basil, salt, pepper. Heat in butter. Add 1 glass of champagne, 6 tablespoonfuls of reduced espagnole sauce, and cook. Remove the plovers and truffles. Skim the fat off the sauce, reduce it, pass through a sieve, add the juice of 1 lemon. Arrange the plovers on a platter, the truffles on top and serve.

POMEGRANATE. A fruit much sought after to garnish baskets of dessert fruit, which it greatly embellishes.

"There are no beautiful dessert baskets without pomegranates," says M. Gohier du Lompier, "any more than there can be any without oranges. The open pomegranate, like a treasure of rubies or shining garnets, is the finest jewel of our great fruit baskets. But we must admit that aside from this important role as decoration for the table or the buffet, it is next to good for nothing in this temperate climate where the four red fruits are abundant and excellent."

A syrup called grenadine is made from the pomegranate. It is very good for a dry cough or throat irritation.

PORK. "He is the king of unclean beasts," says Grimod de la Reynière in his eulogy of the pig. "His empire is the most universal and his qualities less contested than any other. Without him, no bacon, and therefore no cooking; without him, no ham, no sausage, no *andouilles*, no black puddings, and no pork butchers.

"Foolish physicians! You condemn the pig, and his indigestibility is one of the finest ornaments in your crown!

"Pork products are far better at Troyes and at Lyon than anywhere else. The hams and shoulders of pigs have made the fortunes of two cities: Mainz and Bayonne. Everything in a pig is good. What ingratitude has permitted his name to become a word of opprobrium?"

And by what ingratitude is M. Grimod de la Reynière capable of forgetting that we owe truffles to the pig's delicate sense of smell? And how the pig is rewarded for each truffle it finds and permits a man to put into his basket? And how we admire the persistence of this gastronomic searcher which is always cheated, not in its search, but of its reward! It persists in searching just to be beaten and to have the truffle stolen from under its snout!

Pigs were the principal nourishment of the Gauls, who had great herds of them. The Romans cooked them whole, in two ways. One was to boil them on one side and roast them on the other. The second method was called the Trojan, an allusion to the famous horse. It was stuffed with figpeckers, oysters, and thrushes and basted with good wines and delicate juices. This dish became so extravagantly expensive that the Senate enacted a sumptuary law forbidding it.

Humbert, Dauphin of Vienne, leaving for the Crusade in 1345 (we leave it to the savants to say what Crusade that was), set up regulations for the management of his wife's house in his absence, limiting it to thirty persons. For these thirty persons he allotted one pig a week, plus thirty salted pigs a year, which made it three pigs per person.

The pig and the rabbit are the most prolific animals in the world. Vauban, an excellent mathematician, wrote a treatise on pigs that he called *La Cochonnerie*. He calculated the progeny of a single sow over twelve years. His figure was 6,434,838 pigs.

The pig is of all animals the one whose flesh is most employed in cookery. In almost every dish one uses either bacon or ham. The other portions are less popular. But pig's head is a distinguished dish when prepared by a man who knows his business. The feet are served *à la Sainte-Menehould* or stuffed with truffles. The ears are on kings' menus. The breast is used in stews. Pork should be young and fat, but take care it is not infested with the trichina parasite. Nothing of this animal is discarded. From his blood one makes blood pudding; from his intestines, casings; from the trimmings of his flesh, sausages and headcheese.

Pig's Head. Since the famous Beauvilliers and the illustrious Courchamps give exactly the same recipe for pig's head or boar's head, we can do no better than concur with these great masters of the art of eating.

Cut off the head to include half the shoulders. Singe it thoroughly. Clean inside the ears with a nearly red-hot poker. Wash well, pluck again, scrape. Remove the bones, taking care, however, not to pierce the skin. Rearrange the flesh in even layers inside the skin. Put into a large crock and cover with cooled salted water. Add 1 handful of juniper berries, 4 bay leaves, 5 or 6 cloves, 2 or 3 cloves of garlic cut in two, ½ ounce of powdered saltpetre, thyme, basil, and sage. Cover with a cloth and a weight. Let stand 8 or 10 days. Drain. Remove all the added ingredients.

Make the following forcemeat: take fresh pork and remove the rind and sinews, add a similar quantity of bacon, season with salt and fine spices, chop and mix finely and thoroughly. Pound in a mortar. Add 5 or 6 eggs, one at a time. Taste and improve the spicing if necessary.

Cut long narrow strips of bacon and roll them thoroughly in salt, pepper, four spices, aromatic herbs, parsley, and scallions – all chopped fine, of course.

Rearrange the flesh inside the head, and line it at intervals with your bacon strips, with forcemeat between them, to the thickness of about 1 inch. Add the tongue, scalded, skinned and cut in strips, interspersed with shelled pistachios. Repeat the process until you have no more ingredients. Sew up the skin of the shoulders to close the opening, making sure you press the head into its original form. Put meat trimmings (especially veal), onions, carrots, 3 bay leaves, 2 bouquets of parsley and scallions, some cloves, garlic, and 3 bottles of red Burgundy into the bottom of a large, heavy pot. Wrap the head in several thicknesses of cheesecloth, sew, and tie up with string. Put it in your pot and add bouillon to cover. Bring to a boil. Cover with 2 pieces of strong buttered paper, then the pot cover. Bake 5 or 6 hours, depending on the size of the head and the age of the pig from which it comes. When you can easily penetrate it with a skewer, let it cool in its own juice until nearly cold. Take out of the pot. Allow to cool completely before unwrapping. Take off any fat that may be clinging to it, trim around your sewing. Arrange on a napkin and serve.

Braised Ham. Trim off the fat, remove the large bone, and parboil to remove the saltiness. Wrap in a cloth and tie up. Put into a large, heavy pot over scraps of beef and veal, carrots, onions, scallions, parsley, cloves, bay leaf, thyme, etc. Cover with water and bring to a boil. Halfway through the cooking add 1 bottle of white wine (champagne fortified with brandy, or, better still, straight Malaga). Do not cover. Let the liquid cook down. Drain, remove the rind, glaze with reduced veal stock. Serve on a platter with vegetables of choice.

Pork Chops. Grill and serve with *sauce Robert.*

Pigs' Ears. Singe and clean with a nearly red-hot poker. Scrape, clean, blanch. Cook in a braising pot, fire under and over. Let cool. Cut into thin strips and cover with sliced onions cooked in butter and veal broth, adding a dash of vinegar just before serving.

Pigs' Feet à la Sainte-Menehould. Singe as many feet as a pig has, generally 4. Scrape and wash in hot water. Split them in half. Tie the pieces together with a tape as a hairdresser ties a queue. Sew the ends of the tape together. Braise, or cook in bouillon. Drain, let cool, remove the tape, and separate the pieces. Dip in melted butter, bread, grill, and serve without sauce.

Suckling Pig. Care should be taken in cleaning not to make too large an incision. The smallest possible to enable you to remove the entrails and everything else except the kidneys is large enough. Before putting on the spit, pass a skewer to hold the hind legs trussed, another to do the same for the forelegs, and a third over the kidneys to prevent the pig from making a camel back. Make 4 incisions on the rump through which to thread the tail between the skin and flesh. After the spit has turned 3 or 4 times, brush the pig with oil. Repeat this operation several times so that the skin will be crisp. When it is done, take it off the spit, cut an incision around the neck so that the skin will remain crisp, and serve very hot.

Suckling Pig Stuffed English Style. Exactly as above, but stuff with chopped liver, white of bread dipped in milk, butter, calf's udder, eggs (especially egg yolks), herbs and spices, etc.

Smoked Pork Tongues. Trim most of the root from the tongues. Scald. Remove the outer skin, squeeze them tightly together in an earthenware crock, sprinkling each layer with salt, a little saltpetre, a bit each of basil, thyme, bay leaf, juniper berries, and shallots. Cover. Keep in a cool place 8 days. At the end of that time, remove them from the brine, drain them. Stuff them tightly into pork, beef, or veal casings. Tie up both ends. Smoke them. To use, cook in water with a little wine, seasoned with a bouquet of parsley and scallions, several onions, thyme, bay leaf, basil. Let cool before serving.

POTATOES. Are a truly healthy, convenient, inexpensive, and nourishing food. The eagerness with which children devour potatoes baked in the ashes shows how digestible they are for anyone.

Potatoes à la Maître d'Hôtel. Boil, peel, cut in slices, fry. Then put into a pot with fresh butter, chopped parsley, salt, pepper, the juice of 1 lemon. Mix well together. Add a little cream, and serve.

Potatoes à la Parisienne. Melt a piece of butter or fat in a pot with 1 or 2 onions, diced. Add a glass of water and peeled potatoes, salt, pepper, and *bouquet garni*. Cook on a slow fire.

Potatoes à la Provençale. Put 6 tablespoons of oil in a pot with the zest of $\frac{1}{2}$ lemon, garlic and scallions well chopped up, a little grated nutmeg, salt, and pepper. Add your peeled potatoes and cook. Just before serving add the juice of 1 lemon.

Potatoes à l'Italienne. Boil, peel, and mash, adding butter and crustless bread soaked in milk. Add milk to make a workable paste. Add 7 or 8 fresh egg yolks and five whites beaten stiff. Mix well and arrange in a pyramid on a platter. Pour a little melted butter over the pyramid, put into the oven until it has a fine golden colour, and serve.

QUAIL. This is the most darling and lovable of game. A fat quail gives equal pleasure by its flavour, colour, and form. It is an act of culinary ignorance to prepare quail in any way except roasted in buttered paper, for when they are in contact with a liquid their flavour is dissolved, evaporated, and lost.

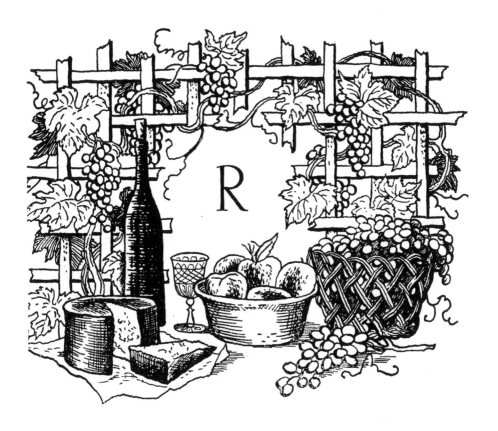

RABBIT. Rabbits originated in Africa. From there they migrated to Spain and thence to France. Pliny and Varro say that they were so numerous in Tarragona, a city of Spain, and had dug so many tunnels under the houses, that twenty-five or thirty of the latter tumbled down. Rabbits ate all the crops of one of the Lipari Islands, and the inhabitants were reduced to famine. At one time they were so abundant in the South of France that Beaujeu tells of a Provençal gentleman who went out with a few of his vassals and three dogs, in 1551, and returned with six hundred rabbits.

Winter is the best time to eat rabbits. They must be neither too young nor too old. To check on the age of a rabbit, palp the outer side of the front leg joint. In a young rabbit there is a little lump the size of a lentil under the skin. Wild rabbits have reddish hair on their paws and under their tails. Domestic rabbits are treated to imitate this characteristic by frizzling these portions with fire. This can be recognized by the odour. The flesh of a young rabbit stands between a chicken that isn't too fat and one that is, for digestibility.

Wild rabbits are usually the best, especially if their warren is exposed to the east or south. A warren that is owned by a hunter should be planted with wild plums, mulberries, broom, currants, rosemary, and especially juniper, of which partridges and thrushes are very fond. For rabbits there is no problem of water or lodging. The rabbit makes his own home, and he hates water. A warren is stocked by putting a dozen pregnant females there. At the end of the first year it will have five hundred rabbits; five thousand by the end of the second.

In this connection, I shall always remember a model warren where I first hunted with one of the finest men and most original hunters I have ever known. The Abbé Fortier was vicar and teacher of the village of Béthisy, near Compiègne. I called him my uncle. I don't know why.

The day before the season opened, he warned his flock: "My good friends, you know that the only diversion I have, living among you fools, is hunting. Now, if I said two Masses tomorrow at the usual times, it would be eleven-thirty or twelve before I could start hunting, and since you are all poachers and vagabonds, the whole territory would be denuded by that time. Therefore, I shall say the first Mass at six in the morning, and I suggest you attend. I shall take note of those who don't appear and deal with them later."

At half-past five the Abbé Fortier began to say Mass, and it was half done when his parishioners arrived. At a quarter past six Low Mass was finished. The parishioners stirred.

"Oh, no," said the Abbé. "Since you are here, it would be foolish to have you return at ten for High Mass. I shall say that now."

Three quarters of an hour later, High Mass ended, and everyone started to go.

"Now wait," said he. "Don't imagine I'm going to quit the hunt at its finest moment, about two in the afternoon. I'm not that stupid. We're going to get through with vespers as we did with High and Low Mass. It will take fifteen minutes."

And he went through the vesper service, so that by half-past seven, a beautiful hour to start hunting, he had finished all his services. Poor abbé! May God give his soul peace! Never was a human creature a better man or a worse priest.

He died at the age of ninety, and none of his flock ever forgot his last sermon.

"I'm going to leave you, my children," he said. "God gave you to me stupid, and stupid I return you. He will have nothing for which to reproach me."

Old-fashioned Stewed Rabbit. Cut a rabbit into pieces and a medium-sized eel into slices. Put into a *roux* and heat. When they · have a good colour, add mushrooms and small onions. When all are hot, add ⅓ white wine, ⅔ good bouillon. Season with salt, pepper, parsley, scallions, and thyme. Remove the eel and the onions. Cook over a hot fire. When the liquid has been reduced by ⅔, put back the eels and onions, finish cooking on a slow fire, skim off the fat, and serve.

Escalopes of Young Rabbit. Skin 2 young rabbits. Remove the fillets, the other large pieces of flesh, and the kidneys. From these remove all sinews and membranes. Cut into pieces of equal size. Flatten with the side of the cleaver. Trim. Melt butter in a skillet, arrange your *escalopes* in it, salt and pepper lightly, cover with a piece of buttered paper, and leave until almost ready to serve.

Break up the rabbit carcasses and put into a pot with 1 carrot, 2 onions (1 with a clove stuck in it), a bouquet of parsley and scallions, 1 bay leaf, 1 slice of ham, and some scraps of veal. Cover with consommé, bring to a boil, skim. Boil for 1 hour. Skim off the fat and strain. Reduce by ¼. Add 2 tablespoonfuls of reduced espagnole sauce. Heat your sauce, stirring constantly, until it has the consistency of a thin glaze. Just before serving, put your *escalopes* on the fire in their butter, sauté them until brown on both sides. Pour off the butter, put them into the sauce, heat again, arrange on a platter, and serve.

In season, you might sauté some slivers of truffles in butter, drain them, and add them to your *escalopes* just before re-heating.

Rabbit en Casserole. Cut rabbits in quarters, keeping the livers aside. Lard with seasoned strips of bacon and with strips of ham. Line the bottom of a heavy pot with slices of bacon and veal, with salt, pepper, *fines herbes*, fine spices, onions, scallions, parsley, carrots, and parsnips. Arrange the rabbit quarters on top of this, cover, and bake.

Make a cullis as follows:

Put beaten slices of ham and veal in the bottom of a pot with 1 onion, a piece of carrot, and sliced parsnips. Heat slowly. When they begin to stick, add melted lard mixed with flour, stir, add ½ gravy and ½ bouillon, season with mushrooms, truffles, parsley, whole scallions, 3 or 4 cloves, a few crusts of bread. Simmer the whole together.

Take your rabbit livers, crush in a mortar, mix with some of the juice from your cullis, heat, add to the cullis, strain.

Your rabbits cooked, put them into the cullis. Simmer. Arrange on a platter, pour the cullis over them, and serve very hot.

Young Rabbits à la Saingarac. Lard young rabbits well and roast on the spit. Take some beaten slices of ham, add a little bacon and a little flour, heat. Add a bouquet of *fines herbes*, good unsalted gravy, cook all together. Add a dash of vinegar. Thicken with cullis and bread. Cut your rabbits in quarters, arrange on a platter, skim the fat from the sauce and pour it, with the slices of ham in it, over them, and serve hot.

Young Rabbit Fricassée. Cut 2 very young, tender rabbits into pieces, wipe off the blood. Put into a pot with water, a few slices of onion, a bay leaf, a sprig of parsley, a few scallions, and a little salt. Bring to a boil. Drain. Wipe dry. Trim.

In another pot, sauté the pieces in butter, sprinkle lightly with flour, add some of the water in which they were parboiled, being careful to stir so that no lumps are formed. Bring to a boil. Add mushrooms and morels, cook. Reduce the sauce. Thicken it with 4 egg yolks, mixed with butter or cream or with some of the sauce, chilled. Finish with the juice of a lemon, or a dash of verjuice, or a dash of white vinegar, and serve.

Young Rabbits au Gratin. Dress and dismember a young rabbit. Put slices of veal, bacon, and five or six slices of ham cut uniformly, in the bottom of a pot. Put the pieces of rabbit on top, with very little salt, cover with slices of bacon, add a *bouquet garni*, a clove, basil, and bay leaf, and braise.

Chop up the liver with parsley, scallions, and mushrooms. Mix in 2 egg yolks. Add grated bacon, salt, and pepper. Put this mixture on a platter and let it cook on a very low heat. When it seems cooked, pour off the fat. The rabbit cooked, take it and the ham slices out, skim the fat from the gravy, add a little cullis and gravy, bring to a boil. Skim off the fat again and strain. Arrange your pieces of rabbit on top of the mixture in the platter, with a piece of ham between each. Pour your sauce over. Reheat and serve.

Mayonnaise of Young Rabbit. Broil 2 young rabbits on a spit. Let them cool. Dismember them. Trim. Sauté in mayonnaise and serve.

RAGOUTS. Ragouts made the ancient French cuisine shine. On the other hand, all other cuisines, and especially the English, are sinful in this respect. No other cuisine will ever rise to the same heights.

Salpicons. These are made of all sorts of vegetables and meats, such as sweetbreads, truffles, mushrooms, artichoke bottoms, etc. But each meat or vegetable must be cooked separately for its own length of time.

Ordinary Salpicon. This is composed of veal sweetbreads, *foie gras*, ham, mushrooms, and truffles if they are in season. Each ingredient should be diced fairly small, and all the same size. Just before serving, have a well-reduced espagnole sauce, of sufficient quantity in proportion to your other ingredients, hot on the stove. Put the ingredients in, stir on the stove but do not let boil, and serve.

Salpicons may be made with all sorts of other ingredients, such as quenelles, *godiveau*, breast of roasted fowl, cockscombs, etc., depending on the season and what you have on hand.

Truffle Ragout with Champagne. Wash the truffles several times in warm water. Scrub them. Cover the bottom of a pot with slices of bacon. Put in your truffles with salt, bay leaf, and 1 bottle of champagne. Cover the pot tightly. Boil ½ hour. Serve the truffles on a napkin. Baron Thiry, a distinguished gastronome, prefers Collioure to champagne, and M. Bignon, another authority, prefers Madeira or sherry. Since one can eat truffles on a napkin more than once in a lifetime, I suggest trying all three in succession.

But when you want to conserve the pure, natural flavour of truffles, you wrap each one in a piece of buttered paper, put them into a colander, and steam them over boiling water.

To all these methods of preparing truffles, you may prefer truffles cooked in hot ashes. Wrap them in buttered paper. Eat them with butter. (Vuillemot.)

Celery Ragout. Chop up celery as you would spinach. Cook it in a good bouillon with salt, pepper, nutmeg. Serve it with golden croutons. If you are a very special type of gourmet, put a few ortolans or a few breasts of partridge on a bed of this ragout. Try this dish, fellow gourmands, and you may be well satisfied with it. (Recipe from Dr. Rocques.)

Stuffed Tomatoes à la Grimod. Take the seeds out of your tomatoes and stuff them with sausage meat seasoned with garlic, parsley, scallions, and tarragon. Bake them in a shallow earthenware dish, sprinkle with lemon juice, and serve in the same dish.

Mushroom Ragout à la Cussy. Slice firm, fresh mushrooms and truffles as thin as cardboard. Put on a hot stove with butter and a little fine-chopped garlic. Stir. When the butter has melted, add the juice of 2 lemons, salt, coarse pepper, nutmeg, 4 tablespoonfuls of espagnole sauce and a similar quantity of reduced consommé. When the ragout comes to a boil, add 1 glass of sauterne or sherry, cook another 20 minutes, and serve.

Cucumber Ragout. Peel 3 cucumbers. Quarter lengthwise. Take out the seeds. Slice into shell shapes with a curved knife. Cook in boiling water with a little salt. Put 3 or 4 large tablespoonfuls of *velouté* into a saucepan. Add your cucumbers. Cook and reduce. Skim off any fat. Adjust the seasoning. Stir in a piece of butter. Grate a little nutmeg over the ragout and serve.

Chipolata Ragout. Put into a pot 2 ladlefuls of reduced espagnole sauce, $\frac{1}{2}$ bottle of Madeira, fluted mushrooms, cooked little white onions, a few cooked and peeled chestnuts, little chipolata sausages cooked in bouillon, quartered truffles, and a little coarse pepper. Cook and reduce, skim off the fat and serve.

Endive Ragout in Brown Sauce. Trim 12 heads of endive, removing all green leaves. Wash well, holding them by the root and plunging up and down, making sure to remove any worms that may have made the endive their home. Drain. Blanch in boiling, salted water. They are sufficiently blanched when they can be crushed easily between finger and thumb. Remove, drain, plunge into a pail of cold water. Drain. Press between the hands to remove as much water as possible. Cut off the roots. Chop. Put into a pot with a piece of butter, and put on slow heat to dry out well, about ¼ hour. Add 2 tablespoonfuls of espagnole sauce and 1 of consommé. Cook at least 1 hour, stirring frequently with a wooden spoon to avoid scorching and sticking. When properly reduced, add salt and serve.

RAVIGOTE. The name of a *sauce piquante* made mainly with chopped chervil and tarragon, to which are added burnet, scallions, salt, pepper, and the four spices. These are mixed and heated in white veal stock, with vinegar and fresh butter.

Oil Ravigote. Take the same basic ingredients, but instead of heating in stock mix cold with oil, vinegar, and cold bouillon. Stir long to mix well.

Green Ravigote. Take equal quantities of chervil, burnet, and tarragon, a little chives, parsley, garden cress, and water cress. Blanch in boiling water. Plunge into cold water, drain, and press. Crush the whole in a mortar, adding a little cold allemande sauce. When the whole makes a sort of paste, squeeze it through a sieve with a wooden spoon.

Use this to put into sauces, ragouts, and as thickening for dishes that require it.

REMOULADE. A sauce composed of anchovies, capers, chopped parsley and scallions, all heated in a good gravy with a drop of oil, a clove of garlic, and the usual seasonings.

Remoulade à la Provençale. Chop parsley, 2 shallots, and a little onion and press in a cloth to extract the juices. Chop gherkins, capers, and an anchovy. Crush completely in a mortar with four hard-cooked egg yolks, a little blanched parsley, and some garlic. When well crushed, add 1 raw egg yolk. Drop by drop, stirring, pour 1 good glass of oil into the mortar. Season with salt, pepper, mustard, 1 tablespoonful of good tarragon vinegar, and the juice of 1 lemon. Stir the whole well together.

RICE. Turkish Rice. Clean and blanch 10 ounces of Carolina rice. Cook in 4 glasses of milk, 2 ounces of sugar over which you have grated the zest of 1 lemon, 2 ounces of butter, 6 ounces of well-washed dried currants, and a pinch of salt. When the rice has cooked, take it off the fire, stir in 4 egg yolks, pour into a silver dish, and bake 20 minutes. Sprinkle with powdered sugar and brown. Serve at once.

Turkish Rice (Another Method). Wash 1 pound of rice in several waters, drain, cook in consommé. Use no more liquid than necessary. When nearly done, add a little powdered saffron, a piece of butter, melted beef marrow, and a little poultry glaze. Mix well, finish cooking. Serve with clarified consommé.

Indian Rice. Prepare and cook as in the first recipe above. After cooking, add ½ glass of rum and a little infusion of saffron, enough to give it a good yellow colour. Sprinkle with powdered sugar, put into a silver dish, and glaze.

French Rice. Wash, blanch, and cook with butter, sugar, and milk. Then stir in some bitter macaroons, a little orange-flower water, sliced pralines, diced candied orange peel, 20 candied cherries cut in half, as many seeded dried muscat raisins, and a few slivers of candied angelica. Finish as above. Serve with a sweet sauce in which use Alicante wine.

Rice à la Ristori. Cook 1 pound of rice. Grate ½ pound of bacon, shred a Savoy cabbage, add salt, pepper, parsley, and a few fennel seeds. Cover all together (not the rice) and steam for 45 minutes. Add the rice and enough bouillon or consommé barely to cover. Cook another 15 minutes and serve with grated Parmesan cheese.

Rice à la Cochinat. Cut 2 pullets into serving pieces. Brown in butter with a *bouquet garni*, 2 cloves, crushed hot peppers, and a pinch of saffron. Slice 30 onions, removing the ends and hearts. Fry but do not brown. Add to the pullets. Cover with bouillon. Boil over a hot fire. Cook 1 pound of rice, but be careful not to overcook. Serve the pullets in one dish, the rice in another. Make sure the liquid is not too thick.

ROASTS. Some people consider roasted meats to be less healthful and nourishing than boiled meats. "Fire acting directly upon meat," they say, "dissipates all the juices that made it healthful, dries out all its fibres, and, concentrating all the liquids that have not been dissipated, ferments and distills them into a saline juice that heats the blood and excites the bile.

"Boiled meats, on the contrary," their argument continues, "are only affected by the fire through the medium of water, which moderates and corrects it. It is no longer a hot fire that cooks. It is a gentle and moderate heat that cooks without toughening or hardening, and penetrates without drying out. It is similar to the digestive processes within the body, and is the best preparation for the foods that nourish it. Finally, a roast is possibly more invigorating because it stirs the spirit more, affects the palate more agreeably, but it supplies less nourishing juices because the direct heat of the fire has destroyed more."

This is an error. Nothing, in fact, will rob meat of its juices more efficiently than water. Water is the most powerful solvent. It empties the pores of the meat, preparing it to absorb all sorts of salts and oily substances. How could meat, staying for long periods in boiling water, fail to lose the best part of its juices? It loses them so effectively that the bouillon absorbs all the jelly from it. If a roast has a better flavour than boiled meat, it is because it retains all its juices, which in the other case pass off into the boiling water.

Roasted meats must not be started on too hot a fire, any more than they should be overdelayed in browning. Dark meats should be roasted rare, to preserve their juices. But white meats require a more even cooking through, and there should remain not a trace of pinkness. As for a hard-and-fast rule about roasting time, this is pretty difficult. It depends on the quality and quantity of the meat. But there are certain things it is essential to consider in the procedures to be followed. First, the way to build and keep up the fire, then the quality of the meats, and the different treatment for light and dark meats.

We borrow the following on the roasting of meats from M. A. Gogué, author of *Les Secrets de la Cuisine Française*:

Dark meats such as beef or mutton should be put on a lively fire. The fire should be clear, and mostly at the two ends of the spit. Do not cook too fast. Tend your fire so as gradually to diminish the heat. A large joint, a mutton or beef roast weighing eight to ten pounds, for example, will require an hour to an hour and a half of roasting. The signs by which one recognizes that the meat is properly cooked are: (1) a light steam rising from the meat; (2) a certain resistance one feels on prodding the meat with the finger; (3) drops of blood that begin to ooze and drip. Dark meats baste themselves. Never baste them. The contrary goes for white meats.

White meats, such as veal, lamb, turkey, and certain other poultry are treated quite differently. They should be basted with butter from time to time, because they are not so juicy as dark meats, and would dry out without this treatment. One recognizes that light meats are done by their tenderness under the interrogating finger, and by a light steam that rises from them. Aside from that, all that is required is the acquisition of a little experience in roasting light meats properly. In this respect an inexperienced cook can, in a few months of practice, become as clever as one who has grown old in his profession.

This is not so in regard to dark meats. The true talent of the roaster is revealed in the manner in which he cooks these meats, which must conserve all their juices until they arrive at the table, and yield tender, succulent slices under the carving knife.

Times Required for Various Roasts. *In dealing with butcher meats (beef, mutton, etc.), and with poultry and game, we have had occasion to give special recommendations in regard to each type of meat, and we have worked out with reasonable exactness the times required for their cooking, given always a spit to roast on, and a properly cared-for fire. With the apparatus known as a* cuisinière [reflector], *less time is required. With this apparatus, plus a grate for the fire, the time is reduced even more. Some kitchens simply use a spit and the grate set at a proper distance from each other. This may be the best system.*

TYPE OF MEAT	COOKING TIME
Beef, 5 lbs.	1½ *hours*
Beef, 10-11 lbs.	2½ *hours*
Veal, 4 lbs.	1 *hour*
Mutton leg or shoulder, 4 lbs.	1 *hour*
,, ,, ,, ,, 6 lbs.	1½ *hours*
Lamb, large quarter	1 *hour*

TYPE OF MEAT	COOKING TIME
Lamb, small quarter	¾ *hour*
Fresh pork, 4 lbs.	2 *hours*
Suckling pig	2½ *hours*
Capon or fat pullet	1 *hour*
Chicken	¾ *hour*
Turkey	1½ *hours*
Pigeon	½ *hour*
Duck	¾ *hour*
Duckling	½ *hour*
Fat goose	1¼ *hours*
Pheasant	¾ *hour*
Partridge	½ *hour*
Woodcock	½ *hour*
Lark (wrapped in bacon)	20 *minutes*
Venison, large haunch	3 *hours*
Hare	1½ *hours*
Young hare	½ *hour*
Young rabbit	½ *hour*

Roast à l'Impératrice. The Trojan roast pig, stuffed with fig-peckers, oysters, and thrushes, and the whole basted with good wine and fine meat broth — which the Roman Senate felt itself obliged to forbid by sumptuary law because of its extravagance — must yield to the luxury of this recipe.

Take the pit out of an olive and replace it with an anchovy. Put the olive into a lark, the lark into a quail, the quail into a partridge, the partridge into a pheasant. The pheasant in its turn disappears inside a turkey, and the turkey is stuffed into a suckling pig. Roasted, this will present the quintessence of the culinary art, the masterpiece of gastronomy. But don't make the mistake of serving it whole, just like that. The gourmand eats only the olive and the anchovy.

SALAD. [See the Letter to Jules Janin in the front of this book.]

SALMON. A fresh-water fish in the summer months, a salt-water fish the rest of the year. In spring it leaves the sea to spawn, and travels in huge numbers. These nomads preserve a remarkable order, proceeding in a double file united at the front end, like migratory birds in the air. They usually travel slowly and are very playful. But when they think they are in danger, the eye cannot follow the speed of their flight, which is matched only by lightning. Neither dams nor falls can stop them. They lie on their sides on the stones in shallow water, arch themselves, then, straightening out violently, go flying through the air over any obstacle. They often go as much as eight hundred leagues upstream from the river mouths. Salmon are caught from February to October.

Rolled Salmon Irish Style. Bone and blanch half a salmon. Sprinkle the inner surface with a mixture of pepper, salt, nutmeg, chopped oysters, parsley, and bread crumbs. Roll it up. Put into a shallow baking dish and bake in a hot oven. Serve in its own juice.

Salmon à la Genevoise. Cook your salmon in a pot with the jowl tied up, sliced onions, carrot parings, a bouquet of parsley and scallions, bay leaf, 1 or 2 cloves, salt, fine spices, and red wine. After cooking, pass a portion of the liquid in which it has cooked through a very fine sieve, add an equal amount of *roux*, reduce to the consistency of a sauce, add a bit of butter, and stir. Drain the salmon, garnish with fried croutons, and serve with the sauce.

The Genevans never use this recipe. They would rather drink their wine than use it for cooking.

Grilled Salmon. Clean the tail half of a salmon. Marinate in oil, salt, bay leaf, parsley, and scallions cut in half. Turn over. Slip the fish on the grill. Baste from time to time with the marinade. Turn over. When cooked, which you will know by examining the flesh near the backbone (if it is still red, it is underdone), skin. Pour a butter sauce over it, sprinkle with pickled capers or pickled capuchin capers.

SAMPHIRE (Crithmum maritimum). This plant grows by the seashore among the rocks. I have picked it in Normandy. The stems are crisp, with fleshy leaves. The flowers are white. Its flavour is sharp, salty, aromatic, but very pleasant. The stems are pickled and eaten like cucumbers.

SARDINE. A small, delicately flavoured, salt-water fish. It is found everywhere, but especially off the shore of Brittany, where the sardine fisheries are a source of wealth for the inhabitants. It is said that in the eighteenth century they already produced an immense revenue, and in the city of Port-Louis alone, four thousand barrels were put up each year. Sardines are abundant in the Mediterranean, especially around Sardinia, from which they derive their name.

Only inhabitants of the coast can eat fresh sardines, and even so the sardines must be salted as they are taken from the water, for of all fish these keep the shortest time.

Sardines are prepared by salting and smoking. Those from the North are the most highly esteemed because aromatic herbs and spices are added to their brine, giving them a very pleasant flavour. But these sardines do not keep very long. When they have spoiled, they are used as bait for mackerel and other sea fish.

Pisanelli claims that sardines love the sound of musical instruments, and will stick their heads out of the water to listen. Drinkers especially are fond of sardines, which stimulate their thirst and, they say, help them distinguish which is the best wine.

SAUCES. [*See Index for other sauces that appear under various headings throughout this book.* – Ed.]

Beef Gravy. Butter the bottom of a pot, put in slices of bacon and ham, sliced onions and carrots. Cover with slices of beef about 2 fingers thick. Add 1 ladleful of good bouillon. Put on a very hot fire. When it begins to stick, prick the meat with the point of a knife and remove to a more gentle heat. Take care it doesn't burn. Cover with bouillon, bring to a slow boil, skim, season with a bouquet of parsley and scallions and a few mushroom stems. Simmer. When the meat is cooked, skim off the fat and pass the broth through a cloth. Use it to colour soups and sauces, or other dishes that require its use.

Espagnole Sauce. Put slices of bacon and even more of ham on the bottom of your pot. Add slices of veal rump, 1 tablespoonful of consommé, 5 or 6 onions and carrots. Bring to a boil and set on low heat until the meat juices start to collect. When the liquid in the pot is a fine golden colour, take off the fire. Stick the veal with the point of a knife to facilitate the flow of juices. Cover with a consommé in which partridge, rabbit, or chicken has been cooked. Add a bouquet of parsley and scallions seasoned with 2 cloves, ¼ bay leaf, 1 clove of garlic, a little basil and thyme. Bring to a boil. Take off the heat and skim off the fat. Simmer. After 2 hours, thicken with a *roux*, but leave it rather thin than thick. Boil ¾ hour so that the *roux* becomes incorporated into the sauce. Skim off the fat again, pass through a sieve into another pot, and return to the heat to reduce by a quarter.

Do not add wine until ready to use the espagnole. Then you will add the variety required, whether Madeira, champagne, or Burgundy, spices to make it tasty or sharp if needed, and reduce just before using.

Velouté or White Cullis. Start as above, in a buttered pot, with veal, 1 ladleful of consommé, carrots and onions. When it is about to stick to the pot, add enough consommé, depending on strength and the amount of meat. Bring to a boil, take off the fire, add shallots and mushroom parings (*but no lemon*), a seasoned bouquet that you will take out when it is cooked, squeezing the juice from it between 2 spoons. Remove the meats also. Have ready a white *roux*. Add the above liquid to it gradually, stirring constantly. Skim off the fat, strain, return to the heat, skim again, reduce once more, pour into a bowl, and spoon until it is quite cold.

Allemande Sauce. Cook chopped mushrooms in butter, add 3 skimming spoonfuls of whipped *velouté* and 1 of consommé. Reduce. Add butter, chopped blanched parsley. Strain and spoon the mixture. Add the juice of ½ lemon, pepper, strain and serve.

Béchamel Sauce. Heat 1 quart of *velouté* and a little consommé, stirring, until it is reduced by a third of its volume. Reduce ½ pint of heavy cream and incorporate it little by little into your sauce, stirring constantly until it is reduced to the same volume it had before adding your cream. This sauce should have the consistency of thin porridge. Strain through a cloth and heat in a double boiler before serving.

Sainte-Menehould Sauce. Mix butter and flour in a saucepan, stir in milk or cream. Season with a good bouquet of parsley and scallions, ½ bay leaf, a few mushrooms and shallots. Heat. Stir constantly. Strain through a cloth. Return to the fire, adding a little chopped parsley and pepper.

Sauce Italienne, Brown. Put into a pot chopped mushrooms, slices of lemon (no seeds), diced ham, 1 tablespoonful of chopped shallot washed and squeezed in a cloth, ½ bay leaf, 2 cloves, and ½ pint of oil. Heat. When you see your ingredients are about cooked, take out the lemon slices. Add 1 tablespoon of chopped parsley and 1 of espagnole sauce, 1 pint of good white wine, and a little pepper. Reduce. Skim. Remove the ham. When sufficiently reduced, take off the heat.

Sauce Italienne, White. As above, but use *velouté* instead of espagnole sauce.

Maître d'Hôtel Sauce, Cold. With a wooden spoon mix butter, chopped parsley, a few chopped tarragon leaves, 1 or 2 balm leaves, some salt, juice of 1 or 2 lemons, or a dash of verjuice, until thoroughly wed.

Maître d'Hôtel Sauce, Thickened. Take 2 tablespoonfuls of *velouté*, butter the size of an egg, finely chopped parsley, and 2 or 3 chopped tarragon leaves. Heat, stirring constantly until the butter is completely incorporated into the *velouté*. Just before serving, strain and spoon your sauce, adding the juice of 1 lemon or a dash of verjuice.

Poivrade Sauce. Dice a slice of ham, heat in a pot with a little piece of butter, 5 or 6 sprigs of parsley, 2 or 3 scallions, bulb and all, sliced in half, 1 clove of garlic, 1 bay leaf, a little basil and thyme, 2 cloves. When well cooked, add a pinch of fine ground pepper, 1 ladleful of vinegar, 4 of unreduced espagnole sauce. Stir all together, bring to a boil, simmer ¾ hour, skim, and strain.

Sauce Piquante. Chop 1 onion and cook in butter without letting it brown. Add ½ glass of vinegar, a bouquet of parsley, 2 bay leaves, a little thyme, pepper, and clove. Reduce liquid to half. Stir in 1 glass of broth or bouillon and the same amount of sugar. Bring to a boil and put on a low fire. After 15 minutes, skim and pass through a sieve, add 2 tablespoonfuls of whole capers and the same amount of chopped gherkins.

Périgueux Sauce. Brush, peel, and dice 2 or 3 truffles. Keep them aside, covered. Into a pot put 1½ glasses of brown sauce, a few tablespoonfuls of good veal broth, add part of the truffle peelings, put on a lively fire, stir, and reduce by one third. Stir in, slowly, ½ glass of good Madeira, add the truffles, boil 2 minutes, and take off the fire.

Sauce Robert. This is one of the tastiest and most appetizing of sauces. Rabelais refers to it as "so salubrious and so essential."

However, its fame is not merely culinary. It is as much religious as anything else, which does not mean that cookery is a stranger to religion.

The historian Thiers (not to be confused with the minister) was curé of Champrod, in the diocese of Chartres. He fought against certain ecclesiastical charlatanries that had been authorized by the chapter of the church of Chartres. Among his adversaries was Robert, vicar-general of the bishop of Chartres. The pastor of Champrod wrote a satire entitled *Sauce Robert*, alluding to the famous culinary preparation. The satire was denounced. Thiers' arrest was ordered, and he was obliged to flee.

This is how the sauce is made:

Slice 6 big onions and wash them to remove the bitterness. Put into a pot with a proportionate amount of butter, sprinkle with flour, and brown. Add bouillon and let it cook. Add salt and pepper and, when your sauce is quite ready, mustard, and serve.

Poor Man's Sauce. Chop 5 or 6 shallots, add a pinch of finely chopped parsley, put into a pot with 1 glass of bouillon or $\frac{1}{2}$ gravy and $\frac{1}{2}$ water, and 1 ladleful of good vinegar, salt, a pinch of coarse pepper. Bring to a boil and cook until the shallots are done, then serve.

Cooked Marinade. Into a pot put a piece of butter the size of an egg, 1 or 2 sliced carrots and onions, 1 bay leaf, $\frac{1}{2}$ clove of garlic, a little thyme and basil, parsley leaves, 2 or 3 whole scallions cut in half. Heat over a good fire. When your vegetables begin to brown, add 1 part white vinegar and two parts water, salt, coarse pepper. Let it cook well. Strain. Use as needed.

Mirepoix Sauce. [*Not to be confused with the mirepoix called for in several recipes in this book, which is the mixture of diced vegetables, bacon, etc., used in the bottom of the braising pot. –* ED.]

Dice 4 pounds of veal round, $1\frac{1}{2}$ pounds of ham. Add $1\frac{1}{2}$ pounds of grated bacon, 5 or 6 diced carrots, 8 whole medium-sized onions, a good bouquet of parsley and scallions in which you will enclose 3 cloves, 2 bay leaves, a little thyme and basil, 3 sliced, peeled lemons (seeds removed), 1 pound of butter. Heat slowly. Add bouillon or consommé and 1 quart of champagne or other good white wine. Bring to a boil, skim, simmer 4 or 5 hours, pass through a sieve, and use as needed.

Sauce Colbert. Recommended by Urbain-Dubois, author of *Cuisine de Tous les Pays*. Because of its nature, he says, this sauce may be used with equal success with meats, fish, or a variety of vegetables. It may be served with roast, grilled, or fried dishes. In this respect no other sauce, ancient or modern, can compare with it.

In passing, let us note that its preparation requires neither great skill nor much work. I recommend it as very useful.

Mix 8 ounces of butter with 1 tablespoonful of chopped parsley, a bit of nutmeg, and the juice of 2 lemons. Bring to a boil ⅔ glass of melted meat glaze. Take off the fire and incorporate the butter into it bit by bit, on low heat, stirring vigorously with a spoon. For this purpose the butter should be cut into little pieces beforehand. Do not let it boil. When the sauce is well mixed, add 1 tablespoonful of cold water, stir, and remove from the heat. The primary purpose of this sauce is for use with sole *à la Colbert*.

So-called Sauce Genevoise. Put into a pot 1 bottle of red wine, onions, parsley, shallots, garlic, bay leaf, thyme, and mushroom parings. Reduce by a quarter. Add a ladleful of consommé, and liquor from boiled or steamed fish. Reduce again, stirring to mix well but taking care not to crush the vegetables. Strain. Finish with anchovy butter. Make sure this sauce is thick enough to stick to the freshwater fish over which you use it.

We quote here, without taking any responsibility for the truth of it, the commentary of an ill-humoured gastronome.[1] (It is bad enough to have one city of the Swiss Confederation against me, without rousing the capital itself.)

"You should know," says this gastronome, "that when one asks a Genevan for this simplest and most economical of recipes, he subjects you to an interminable, boastful panegyric. He tells you especially that it is essential to use half champagne and half Bordeaux for the court bouillon of any fish that is to be served *à la Genevoise*. We warn all travellers not to be taken in by this recipe, which is used in Geneva only to tell to foreigners. When a Genevan makes up his mind to treat himself to two bottles of champagne or Bordeaux, it is to drink them in company, never to pour them into a fish kettle."

Sauce Suprême. Put 2 or 3 tablespoonfuls of reduced *velouté* and 2 or 3 of chicken consommé into a pan and reduce to the original amount of the *velouté*, stirring. Just before using, add a good piece of butter. Stir on a hot fire. When it is sufficiently thickened, remove it. Strain. Add the juice of 1 lemon or a dash of verjuice, spoon it, and use as needed.

[1]Comte de Courchamps.—ED.

Garlic Butter Sauce. Crush 2 fat cloves of garlic, mix well with butter the size of an egg. Force through a fine sieve. Use either in *velouté* or in a reduced espagnole sauce.

Provençal Butter Sauce. Prepare garlic butter as above, but use 6 cloves of garlic to the same amount of butter. Put into a porcelain bowl. Pour a little virgin oil on it and keep stirring, adding oil drop by drop and a pinch or two of salt. Keep working until it is like butter.

Tartar Sauce. Chop very fine 2 or 3 shallots, a little chervil and tarragon. Add mustard, 2 egg yolks, a dash of vinegar, salt, and pepper. Stir, adding a little oil. Keep stirring. If it seems to get too thick, add a little vinegar.

Fennel Sauce. Chop a few leaves of fennel; blanch; drain. Put into a pot 2 skimming spoonfuls of *velouté* and the same amount of butter sauce. Heat, stirring. Just before serving, add the fennel. Stir it in well, add salt and nutmeg.

Sauce Duxelles. Chop equal amounts of mushrooms, scallions, parsley, and shallots. Season with salt, coarse pepper, fine spices, a little nutmeg, and 1 bay leaf. Stir over heat into equal quantities of butter and grated bacon. Add a few tablespoonfuls of espagnole sauce or *velouté*. Simmer, stirring, until all the moisture from the herbs has evaporated. To use, stir into a bland sauce, but do not boil. If you wish, add the juice of 1 lemon. Keep this in a bowl or jar and use as needed, especially for meats to be cooked in paper covers.

Orange Sauce. Squeeze and strain the juice from some oranges. Remove the zest and cut into tiny slices. Blanch them, drain them. Put into beef gravy sharpened with coarse pepper. Simmer. Just before serving, add the orange juice.

Matelote Sauce. Into a pot with a ladleful of reduced espagnole sauce put little onions cooked and browned in butter, mushrooms, and artichoke bottoms. Just before serving, add a piece of butter the size of a small nut. Stir in carefully so as not to crush the other ingredients.

Raisin Sauce. (To serve with beef tongue à l'écarlate.) Put into a pot 1 glass of vinegar, a bouquet of parsley, thyme, bay leaf, whole pepper, cloves. Reduce by half. Add 2 glasses of gravy, boil, thicken with 1 tablespoonful of starch mixed with cold water. After 5 minutes' simmering, put through a sieve into another pot. Add 2 tablespoonfuls of currant jelly and 2 handfuls of dried seeded raisins (washed in hot water), boil gently 5 minutes, and pour over the sliced tongue.

Pluche Sauce. Pluck parsley leaves from their stems. Blanch them, freshen in cold water, and set aside to drain. Put 3 tablespoonfuls of reduced *velouté* and 2 of consommé into a pot. Reduce and add the parsley leaves just before serving. If it is too salty, add a bit of butter, strain, spoon, and serve.

Lobster Sauce. Remove the flesh and coral from a cooked medium-sized lobster. Dice the meat. Remove the membrane from the coral. Put both aside in a covered dish. Wash the shells, discarding the little legs. Dry out in a warm oven. Crush fine in a mortar. Mix with butter and force through a sieve. Add this to a white sauce. Heat without boiling, stirring. Add a little cayenne or plain coarse pepper, pour over the meat and coral. Stir and mix well and serve in a sauceboat.

Cold Polonaise Sauce. Put the juice of 4 lemons and 1 bitter orange into a sauceboat. Add a good pinch of fine pepper, 3 coffee spoonfuls of good mustard, 6 full tablespoonfuls of sugar. Stir until the sugar is melted. Serve with cold game.

Sauce à la Provençale. Stir together 2 raw egg yolks, a tablespoonful of gravy or reduced consommé, garlic, hot pimento, and the juice of 2 lemons. Thicken in a double boiler, stirring constantly. Add and stir in well a little olive oil. Serve with fish entrees.

SAUERKRAUT. All the peoples of the North and the East use it in great quantities, and navigators on long voyages put in great stores of it. The Germans are mad about it. It has become proverbial that a sure way to get oneself murdered in Italy is to say the women are not pretty; in England to tease the inhabitants about the degree of liberty they enjoy; in Germany to question whether sauerkraut is a dish for the gods.

The famous Captain Cook attributed the health of his crew in great part to the large quantity of sauerkraut he fed them, sauerkraut being more easily digestible than ordinary cabbage, which, according to a Greek proverb, kills on the second round.

To Prepare Sauerkraut. Wash in several waters and drain well. Put it into a casserole with smoked pork, sausages, cervelat, fat from roast beef, juniper, white wine, and bouillon. Cook for 6 hours on a slow fire. Serve with the pork on top, mixed with your sausages and cervelat.

SHAD. An excellent fish that goes up the rivers from the sea at certain seasons of the year. During its journey upstream it fattens and loses its saltiness. It may be cooked, without scaling, in court bouillon, like salmon or Rhine carp, and served with fresh parsley and grated horseradish. Or it may be scaled and served with various sauces, such as sorrel, caper, or tomato.

Shad with Sorrel. Scale, gut, and wash your shad, and wrap in buttered paper after sprinkling with *fines herbes*. Cook on grill and serve on chopped cooked sorrel or on maître d'hôtel sauce.

Shad on the Spit. If, in the course of your fishing, you catch a very big shad, which can well happen towards the end of summer, it is better spitted than grilled, as it cooks more evenly this way. Cut light incisions slantways on the back and marinate in oil with salt, parsley sprigs, and chopped scallions. Turn it several times in its marinade. Cook it on the spit, basting with your seasoned oil. It should be eaten with an oil or a vinegar sauce.

SHALLOTS. *Ascalonia* in Latin. This indicates their origin. They came from Syria to Europe with the homing Crusaders.

Like onions and garlic, the shallot is used in sauces, but it brings to them a quite distinctive flavour, much more delicate than the other two condiments named. Shallots are excellent in oil and vinegar sauces served with artichokes hot or cold. It is impossible to make a good *sauce piquante* without shallots. [*But see Dumas' recipe for this sauce, above, p. 216.*–ED.]

SHARK. For people who like shark, or would like to try it, we recommend the recipe below, given to us by M. Duglerez, chief kitchen steward of the House of Rothschild, to whom we owe a number of recipes of this type. But we warn the diner in advance that we have no personal opinion on this dish. We have never eaten it. We have never had any desire to do so.

Shark flesh is tough, leathery, dry, gluey, and hard to digest. This does not prevent the Norwegians and Icelanders from drying it, later actually to cook and eat it. We recommend this recipe to them also.

Young Shark Stomachs. Soak 15 young shark stomachs for 24 hours. Drain. Parboil 20 minutes in lightly salted water. Drain. Freshen with cold water. Dry with a cloth.

Line a pot with strips of bacon and add the shark stomachs. Add 1 bay leaf, 2 cloves, 3 peeled and pitted slices of lemon, 1 ladleful of good poultry consommé, 3 ounces of butter. Simmer until well done.

Just before serving, make a sauce with 1 ladleful of *sauce suprême*, 1 tablespoonful of soubise sauce, 2 good pinches of Indian curry. This sauce should be reduced, but not pasty.

SHEEP AND MUTTON. [See also LAMB.] In the mountains of Greece and on the islands of Cyprus, Sardinia, and Corsica, there is a breed of sheep, now rare because they are hunted avidly, believed to be the original variety from which the various sheep of today are descended. They are about the size of a fallow deer and have enormous horns. The sheep of the Cape of Good Hope, of Astrakhan, and of the Caspian region have tails that weigh up to twenty pounds, which they drag around on little carts so the wool will not be ruined by dragging on the ground.

Pedro the Cruel, King of Castile, introduced Barbary sheep, which have brought such fame to Spanish wool, to his people. The profits from these animals were so enormous that the King and all his nobles visited their flocks and personally superintended their care and breeding. Shearing time was celebrated with feasting. For this reason sheep, bringing in revenues of thirty million to Spain, were called the jewels of its crown. A pure-bred ram was priceless, and some have sold for as much as five hundred francs.

In the fifteenth century, the King of Spain gave Edward IV of England three thousand of these highly bred sheep. The change of climate made the wool longer and coarser. Since then, English woollens have been sought after, and it is to remind the nation of the importance of its commerce in this product that a woolsack was used — and I believe is used to this day — for the Lord Chancellor's seat in the House of Lords.

The sheep is an important item of food in every country, but especially in those which have neither inns nor kitchens. I refer to Spain, the banks of the Nile, and Arabia. When one travels in the desert with four to six Arabs, the price is arranged beforehand, based on whether you will feed them or they will feed themselves. In the latter case, they lunch on one date, dine on two, and tighten their belts after every meal. In the former, they are always hungry, and there is no way to satiate their appetites.

In 1833 I travelled through Tunis to visit a Roman amphitheatre twelve or fifteen miles in the desert. I bargained with four Arabs to conduct me to this ruin, called Djem-Djem. They agreed to furnish me with my mount, a camel, and to feed themselves. I had brought a sort of a tin valise containing a piece of roast meat, bread, fruit, wine, dates, brandy, and water. When we came to our first night stop, I saw with astonishment that the Arabs were dining on a few dates and a banana. I was ashamed of the relative sumptuousness of my meal, and gave them most of my food. I told them that next day we should all lunch together, and they should buy a sheep for that purpose.

Next morning, I found they had bought a fifty-pound lamb. Two hours later, we arrived at Djem-Djem. I ascertained that the lamb would take about two hours to cook, and that the same amount of time would suffice to visit the amphitheatre. Since I was very curious about desert methods of preparing lamb or mutton, I stayed to watch all the preliminaries.

First the Arabs killed the lamb as prescribed by the Koran. They opened its belly and discarded the intestines, but put back the heart, liver, and lungs. Then they filled up the opening with dates, figs, dried raisins, honey, salt, and pepper. Then the stomach was carefully sewn up again. Meanwhile two of the Arabs had been busy with their swords, digging a pit two feet deep, which they filled with dry wood that was set on fire. The lamb was laid on the bed of coals, and another pile of dry wood placed over it, which immediately caught fire. When that was reduced to coals, they covered them with some of the earth from the pit.

I left then, to visit the amphitheatre, but I got very hungry and was eager to taste my guides' cooking. They were apparently as eager as I, for no sooner had I returned than they began to haul the lamb out of the pit.

It was roasted like a potato whose skin is charred by the coals. Scratched with a knife, the wool fell away completely, revealing a golden skin. Behind this skin, which had retained every drop of juice and fat, evidently lay the most tender, succulent meat. I did not know how to carve this lamb, so I gave the chief of the Arabs the signal to start.

He didn't wait to be begged. His thumb and index finger plunged into the meat like a vulture's beak, and he pulled off a ribbon of meat. The others did the same, and I saw that if I did not hurry there would be nothing left. So I cut off a shoulder with my knife and, not being particularly desirous of watching the manner of the Arabs' feasting, put it on a platter and carried it off to eat by myself, like a child being punished.

I must say that I have eaten lamb prepared in some of the most renowned kitchens of Europe, but I have never eaten any meat more savoury than this which was cooked in the coals. I recommend it to all travellers in the Orient.

Braised Leg of Mutton. Bone a leg of mutton, leaving only the shank bone. Lard it with fairly thick strips of bacon rolled in fine spices, salt, basil, pepper, parsley, and scallions. Tie it up into its original shape. Put into the bottom of an iron pot a few scraps of butcher's meat, 5 or 6 onions and carrots, and your leg on top of them. Pour over it a little consommé with brandy, bay leaf, cloves, a clove of garlic, and some thyme. Bring to a boil slowly. Cover tightly and cook slowly in the oven 4 or 5 hours. Drain and glaze and serve on any vegetable base you choose or simply with its own gravy.

Leg of Mutton English Style. Bone a leg of mutton as above. Flour it. Wrap it in a cloth tied at the four corners. Put it into a kettle of boiling salted water with a bunch of sliced turnips. Keep it boiling, turning it over at least once, for 1½ hours. Meanwhile, when the turnips are done, take them out, drain, mash, and season with butter, salt, pepper, adding a little cream or boiled-down milk. The turnip purée should be thick enough to be piled on a platter in the form of a pyramid. Arrange the leg of mutton on a platter, pour a butter sauce over it, sprinkle with capers. Serve with the turnips and a sauceboat of white sauce with capers. (Recipe from Vuillemot.)

To Make Leg of Mutton like Venison. Have your leg of

mutton well seasoned. Beat it. Remove the membrane. Lard it. Put it into an earthenware vessel with a handful of juniper berries and a pinch of melilot. Cover with a strong marinade made with a good proportion of red vinegar. Marinate 5 or 6 days. Drain. Roast on the spit and serve with a poivrade sauce.

Ratonnet of Lamb or Mutton. Slice a leg of lamb. Flatten the slices, season with salt, pepper, chopped *fines herbes*, parsley, scallions, garlic, 1 glass of oil, the juice of 1 lemon, all mixed together. Let them marinate 2 hours. Cover each slice with a layer of chopped chicken. Roll, fasten with a skewer, with a slice of bacon over each end to prevent the stuffing from spilling. Attach to a spit and broil, basting with the marinade, mixed with 1 glass of white wine. Arrange on a platter. Add a little cullis and meat broth to the drippings, skim off the fat, and sauce your *ratonnets*, or serve with an italienne sauce.

You can do the same with well-hung veal or beef.

SMELTS. One of the most delicate of eating fish.

Fried Smelts. Clean and scale a sufficient quantity of smelts. Wipe each one carefully. String them through the eyes on a skewer, dip in milk, then flour. Fry in deep fat to a fine colour. Put a napkin on your platter, arrange them on top, and serve.

Smelts English Style. Into a saucepan put 2 tablespoonfuls of oil, salt, pepper, ½ peeled lemon (sliced and the seeds removed), 2 glasses of white wine, 2 glasses of water. Boil for 15 minutes or thereabouts. Add your cleaned, scaled, and wiped smelts. When cooked, drain and serve with the following sauce:

Blanch 1 clove of garlic and crush. Put it into a pan with well-chopped scallions and parsley and 2 glasses of champagne. Boil 5 minutes. Add butter mixed with flour, salt, and a pinch of coarse pepper. Stir and thicken. After cooking add the juice of 1 lemon, taste, and serve.

SNAILS. The only distinction gourmands make between snails concerns where they are picked. Those found on grapevines are the most sought after and the best. The Romans were so fond of them they built special enclosures in which the snails were fattened on wheat and old wine to make them more digestible. They are seasoned vigorously. A broth that is very soothing to consumptives is made from snails.

Snails à la Provençale. Soak 36 snails in cold water and brush with a stiff brush. Meanwhile, bring water to a boil in a large pot. Sift a handful of wood ashes, tie up in a cloth, and put to boil in the water 15 minutes. Add your snails and boil until they come out of their shells readily. After 12 or 15 minutes put the snails into fresh cold water and take them out of their shells, putting them into warm water. Meanwhile, in 2 tablespoonfuls of good oil, sauté lightly parsley, mushrooms, shallots, ½ clove of grated garlic, salt, grated nutmeg, and a little green pepper, all chopped fine. Stir in ½ tablespoonful of flour and add 1 glass of good white wine. When this sauce begins to simmer, drain your snails and add them, letting them simmer until completely cooked. Add 2 or 3 raw egg yolks to bind the sauce. Fill the shells with this mixture, cover with bread crumbs, sprinkle with oil, and bake 15 minutes. Serve piping hot.

SOLE. The best sole is the grey. It is caught in the waters off Dieppe. The soles caught at Calais or Roscoff are not so fine.

Fried Sole. Just before serving, flour and fry in a hot skillet. These, like other fried fish, should be firm when taken from the skillet. When they have browned nicely, drain on a cloth, sprinkle with salt, serve on a neatly folded napkin on a platter. Serve whole lemons or bitter oranges alongside.

Sole Fillets Flemish Style. As above. Then place in a fish-poaching pan, simmer in salted water, drain, and serve with a sauce-boat of melted butter or with oyster sauce.

Baked Sole. Split down the back, stuff with *fines herbes* lightly fried in butter and cooled. Butter the bottom of a dish, arrange your soles on it. Brush with melted butter, sprinkle with a little salt and fine spices. Bread with white crumbs, add a little white wine or bouillon to the pan, and bake to a good colour.

Deep-fried Sole Fillets. Marinate with salt, pepper, lemon juice. Just before serving, dip in beaten egg, then in bread crumbs. Deep-fry. Serve in a ring with remoulade or *sauce Robert* in the centre of the platter.

Sautéed Sole Fillets. Cut each fillet into 4 pieces. Marinate in salt, pepper, a chopped shallot or onion, chopped parsley and truffles, the juice of 1 lemon. Butter a skillet. Place the fillets in it. Put on the fire. Turn when firm on one side. Arrange on a platter. Pour the butter out of the skillet and replace it with ½ glass of dry white wine. Add slices of truffle and reduce the liquid to half. Add a little espagnole sauce. Skim off the fat. Pour over the fillets.

Sole Fillets au Gratin. Spread a thin layer of prepared fish or meat forcemeat stuffing on each fillet. Roll up, starting with the thin end. Make them all the same size by putting a thicker layer of stuffing on the thinner fillets. Put a finger-thick layer of the force-meat on the bottom of your platter. Arrange the rolled fillets on this in the form of a crown, leaving the centre empty. Fill the spaces between each fillet completely with the stuffing. Smooth the surface with a knife dipped in warm water. Bread with white crumbs, pour a little melted butter over them. Bake to a good colour. Fill the centre with Provençale or italienne sauce and serve.

Sole Fillets à la sauce de Provence. Cut 4 fillets into 2 pieces each. Season, flour, plunge into deep hot fat. When they are done, drain, arrange on a platter with parsley between them. Send to the table with a sauceboat of the following:

Simmer the fishbones in white wine and aromatic herbs. Skim, strain, and reduce to a thin glaze. Add 1 tablespoonful of strained, plain tomato purée and 1 tablespoonful of espagnole sauce. Reduce a few minutes, then put on the side of the fire. Stir in bits of butter amounting to about 6 ounces. The sauce must be stirred constantly during this process. When it is well blended, finish with the juice of 1 lemon and a dash of cayenne pepper.

Sole à la Mode de Trouville. Remove the black skin from 2 fresh soles and divide them into 2 or 3 pieces. Butter a pan, sprinkle with 2 tablespoonfuls of chopped onions, arrange your pieces of sole on these. Season them, and just cover with cider. Bring to a quick boil for a few moments, then put into a hot oven for 10 minutes. Remove to a platter. Boil the liquid rapidly for 2 minutes, take it off the fire, stir in a piece of butter mixed with flour, incorporate a bit of fresh butter and a pinch of parsley. Serve over the sole.

SORREL. A potherb that owes its flavour to the presence of oxalic acid. It is useful to cooks and physicians. It is used for soups, purées, etc.

Sorrel Purée. Chop together sorrel, chard, lettuce, and a little chervil. Stir without moisture over the fire until well softened. Add a piece of butter and continue to stir until quite cooked. Season with salt and coarse pepper. Thicken with egg yolks and cream.

Another Recipe. Use gravy, the liquid from a meat braise, or reduced bouillon instead of egg yolks and cream. Use this purée as a bed on which to serve meats.

SOUPS. Bouillabaisse. Take 6 or more varieties of fish and cut them into pieces. Heat in a casserole 1 or 2 glasses of oil, depending on the size of the bouillabaisse you wish to make, with chopped onions, garlic, parsley, tomatoes, bay leaf, some orange peel, pepper, and fine spices. Add your fish, a pinch of salt, and a pinch of saffron. Cover with boiling water and boil hard for ¼ hour, by which time the water should be reduced by a quarter. To serve, pour the bouillon over pieces of bread in the soup tureen and serve the fish in another platter. (Recipe from M. Roubion, restaurateur at Marseille.)

Bouillabaisse à la Nîmoise. First make fish bouillon by boiling all sorts of fish (including those which are well flavoured but too bony to eat) with 1 onion, 1 sliced carrot, celery, heart of lettuce, chervil, parsley, 2 cloves, ½ bay leaf, and a little fine oil or butter. Strain. This will serve for making fish soups and sauces.

Take a number of varieties of fish, those which take longer, like eels, half cooked in advance, cut them into pieces, put into a pot with a piece of butter, sprinkle well with *fines herbes*. Cover with the fish bouillon above and 1 glass of Madeira or dry white wine. Boil hard so that the bouillon will reduce fast.

Take the liver of an angler or fishing frog, crush it completely in a mortar, mix with 3 raw egg yolks and ½ glass of good oil. Arrange your fish in a dish, reheat its bouillon, thicken with the liver, etc., pass through a strainer over the fish. Edge the dish with croutons fried in butter.

Veal Soup. Butter the bottom of a pot. Put into it a few slices of ham, 4 or 5 pounds of good-quality veal, 2 or 3 carrots, the same number of onions. Pour over it 1 tablespoonful of fine bouillon and let it stew on a low fire until the liquid is reduced to a glaze and has turned a fine yellow colour. Remove from the stove, cut the meat with the point of a knife to let the juices flow. Cover. Let it stew another 15 minutes. Then cover with good bouillon, add a bouquet of parsley and scallions with ½ clove of garlic and 1 clove stuck into them. Bring to a boil. Skim. Let it simmer until the meat is done. Skim off fat, strain, and serve with rice or vermicelli, or use the broth to make your sauces.

Soup à la Reine. Roast 2 or 3 chickens. Remove the skin and bones, which put into a good bouillon and simmer. Crush the meat in a mortar, mixing in 5 or 6 almonds to make it white and a piece of crustless bread the size of an egg which you will have dipped in your bouillon. Add some of the bouillon and continue to macerate with the pestle. Pass through a strainer, adding bouillon as you go to obtain the thickness of a purée.

When ready to use, heat this purée in a double boiler. Pour into a soup tureen and garnish with croutons fried in butter.

Note. This purée may be made with any sort of fowl or game, leaving out the almonds.

Cabbage Soup. There are various ways of making cabbage soup. The simplest is to put your cabbage into a *pot-au-feu*, remove it when you think it is done, and serve it with the bouillon in which it cooked.

We shall indicate a few refinements we have worked out for this, it seems to us, too-simple recipe.

Make a hash of all the left-over poultry and game you may have. Make a bouillon by cooking your beef today in a bouillon you made yesterday. Line the bottom of a pot with fine smoked ham. Spread the leaves of the cabbage and fill between them with the hash. Tie up the cabbage in its original form. Cover with bouillon and cook

2 hours, replacing any bouillon that may evaporate. Let it simmer another ¾ hour. Bring to a boil once more.

Now you have the choice of serving the cabbage in the soup, or serving the bouillon separately as a soup to dip your bread into and using the cabbage with the next course.

Another Method. Line the bottom of a pot with 1 or 1½ pounds of smoked ham. Cut your cabbage into quarters to remove the core and any little animals that may have crept into it – whose meat is superfluous to the preparation of this bouillon. Tie it up carefully again so that the leaves don't fall off and place it delicately on the slices of ham. Fill your pot to the top of the cabbage with a bouillon that has *smiled* for 6 or 7 hours.

The bouillon should have been prepared as described in the article under that title. To *make the pot smile* is a common French expression for the slow process of simmering described there. You will not find it in any dictionary. But if ever I become one of the Forty [Immortals of the French Academy] I promise I shall have it included in the *Dictionnaire de l'Académie.*

Back to our cabbage. Now that the ham is the only meat in the *pot-au-feu,* make it boil hard. After 20 minutes your pot will be almost dry. The cabbage will have absorbed all the bouillon and will now be a third larger than when you started. You fill the pot again and boil hard until half the bouillon has disappeared. Then fill again.

After 2 hours of cooking, you serve the cabbage on the slices of meat, on a platter, and the bouillon in which it has cooked in the soup tureen.

And that is the famous, excellent cabbage soup for which every guest will demand the recipe once he has tasted it.

Salsify Soup Lyonnaise. Scrape large salsify roots and cut them into pieces as long as your finger. Blanch a few minutes in boiling water. Drain and cook in a good bouillon. Thicken with 6 raw egg yolks and pour over bread crusts in the soup tureen.

Refreshing Veal Bouillon. Dice ¼ pound of round of veal, and boil with 3 pints of water, a head of lettuce, and a handful of chervil. If you wish, add a little wild chicory. Put this bouillon through a very fine sieve, reheat, and serve.

Wooden Leg Soup. Cut both ends off a beef shinbone, leaving it about 1 foot long. Put into a big kettle with good bouillon and a good slice of fresh beef, some cold water. Bring slowly to a boil. Skim. Season with salt and a couple of cloves. Add 24 to 36 carrots, 12 onions, 12 stalks of celery, 12 turnips, 1 hen, and 2 old partridges. (Take note that you should allow yourself plenty of time for this dish, so that it will cook slowly and be that much better.)

Now take a slice of veal round, about 2 pounds, warm slowly in a pot, and fill with bouillon from the above. Skim off the fat. Add 12 little onions, a few small stalks of celery, add the whole to the big kettle and cook about 1 hour. Correct your seasoning. Skim off all fat again. Put grated stale white of bread into a pot. Add bouillon. Simmer. Put into the tureen for serving, add the cooked vegetables, put the bone on top, pour the bouillon over. Serve very hot. (Recipe from Grimod de la Reynière.)

Mussel Soup. May be made with prawns, shrimps, crayfish.

When tomato time comes around, I recommend this soup, which I myself invented and perfected.

At eleven o'clock in the morning start a *pot-au-feu* as I have described (see p. 66), but in a small proportion since, as you will see, the bouillon is only a third of the preparation for this soup.

At four in the afternoon, put 12 tomatoes and 12 white onions to boil for 1 hour in the bouillon you have made. Then put the whole through a sieve fine enough so the tomato seeds won't pass through. Put this purée on a slow fire, adding salt, pepper, and 3 or 4 ounces of meat glaze, and let it reduce.

Put your mussels or prawns into a pot on the fire without water. If you use shrimps or crayfish, put them on in the following sauce: 1 bottle of white wine, a bouquet of herbs, chopped carrots, salt, pepper, and 1 glass of good vinegar.

After 15 minutes, your mussels or prawns will be cooked. After 30 minutes your shrimps or crayfish will be cooked.

Put their juice or sauce into your tomatoes. Bring to a boil. Remove from the fire immediately.

Put a crushed ½ clove of garlic into a pot with a little oil and brown lightly. Pour the liquid into this, stirring constantly, and cook 15 minutes to homogenize. Add the mussels or the shelled shrimps or prawns.

If you are using crayfish, pound the whole crayfish very fine in a mortar, boil it in a portion of your sauce, and when the flavour and aroma have been extracted pour into the whole sauce.

Pardon my prolixity. I am saying all this less for the benefit of cooks among my readers than for that of those who have no notion at all of cooking and must have everything explained carefully.

Now we come to a soup beloved of huntsmen and venerated by drunkards.

Onion Soup. There are two types of onions, the big white Spanish and the little red Italian. The Spanish has more food value and is therefore chosen to make soup for huntsmen and drunkards, two classes of people who require fast recuperation.

Chop fine 20 big Spanish onions. Brown in a skillet with 1 pound of butter. Add 3 quarts of milk still warm from the cow – any older milk would turn. When the onions have boiled in the milk, put through a coarse sieve to make a purée. Salt, pepper, and stir in 6 raw egg yolks. Add pieces of toasted bread crust. And there you have it.

Herb Soup à la Dauphine. Chop together 4 handfuls of spinach, 3 hearts of lettuce, the white of 1 leek, 2 onions, 2 handfuls of sorrel, 2 of garden orach, 2 of chard, a good pinch of chervil, a few tansy leaves, a few stalks of purslane, and finally some marigold petals – be sure to use only the petals; the ovaries and calyx are very bitter. Heat with butter until all is wilted. Add hot water, or water in which root vegetables have cooked, or rice water, or fish bouillon, and bring to a boil. Put bread without crust in the bottom of the tureen. The flavour of the crust would spoil the fine, simple delicacy of this vegetable combination.

SPANISH COOKING. In Spain there is one dish everybody eats. It is called *puchero*. These are the ingredients of a good *puchero*: 1 pound of beef, ½ pound of smoked ham with the bones. The older the ham, the better. The best is from Galicia. Boil these meats in 1 gallon of water until it is reduced to 2 quarts. Add ¼ pound of *garbanzos*.

Before going any further, we must explain what a *garbanzo* is. It is an enormous chick-pea. Its goodness depends on the ground in which it grows. A *garbanzo* that cooks in ½ hour is priceless. But if it comes from poor soil it is harder after 1 hour of cooking than it was to start with. The *garbanzos* must be soaked overnight in salted water before cooking. It is a legume capricious as to both physical and moral properties. If a single drop of cold water is added while it is cooking, it refuses to cook at all. It is hastier than the bean, producing rumblings in the stomach that the bean waits to develop until it reaches the intestines.

Let us return to our unfinished *puchero*. The time has come to add the *chorizo*. This is a hash of veal and pork seasoned with red pepper and other strong flavourings. With the liquid reduced to 2 quarts, you take 1 ounce of ham, 1 ounce of bacon, a pinch of parsley, ½ clove of garlic, and chop it all up with 1 tablespoonful of bouillon taken from the pot. Then you beat 2 eggs, crumble a small piece of bread into them, mix the whole together, divide into as many parts as there will be people to eat, dry them well, add to the *puchero*, and cook for another ½ hour.

This is the invariable dinner of every Spaniard, and of any Spaniard who does not have it, one can only say, poor devil!

At eleven o'clock at night, the Spaniard has a supper of *guisado*. This is made of beef and veal with potatoes. It is started cooking at two o'clock, right after lunch. There are two kinds of *guisados*. In one, the potatoes are cooked along with the meat. In the other, they are fried first and added just before serving.

This is in Castile, through which we have wandered with Don Quixote and Sancho Panza, crying like them with horn and voice for milk and for the crows to bring us cheese.

In Galicia, things are different. You don't get *puchero*. You get *caldo*. Also, you don't get the same thick chocolate as in Castile. In Galicia the cups are larger, and the chocolate is thinner.

If you have the good fortune to find a good, recommended hotel in Galicia, you will eat neither better nor worse than in any other part of Spain.

In passing, I have this piece of advice to anyone who plans to tour Spain: let him tour Italy first. Italy is an excellent conditioner between Franch and Spain.

In Italy, where one eats badly, the best hotels will tell you: "We have a French cook."

In Spain, where one eats abominably, the great hotels will boast: "We have an Italian cook."

If by chance you should find a decent hotel in Galicia, you will be served *caldo*. This is a sort of soup made by chopping cabbage, potatoes, and turnips into a big pot of water, adding dried beans. To give flavour, the cook adds ¼ pound of fresh pork and ¼ pound of rancid pork. The more rancid the pork, the better the Galicians like it.

Then will come meat and fish – cooked, they will tell you, in the French or the Italian style. The fish, the poultry, and the game will be excellent, but their seasoning abominable. For lack of spits to broil on, the poultry will be fried in a skillet or roasted in a pan. The same goes for the game. In Spain there is a word for spit in the dictionary, but that is all. This is very unfortunate, for game is plentiful, excellent, and cheap. Hares may be purchased for fifteen to twenty sous. No one eats them, because they are said to scratch up the earth to disinter the dead.

When the unfortunate Spaniards do cook a hare, they have so little understanding of cooking that they immediately bleed it to the last drop. They do not know that a hare's blood does not congeal, that it was put there to season the meat!

As for partridge, which no one cares too much about, the master gives them to the cook. To pluck them more easily she dips them in boiling water and has no idea that this destroys the best part of their flavour. Then she throws them into the olla-podrida, where they cook until they happen to be fished out with a long fork.

This is an olla-podrida, not common at all in Spain, but well advertised in France by novelists who know nothing about it except the name:

An olla-podrida is an immense pot that never comes off the fire and into which every kind of meat that comes into the house, especially gelatinous parts, is thrown. Calves' feet, sheeps' feet, pigs' feet, hogs' noses and ears, for example, all go into the olla-podrida.

In this way, it will not be denied, a very thick and savoury broth is developed, which I would have found excellent, were it not for the eternal tripe, which gives it a flavour I cannot abide.

Salads are generally eaten before the soup. Here are the principal salads peculiar to Spain:

Cauliflower Salad. Boil 4 eggs with cauliflower. Peel the eggs and cut them in quarters. Mix with the cooked cauliflower, season, and serve hot. The eggs cooked with the cauliflower develop a frightful flavour.

Cabbage Salad. Boil cabbage with ham bones, drain, fry in a skillet with oil. At the table this is again seasoned with oil, together with vinegar, salt, and pepper.

Garlic Soup. This is the Spaniard's favourite. In 2 ounces of fat fry 1 clove of garlic until it is burnt. Add 1 quart of water and a pinch of salt. Bring to a boil. In a soup tureen place thin slices of bread and break over them 1 egg per person. Pour the boiling soup over this and serve.

If the meal is an important one, stewed tongue will follow the soup.

Stewed Tongue. Marinate the tongue 3 days in plain water spiced with sweet peppers, a handful of oregano, salt, pepper, and 1 chopped clove of garlic. Drain. Lard with very thin strips of bacon and stew with onions and potatoes.

Chicken Pepitoria. This may replace the tongue. Quarter a chicken, fry in very hot lard, and put lard and all into a pot with water, salt, and 1 bay leaf. Cook well. Crush 3 hard-boiled egg yolks in a mortar with the white part of bread and parsley. Add to the boiling chicken and serve very hot.

It is possible, in Catalonia, to escape the chicken *pepitoria*, but you will not escape chicken with tomatoes and peppers.

Let us imagine you are preparing to feast your friends on this exotic dish.

You fry your chicken in lard as for chicken *pepitoria*. Then you remove it from the skillet and into the boiling lard you put tomatoes and peppers that have already been grilled in the ashes and peeled. Then you return the chicken and fry the whole together until done.

We would be ungrateful to Catalonia if we forgot to mention its national dishes: *longuet* and stews with prunes.

The *longuet* is made with small, long loaves of bread peculiar to Catalonia. These are boiled in milk, hollowed out, filled with chopped meat, and fried in lard.

France stuffs with truffles, Castile with olives, Galicia with chestnuts, and Catalonia with prunes. Ragouts are prepared the same as anywhere else, except that dried prunes are added. A connoisseur at first glance could imagine they were truffles. He would suffer a similar surprise with fat chickens and turkeys, through whose transparent skin he would perceive dark spots to make a gourmand's mouth water. Take care. They are just dried prunes.

SPINACH. A potherb whose leaves are eaten only cooked.

Old-fashioned Spinach. Blanch and chop. Put into a skillet with butter and grated nutmeg. When done, add butter mixed with flour, sugar, and milk. Serve garnished with croutons fried in butter.

Cream of Spinach. Mix a big tablespoonful of cooked spinach, 12 crushed sweet almonds, a little lime juice, 3 or 4 bitter-almond biscuits, sugar, 2 glasses of cream, 1 glass of milk, and 6 egg yolks. Put through a sieve, bake, and serve hot.

Spinach Rissoles. Cook, drain, let cool. Add fresh butter, grated lime rind, 2 bitter-almond biscuits, sugar, and orange-flower water. Crush the whole in a mortar. Then roll out very thin pastry dough, cut into small squares. Put a dab of spinach on each square, turn one corner to make triangles, and seal. Deep-fry in oil. When they have turned golden, drain, put on a platter, sprinkle with sugar, pass under the broiler to glaze, and serve hot.

Spinach Soup. Put well-washed spinach into a pot with water, butter, salt, a little bouquet of marjoram and thyme, 1 onion with cloves stuck in it. Boil all together. When half cooked, add sugar, a handful of raisins and croutons dried in the oven. Finish cooking and serve over slices of bread.

STERLET. A small variety of sturgeon (*Acipenser ruthenus*), for which the Russians have a predilection similar to that of the ancient Romans for red mullet and dolphin.

In Rome, the host showed his guests the live red mullet or dolphin they were to eat. Slaves ran twelve leagues in relays from the fishing port where they were caught to Rome, bearing the fish in tubs of water. The fish nearly always arrived in time for the guests to watch the final agonies tarnish the gold, purple, and azure of their scales.

The Russians are the same, and even worse. The lords of St. Petersburg and the boyars of Moscow prefer the sterlet, above all others, as a dish to place before their guests. They care little for the large sturgeon except for its caviar.

Before there were railways in Russia, a sterlet had to be transported by special carriages — used for this purpose only — as much as two or three hundred leagues. In the winter, when the temperature was thirty degrees or more below freezing, it was quite a trick to keep the water at an even temperature just above freezing to make sure the fish was delivered alive. Sometimes, if two or three sterlets were used to prepare a soup, that soup cost six to eight thousand francs. This sterlet soup was called *ouka*. I have written to Russia to get the recipe, but I have never received it.

Sterlet with Chablis. Scrape the scales from the fish. Clean it. Make an incision in the flesh under the tail and, using a cloth, slowly and carefully draw out the sinew, which is about as thick as a wooden knitting needle and runs along the spine. Cut the fish on the bias into 5 or 6 pieces, put into a buttered pot, add a few pieces of parsley root, a bay leaf, an unpeeled clove of garlic, salt. Cover three quarters with Chablis and the juice of 2 or 3 lemons. Cover. Cook over a quick fire so that by the time the fish is cooked the liquid will be reduced by half. Skim the sauce, add a few tablespoonfuls of liquid glaze and some bouillon, thicken with a piece of butter mixed with flour, add the juice of 1 lemon. Arrange the pieces of sterlet on a long platter, giving it back its original shape. Surround it with truffles, olives, quenelles, and mushrooms. Pour some of the sauce over it and send the rest to the table in a sauceboat. (This recipe is borrowed from Urbain-Dubois' *Cuisine de Tous les Pays*.)

STURGEON (CAVIAR). I spent a month observing the caviar fisheries on the shores of the Caspian Sea from the Ural to the Volga. Nothing is more curious than these fisheries, in which thousands of fish, weighing up to six hundred pounds and twelve to fifteen feet in length, are destroyed in six to eight weeks. They have been caught up to twenty feet long in the Danube, where they come to spawn from the Black Sea. The flesh of the caviar sturgeon has a delicate flavour rare among cartilaginous fish. It can easily be mistaken for veal. But we must admit that the modern nations do not have the same enthusiasm for this meat that the ancients had. They crowned both it, and the servants who brought it to the table to the music of flutes, with flowers.

The greatest sturgeon fisheries are in Russia. They make a *pâté* from its spinal marrow that is highly esteemed. Sealed from the air, the caviar keeps for quite some time. It is shipped in sixteen-, thirty-, and forty-pound barrels the day it is caught.

Sturgeons grow to an enormous size. In 1769 one was caught that was sixty feet long and weighed 2310 pounds.

The sturgeon is very rare and highly esteemed in France. In 1833 I gave a masked ball, which some of my contemporaries may still remember, at which a whole roasted roebuck and a sturgeon cooked in court bouillon were served. Only the bones of the roebuck were left. But though more than four hundred people were served, they were unable to finish the sturgeon.

Once Archchancellor Cambacérès received two enormous sturgeons, one weighing 324 pounds, the other 374, the same day. There was to be a grand dinner that day, and the maître d'hôtel closeted himself with His Highness to resolve the difficulty that arose. If both were served at the same dinner, one would evidently belittle the other. On the other hand, it was unthinkable to serve two fish of the same variety on succeeding days. He emerged beaming from the conference. Here is how the problem was solved.

The smaller sturgeon was bedded on flowers and foliage. A concert of violins and flutes announced it. The flautist and the two violinists, dressed like chefs, preceded the fish, which was flanked by four footmen bearing torches and two kitchen assistants bearing knives. The chef, halberd in hand, marched at the fish's head.

The procession paraded around the table, arousing such admiration that the guests, forgetting their respect for Monseigneur, stood on their chairs to see the monster. But just as the tour was completed, as the fish was about to be taken out for carving, one of the bearers made a false step, fell on one knee, and the fish slid to the floor.

A cry of despair rose from every heart, or rather from every stomach. There was a moment when everyone was talking, giving advice on how to save the situation. But the voice of Cambacérès dominated the tumult.

"Serve the other," he cried.

And the other, larger fish appeared, but with two flautists, four violinists, and four footmen. Applause succeeded cries of anguish as the first fish, weighing fifty pounds less, was taken away.

Sturgeon in Court Bouillon. Take a sturgeon, which need not be so large as the archchancellor's, clean it, remove the gills, and let it drain. Put it into a fish kettle with a court bouillon enriched with grated bacon or butter. Season more strongly than any other fish, because of its thickness, with salt and aromatic herbs. Cook with fire under and over, basting often. Drain and serve with a sauce italienne on the side.

Spitted Sturgeon. Take a cross slice of sturgeon, remove the skin and the bony plates. Lard as you would a veal roast, with bacon or with strips of eel and anchovy. Make a marinade with white wine instead of vinegar, using a great deal of butter. Put on the spit and baste often with this marinade after straining it. Roast to a good colour and serve with a poivrade sauce.

Sturgeon with Croutons. Cut into small slices and put into a casserole with butter, parsley, scallions, chopped shallots, salt, and coarsely ground pepper. When they are cooked on one side, turn them over and let them cook well on the other. Remove. Put a piece of butter mixed with flour into the casserole with 1 glass of red wine. Bring to a boil. Put in a pinch of chopped capers. Reheat the fish in this sauce without boiling, and serve with croutons fried in butter.

Sturgeon Pie. Line the bottom of a dish with pie crust. On top of this put fresh butter, salt, pepper, fine spices, and *fines herbes*. On this lay 2 slices of sturgeon 2 inches thick studded with anchovies and the same seasoning on top as below. Cover with fresh butter, then the top crust and bake. When the pie is done, take the top crust off, skim the fat off, and pour in a rather spicy crayfish [or shrimp] cullis, and replace the top. Serve hot.

SWAN. The domestic swan has an elegance of form that distinguishes it from the goose and the duck, whose near relative it is. A single anomaly brings him especially to the attention of the ornithologist, which is that the naturalists have dubbed him *cygnus musicus* [*sic*]. Anyone who has ever heard the swan song will admit it is the most disagreeable noise he has ever heard. The swan song is a phrase that must be accepted for its poetry, not its reality. What has maintained the position of the swan as a virtuoso is his fine role in *Lohengrin*. But from the point of view of cookery, even this would not give him a recognized position were it not that the flesh of the cygnet or young swan, especially the wild cygnet, is tenderer and more flavoursome than the finest duck or goose. It is made into pies.

SWEET POTATO. This plant originated in India. It is found in Africa, Asia, and even in England and Ireland. The flavour is that of good chestnuts. Sweet potatoes should be cooked in hot ashes, peeled, and a little sweetened orange juice poured over them.

TARRAGON. An aromatic plant, originating in Siberia, much cultivated for seasoning of salads and to flavour vinegar. Everyone knows how often it is used in sauces. I shall go as far as to add that there is no such thing as good vinegar without tarragon.

TEA. It was in 1666, in the middle of the reign of Louis XIV, that tea, after opposition as lively as that which coffee met, was introduced to France. Today, in England and France alone, eight million pounds sterling worth is consumed annually.

The best tea is drunk in St. Petersburg and generally throughout Russia. Since China has a common border with Siberia, tea need not be transported by water to reach Moscow or St. Petersburg. Sea voyages are very bad for tea.

Green tea is rarely used in France. It is lightly intoxicating and affects the nerves when taken too strong or in too great quantity. Tea is made by infusion. A suitable amount is put into a teapot and ½ glass of boiling water poured over it. When the leaves are swollen, the teapot is then filled with hot water. In Russia a custom startling to strangers is that men drink tea in glasses and women in china cups. Here is the legend behind this custom.

It seems that teacups were first made at Kronstadt, and the bottom was decorated with a view of that city. When a teahouse proprietor stinted on the tea, this picture could be seen clearly, and the customer would say to him, "I can see Kronstadt." Since the proprietor could not deny this, he was caught in *flagrante delicto*. It became customary, then, for tea to be served in teahouses in glasses, at the bottom of which there was nothing to see, let alone Kronstadt!

It is the mistress of the house who makes the tea, pours it, sugars it, and adds cream, a slice of lemon, or a drop of cognac. All tea offered to guests is her personal responsibility.

TERRINE. The *Dictionnaire Général de la Cuisine Française* defines this as an entree deriving its name from the fact that meat was often served, formerly, in the terrine (or earthenware casserole) in which it cooked, with no other sauce but its own liquid. Today, a terrine is composed of several sorts of braised meats, and served in a pot called a terrine, either of silver or porcelain, with whatever sauce, cullis, ragout, or purée one may find good to add to it.

The terrines of Toulouse or Nérac duck livers, garnished with truffles and partridge, have a justified reputation.

But all these must yield to the ancient *terrine du Louvre*, in the recipe given by Leclercq.

Terrine du Louvre. Bring to a boil, in bouillon, a fat pullet, a partridge, a saddle of hare, a rump of veal, and a rump of mutton, all larded with medium-sized bacon strips seasoned with *fines herbes* and fine spices. Peel roasted chestnuts and add them. Cover your terrine and seal with paste so that the meats will stew in their own juices. Before serving, skim off the fat from the sauce and add a goblet of canary (sack).

THRUSHES AND BLACKBIRDS. Thrushes, blackbirds, and many other birds should be eaten only at the end of November. After fattening in the fields and vineyards, they are off to the woods to flavour their flesh with juniper berries. If in your haste you kill them too soon, you will find them lacking in this flavour, this incisive aroma, required by the true gourmet.

Horace, Martial, and even Gallus were acquainted with the value of the thrush.

"*Nil melius turdo*," says Horace. The favourite of Augustus and Maecenas ate them whenever he wanted. Not that he was so rich, but that he was invited everywhere.

Poor Martial, on the other hand, often had lean fare, and when a dinner invitation came to surprise him, his joy showed in his eyes as he said: "Perhaps there will be thrushes ... "

Lucius Apicus and all the great gourmands of Rome made much of them. Thrushes were fattened in immense cages, with blackbirds. Each cage contained three or four thousand birds. They were deprived of any view of the woods and fields, so that nothing should distract them from fattening. Varro mentions a country house where five thousand thrushes had been fattened in a single year.

The thrushes of Corsica and Provence are famous, because they eat juniper and myrtle berries. Cardinal Fesch, Archbishop of Lyons and uncle of Napoleon, had them brought from Corsica all through the winter. One dined with His Eminence because of his noble manners, his gracious welcome, and especially because of his thrushes.

Roast Thrush. Pluck but do not eviscerate. Roast on the spit and serve on toast.

Thrush with Juniper. Pluck and singe, truss, cover with slices of bacon and buttered paper, attach to a spit, and roast.

Into a pot put a little gravy and cullis, 1 glass of white wine. Bring to a boil. Add the juice of 1 lemon and 12 juniper berries previously blanched.

When your thrushes are done, take off the paper and bacon, simmer in the cullis, arrange on a platter, skim the fat from the saucer, and serve hot.

Thrush English Style. Pluck and clean but do not eviscerate. Spit them on a skewer and attach both ends of the skewer to the spit. Wrap in paper and cook until half done. Remove the paper. Put a piece of bacon on a long skewer and set it afire. Hold it and let it drip on the thrushes while it burns. Sprinkle with a little salt and bread crumbs, roast to a good colour, set on a platter, and serve with buttered *sauce au pauvre homme*.

TOAD. The toad does not in every country have the evil quality with which we associate it. When African Negroes suffer from the migraine induced by the heat of the sun, they rub their foreheads with live toads, from which they receive a wonderful relief. In the Antilles, toads have flesh as fine and delicate as our frogs, and they are so large that two are enough to make a fine fricassee, of which the aborigines are very fond.

TOAST. Toasts were first drunk in France at the time of the Revolution. The name comes to us from the English, who, when they drank anyone's health, put a piece of toast on the bottom of the beer pot. Whoever drank last got the toast.

One day Anne Boleyn, then the most beautiful woman in England, was taking her bath, surrounded by the lords of her suite. These gentlemen, courting her favour, each took a glass, dipped it in the tub, and drank her health. All but one, who was asked why he did not follow their example.

"I am waiting for the toast," he said. Which was not bad for an Englishman.

When the Earl of Stair was England's ambassador to Holland, he gave brilliant parties to which he invited the ambassadorial corps, who, of course, also invited him to their diplomatic dinners.

One day when they were all the guests of the French ambassador, the host, alluding to the emblem of Louis XIV, proposed a toast to the rising sun.

The ambassador of the Empress-Queen then proposed the moon and the fixed stars, alluding to the various principalities of Germany.

Everyone wondered how the Earl of Stair would propose a toast to his own master that would equal these. He rose gravely and proposed a toast "to Joshua, who stopped the sun, the moon, and the stars in their courses".

Which was not bad, though pretentious.

At an English dinner (it is always at an English dinner that these things happen), toasts were drunk to the ladies, as is the custom. Lord B——, well known for his gallantry, proposed:

"Gentlemen, I drink to the beautiful sex of both hemispheres."

"And I," responded the Marquis de la V——, more realistic than his friend, "I drink to both hemispheres of the beautiful sex."

TROUT. The best are known as salmon trout. Certain naturalists claim that their reddish colour comes from a diet of crayfish. The best of these come from the rivers. They are never very large, but the flavour of their flesh is perfection itself, and their delicacy infinite. On the other hand, the large trout that come from the Lake of Geneva are nearly always dry and coarse.

Trout à la Montagnarde. Soak 1 hour in salted water. Cook with 1 bottle of white wine, 3 onions, a bouquet, 1 clove, 2 cloves of garlic, bay leaf, thyme, basil, and a piece of butter mixed with flour. Boil on a hot fire. Remove the onions and the bouquet and serve the trout with its own sauce, garnishing with blanched parsley.

Trout à la Saint-Florentin. Use the finest trout you can find. Scale and clean. Put inside each trout butter mixed with salt, pepper, and *fines herbes.* Cover, in a fish poacher with a good finger extra, with white wine. Add salt, pepper, onions, cloves, nutmeg, bouquet, crusts of bread. Cook on a live fire so the wine will flame like a punch. When the flames begin to die down, add butter, shake the pan, and serve. (Recipe from the old de la Reynie house.)

TRUFFLE. We have now arrived at the *sacrum sacrorum* of the gastronomes, at the name never pronounced by a gourmand without touching his hat, the *Tuber Cibarium*, the *Lycoperdon gulosorum*, the truffle.

The most learned men have been questioned as to the nature of this tuber, and after two thousand years of argument and discussion their answer is the same as it was on the first day: we do not know. The truffles themselves have been interrogated. and have answered simply: eat us and praise the Lord. To write the history of the truffle would be to undertake a history of civilization, in which they have played a more important role than the laws of Minos or the statutes of Solon. They came to Rome from Greece and Libya.

They were effaced from the time of Augustus to the time of Louis XV, reappearing only in the eighteenth century, and attaining their apogee under the parliamentary government of 1820 to 1848.

The truffle, says Brillat-Savarin, is the diamond of cookery. It arouses erotic and gourmand memories in the sex that wears dresses and gourmand and erotic memories in the sex that wears beards. The truffle is not a positive aphrodisiac, but on occasion it can make women more loving and men more lovable.

Truffle Rock. Wash, brush, and drain your truffles. Season them. Rub them with freshly chopped and crushed bacon, which you will divide into 2 parts. One part is used for a layer over a base of puff paste, on which pile your truffles in the form of a pyramid. Put the rest over the truffles. Cover first with sliced bacon, then with more puff paste, which you shape to the details of the pyramid of truffles, giving it the appearance of a rock. Brush with egg white, make a little hole at the top, and bake 1 hour in a hot oven. Cut the top crust off carefully, remove the slices of bacon, replace the crust, and serve hot. (Recipe by Courchamps and Alexandre Dumas.)

Truffle Salad à la Toulousaine. A very fine French cook, Urbain-Dubois, has given us this recipe and its accompanying eulogy:

"This dish is a recent product of Toulousian skill. It proves that in France the great art of gastronomy is developed everywhere with the same eagerness and always successfully.

"Pick 5 or 6 black truffles, fresh and with a good aroma, and 3 very tender artichokes. Brush the truffles carefully, clean them, wash them, peel them, and slice very thin. Put them aside in a covered bowl. Remove the tough leaves from the artichokes, leaving only those you know for sure will be tender. Split them lengthwise and slice each half leaf as thin as the truffles. Salt. Let stand 10 minutes. Wipe off with a cloth.

"Put 3 hard-boiled egg yolks through a sieve into a bowl. Stir in a little mustard and thin with $\frac{1}{2}$ glass of the best oil and a little of the best tarragon vinegar. Rub a salad bowl with a clove of garlic. Put in the truffles and artichokes, in alternate layers, seasoning each layer with salt, pepper, and a little of the dressing. Ten minutes later, turn the salad to mix with the seasoning. This dish is worthy of bearing a great name."

[*See the Index for other truffle recipes. Truffles are also ingredients in the preparation of many other dishes in this book.* – ED.]

TURBOT. In a single satire, Juvenal has characterized the Emperor Domitian and the turbot on the subject of which he called the Senate into session. There was a long discussion, but the matter was so weighty that the Senate finally dispersed without deciding what sauce should be served with the Emperor's turbot.

The English, who are naturally great fish eaters, have a standard sauce for each variety that they invariably serve.

Thus, with turbot they have a lobster or shrimp sauce; with boiled salmon, a parsley sauce, often accompanied with cucumber salad; with cod, an oyster sauce; with whiting, an egg sauce; with boiled mackerel, a parsley or gooseberry sauce; with fried fish, an anchovy-butter sauce.

Turbot English Style. Choose a fresh, white, thick turbot. Clean and trim. Make a slit on the dark side along the backbone. Soak in cold water 1 hour. Drain. Tie up the head. Put on the rack in the bottom of your turbot pan, black side down. Sprinkle with salt. Cover with cold water. Bring quickly to a boil, then immediately set aside so that it stays just below boiling for 40 to 45 minutes.

Meanwhile, cook a lobster in salted water. Let it cool. Remove the flesh from the body without damaging the shell, slice it, and set aside. Dice the scraps and the meat from the claws, and also set aside, covered. Prepare a smooth butter sauce. Add the scraps of lobster meat and keep the sauce warm over hot water.

When the turbot is ready, drain it, untie it, slip it on to a napkin-covered oval board with two holes in it on a platter. It seems almost superfluous to mention that the white side should be up. Set the lobster shell on top of the fish, and fill with the slices of lobster meat. Stick a skewer decorated with 2 crayfish and a truffle through the lobster shell. Surround the turbot with parsley leaves. Serve the sauce separately.

Turbot Kedgeree. A dish of Indian origin, now commonly served in England, which seems to have become an Indian dependency.

Take raw turbot fillets, cut into large dice, and fry 2 minutes only in butter over a hot fire. Season and remove from the fire. Chop 1 onion. Fry in butter, but do not brown. Add to this 1 pound of rice well washed and drained for 1 hour before using. After a few seconds, add enough fish bouillon so that it is 3 times the height of the rice. Cook over a brisk fire 10 or 12 minutes, then set in the oven until the rice is almost dry. Mix in the pieces of turbot, sprinkle with a pinch of cayenne, put over it 2 tablespoonfuls of sauce, 3 chopped hard-boiled eggs, and bits of butter. Arrange in a dish and pour browned butter over all.

TURKEY. In cookery as in life, turkeys are divided into toms and hens. The hen is always smaller and more delicate than the tom. Turkeys were known to the Greeks, who called them Meleagris because Meleager brought them to Greece in the year of the world 3559. Certain scholars have challenged this fact, maintaining that these were guinea fowl. But Pliny (xxxvII, 2) describes a turkey in unmistakable fashion. Sophocles, in one of his lost tragedies, introduced a chorus of turkeys to mourn the death of Meleager.

The Romans voiced a high regard for turkeys and raised them on their farms. How did they disappear? What epidemic took them off? History does not tell us. But finally they became so rare they were kept in cages as parrots are now.

In 1432 the ships of Jacques Cœur (who started out as one of the biggest brokers in the world and ended up as finance minister and commander of the artillery for King Charles VII) brought back the first turkeys from India. It is therefore clear that, contrary to vulgar belief, we do not owe the turkey to the Jesuits, since the order was not founded by Ignatius of Loyola until 1534, and was not approved by Pope Paul III until 1540.

As a result of the general belief that the followers of Loyola brought the turkey back from America, some cheap wits have got into the habit of calling turkeys Jesuits. Turkeys have just as much right to resent this name calling as the Jesuits would if they were called turkeys.

So our opinion is not that of the majority of scholars, who say the turkey came from America. Discovered by Christopher Columbus in 1492, America could not in 1432 have provisioned the vessels of Jacques Cœur, even though his motto was: "To the valiant heart, nothing is impossible." Its name [in French], *poule d'Inde*, from which *dindon* is derived, would seem to point more naturally to a derivation from India than from America, even though in those days people were in the habit of calling America West India.

Today the turkey is found wild in America, especially in Illinois. Brillat-Savarin, in his *Physiology of Taste*, describes a hunt in the course of which he kills a turkey. A Canadian hunter has assured me that he has killed one of these birds that weighed close to fifty pounds.

Although the meat of the turkey is excellent (especially cold), juicy, and preferable to chicken, there are gourmets who eat no part of it except the *sot-l'y-laisse* — etymology: *sot qui le laisse* ["Fool he who leaves it": the "oyster" — ED.].

One day Grimod de la Reynière, on a business trip, was overtaken by night or bad weather, or some such obstacle so insurmountable that it could force an epicure to stop at a village inn, and asked the host to give him supper.

The innkeeper confessed with shame and regret that his larder was completely empty.

The illustrious gourmand's eyes were attracted to a great fire shining through a glassed door that led to the kitchen. There he saw seven turkeys turning on one spit.

"How dare you say you have nothing to give me to eat!" Grimod de la Reynière exclaimed, "when I see seven magnificent turkeys, just about ready to eat, on your spit!"

"It is true," said the innkeeper, "but they have been reserved by a Parisian gentleman who arrived before you."

"This gentleman is alone?"

"Alone."

"He must be a giant, then."

"No, sir. He is scarcely taller than you."

"Oh! Oh! Tell me this fellow's room number. I'll see whether he won't let me have one of his seven turkeys."

He called for a light and was conducted to the traveller's chamber, where he found him sitting before a fine fire at a table all set up, sharpening one carving knife on another.

"By God!" exclaimed Grimod de la Reynière, "I wasn't mistaken. It is you, my son."

"Yes, Father," said the young man, greeting him respectfully.

"You're the one having seven turkeys broiled for your dinner?"

"Sir," said this pleasant young man, "I can understand that you're painfully affected by seeing me show a vulgar taste so poorly in keeping with my distinguished birth. But I had no choice. There was nothing else in the place."

"Good lord, I don't reproach you for eating turkey instead of pullets or pheasants. When travelling one has to eat what one finds. But I do reproach you for having seven turkeys broiled for you alone."

"Sir, I have always heard you tell your friends that there is nothing edible about a turkey cooked without truffles except the *sot-l'y-laisse*. I had seven turkeys put on the spit to have fourteen *sot-l'y-laisses*."

"That," replied the father, obliged to acknowledge the young man's intelligence, "seems to me a bit spendthrift for a boy of eighteen, but I cannot say it is unreasonable."

The colour red excites the anger of the turkey just as it does the bull's. He flies at anyone wearing that colour and attacks him with his beak. This is what caused the accident that befell the illustrious Boileau.

Boileau, when a child, was playing in a courtyard where, among other poultry, there happened to be a turkey. Suddenly the child fell, his dress went up, and the turkey, seeing the hateful colour, flew at him and with his beak so wounded poor Nicolas that, forever barred from becoming an erotic poet, he became a satiric one and maligned women, instead. The poet was inconvenienced all his life. From this, no doubt, stemmed the aversion he had for the Jesuits, sharing the popular belief that they had introduced turkeys to France.

Turkey with Truffles. Take a fine, young, fat, white hen turkey. Clean and pluck it well. Take 4 pounds of truffles, peel them carefully. Set aside any that are not perfectly formed, to be chopped up (about a handful). Grate 1 pound of fat bacon, put it into a pot with the whole and the chopped truffles, season with salt, coarse pepper, fine spices, and 1 bay leaf. Let the whole simmer ¾ hour. Stir well and stuff into the turkey. Sew it up, truss it, and let it stand 3 or 4 days if the season permits. Then put it on a spit, wrap in strong paper, and roast for about 2 hours. Remove the paper and continue to roast until the turkey has a good colour. Serve in a sauce made from its own juices, to which add a small amount of chopped truffles. (Courchamps' recipe.)

Turkey with Truffles. Prepare your truffles and mix with grated bacon seasoned with salt, pepper, four spices. Let them simmer ½ hour, and with them stuff a freshly killed and eviscerated turkey. Let it hang by its feet in a well-aired larder 3 days, after which pluck and singe, remove the truffles, and replace them with fresh ones prepared in the same manner. (Marquis de Cussy's recipe.)

As you see, de Cussy, like Grimod de la Reynière, will not have his turkey plucked before stuffing. "Note," he says, "that if the bird is not plucked, the pores remain closed, and there is no evaporation. The truffles heat and combine with the aging flesh, and the infiltration of their perfume is more active, more intense, more universal. But in this combination they lose what they bestow." It is because of this, I suppose, that they must be replaced with fresh truffles.

We recommend both recipes. They are excellent. But not everyone can spend forty francs to stuff a turkey with truffles. So here is our recipe, which we can call:

Turkey des Artistes. Chop up veal, chicken, partridge if you have it. Add ¼ pound of sausage meat. Cook in quite salty water with a celery leaf and 15 or 20 chestnuts. Remove the celery. Mash the chestnuts with the meat into a sort of porridge. Add a blood sausage. Chop and mix well. Stuff your turkey with this dressing, putting a bunch of parsley into the very centre of the stuffing. Add a piece of salted and peppered butter and sew up. Put your turkey on the spit and do not remove it until little jets of steam spurt from its body like miniature volcanoes, indicating it is cooked just right.

Above all, never baste any roast with anything but butter mixed with salt and pepper. Any cook who adds a single drop of bouillon to his dripping pan should be sacked immediately and banished from France.

Marinated Turkey. Cut into joints and serving pieces. Marinate for 8 hours in verjuice, lemon juice, salt, pepper, cloves, scallions, and bay leaf. Make a thin paste with flour, egg yolks, and white wine. Dip the pieces of turkey into this paste and fry in deep fat. Serve garnished with fried parsley.

Capilotade of Turkey. Prepare a sauce italienne and put into it a turkey that has been broiled on the spit and cut into pieces. Bring to a boil and let simmer a few moments. Place the pieces of turkey on a platter, pour your sauce over, and garnish with slices of bread fried in butter.

TURNIPS. Vegetables have their own aristocracy and their own privileges. It is well recognized that the finest turnips are from Crécy, from Belle-Isle-en-Mer, and from Meaux. But, for some reason, the only turnips available in Paris today are those from Freneuse and Vaugirard.

The first recipe that comes to hand is for turnips *à la d'Esclignac*. Whatever did M. d'Esclignac do to earn the honour of having a dish of turnips named for him?

Nothing offers a more curious study, in this connection, than books written by cooks, and their strange fancy of saucing, grilling, and roasting our great men.

Here is what you will find under the heading of soups, for example:

Soup *à la Demidov*	*à la Magenta*
à la John Russell	*à la Dumas*
à la Cialdini	*à la Theresa*
au héros de Palestro	*à la Solferino*
à la Lucullus	*à la Mother Goose*
à la William Tell	*à la Rothschild*

And if you go on from there you have:

Patties à la Garibaldi	*Chicken à la Prince Albert*
Timbales à la Titus	*Woodcock à la Prince of Wales*
Soufflés à la Marcus Aurelius	*Hare à la Dante de Castiglione*
Pâtés Omer Pasha	*Red Partridge à la Marshal Ney*

Sticks à la Palmerston

Petits Soufflés à la Cellini

Turbot à la Lord Byron

Sturgeon à l'Ariosto

Turbot Fillets au Prince Hubert

Rump of Beef à la Dante
    Alighieri

Rump of Beef à la Napoleon I

Beef à la Napoleon III

Leg of Mutton à la Jean-Jacques
    Rousseau

Chicken à la Dame aux
    Camélias

Goose à la Don Carlos

Suckling Pig à la Washington

Ham à la Queen Victoria

Beef Fillet à la Julius Caesar

Turtle à la Saïd Pasha

Calf's Head à la Girardin

Breast of Pheasant à l'Impéra-
    trice Eugénie

Suprême of Chicken à la
    Lucullus

Salmon à la Don Juan

Game Pie à la Three Musketeers

Partridge à la Cimarosa

Galantine of Young Turkey à la
    King of Persia

Duck Loaf à la Michelangelo

Game Pie à la Frederick the
    Great

Suckling Pig à la Gemma[1]

Chaud-Froid of Quail à la
    Charles Albert

Timbale of Oysters à la
    Fieramosca

Tuna Mayonnaise à la Vespucci

Lamb Sweetbreads à la Brunel-
    lesco

Lobster à la Borgia

Galantine of Capon à la
    Persano[2]

Boar's Head à la Machiavelli

Goose à la Nelson

Young Turkey Tiberius

We could extend the list indefinitely, and the cook from whose list the above are taken is really excellent. We have used some of his recipes, giving him credit in each case.

Glazed Turnips. Choose turnips of equal size and shaped so they can readily be trimmed into pear shape. Parboil them, drain, put into a buttered casserole that can hold them in a single layer. Brown them lightly with a little sugar. Add a good bouillon and more sugar, a bit of salt, and a stick of cinnamon. Bring to a boil, cover, bake. Uncover, let the juice reduce to a glaze. Arrange the turnips on a platter. Add a little bouillon to the pan to melt the glaze. Take out the cinnamon. Pour the glaze over the turnips.

I see I have skipped over the turnips à la d'Esclignac that

---

[1] Gemma de Vergy, who was forced by her jealous husband to eat her lover's heart.
[2] Admiral Persano, who lost the battle of Lissa in 1866.

started me off on that long parenthesis. I hasten to repair this omission:

Turnips à la d'Esclignac. Choose turnips 5 or 6 inches long, trim off top and bottom, slice in two lengthwise, and carve each half with spirals to resemble a rope. Parboil. Proceed as above, but use no cinnamon. Use espagnole sauce to melt the glaze, add butter, and pour over the turnips.

Turnips Picardy. Cut your turnips into any shape that pleases your fancy. Simmer in a casserole with onions, salt, and butter. Drain. Make a good white sauce, thicken with tapioca, add a pinch of nutmeg, ½ tablespoonful of fine mustard, and pour over the turnips.

Plain Turnip Stew. Carve 30 or 40 turnips into round balls of the same size. Parboil in salted water. Dip in cold water. Finish cooking in a chicken consommé with sugar and marrow. At the end add a piece of fresh butter and thicken the sauce in a double boiler with egg yolks.

TURTLE. When I wrote the article on CALAPÉ I said all I had to say then about the preparation of turtles. But since then I have received some recipes on this subject from M. Duglerez, former chief steward of the House of Rothschild, and I hasten to pass these on to turtle lovers.

In several American countries, says M. Duglerez, the turtle is so common it is sold like fish, very cheaply. In those countries it is prepared without seasoning, except for stimulants.

In England, where the turtle is more highly esteemed, a great amount of it is consumed, though it is generally used only for soup — which apparently can be blamed on the lack of refinement in the culinary arts of that country.

In France, the turtle is more honourably represented, and may be employed in other types of cooking. The most delicate parts are the gelatinous ones, such as the plastron and the carapace, the four fins, and the fat, which is exquisitely delicate.

To Prepare the Turtle. Tie your turtle to a ladder, head down. Attach a 60-pound weight to the neck, cut off the head, and let it bleed for 5 or 6 hours. Then lay it on its back on a table, detach the plastron, remove the intestines, cut off the fins, and collect the fat very carefully because of its delicacy. Cut the plastron and the carapace into 4 to 6 pieces, put them into a large cauldron of boiling water, and cook from 20 to 25 minutes, until the skin separates from the bones. Then take each piece and plunge it into cold water. Drain. The pieces of meat you will have taken out of the cauldron are not very delicate. They will be stringy and tasteless. The larger pieces are like veal rump. They can be larded and served as such, provided you prepare them so as to heighten the flavour. In the culinary art everything is possible.

Turtle Soup. To make a soup you put all the lean flesh into a kettle, with 20 pounds of sliced beef, 2 veal knuckles, 3 old hens, 3 ladlefuls of good bouillon. Over a hot fire let the bouillon reduce to a thin glaze, then fill up the kettle with a rich bouillon, add 4 onions with cloves stuck in them, a bouquet of basil and rosemary. Simmer 6 hours.

Take the skin you have removed from the plastron and carapace and cut it into inch squares. Cut the fins into inch cubes, unless you intend to prepare these separately as described below. Put this diced meat and skin into a pot lined with slices of bacon. Cover with 1 bottle of old Madeira and a sufficient quantity of the bouillon from the above preparation, strained. Cook all together, checking from time to time to see whether the meat is done. It should have a certain firmness, like calf's head, which requires little cooking.

This soup is served in two ways, clear and thickened. It is finished with an infusion of mint, basil, rosemary, and wild thyme in a large glass of dry Madeira, which you should reduce to one quarter. Add a touch of cayenne. Taste to see whether it has a good flavour. It should be pleasantly sharp.

What is so good about turtle soup in England is that our overseas cousins always have fresh herbs and vegetables to make into a purée to finish the soup.

Turtle Fins à la Régence. Put into the bottom of a braising pot slices of bacon and smoked ham, 4 onions with cloves stuck in them, some East Indian aromatic spices. Put the fins on top of this. Sprinkle with a pinch of fine spices, cover with bacon and veal slices, cover with a bottle of old Madeira and a rich consommé. Cover with paper. Seal the lid. Put in the oven 2 hours and check whether it is done. The liquid should be reduced by three quarters. Just before serving, drain the fins, arrange them on a platter around a firm pastry or bread centre against which they will lean. Ornament with a garnish of little bits of pastry, truffles, cockscombs and cock's kidneys, quenelles, etc. Strain the liquid from the braising pot, let it settle, skim off the fat. Put into a large pot for reducing, adding 4 large tablespoonfuls of espagnole sauce and a touch of cayenne. Stir and reduce over a hot fire and keep hot in a double boiler. It should be succulent and highly flavoured.

TURTLEDOVE. A variety of wild pigeon whose flesh is fatter than the ringdove's. It is roasted on the spit, wrapped first in grape leaves and then in a great slice of calf's udder.

VEAL. The finest calves come from Pontoise, Rouen, Caen, Montargis, and Picardy. Those raised in the environs of Paris are not to be disdained, either; veal is juicier in Paris than anywhere else. The special care taken in rearing calves for the butcher is the primary reason for this superiority; a secondary reason is the strict enforcement of the regulation that forbids killing these innocent creatures before they are six weeks old.

Calf's Liver in the Skillet. Slice a fat calf's liver very thin. Melt a piece of butter — according to the amount of liver — in a skillet. Add the liver. Put on a hot fire and keep stirring until the liver is firmed. Sprinkle with flour and stir to let the flour cook. Sprinkle with chopped scallions or shallots and parsley. Season with salt and pepper. Add ½ bottle of red wine. Stir on the fire without letting it boil, else your liver will toughen. If your sauce is too thick, thin with a little bouillon. Finish, if you desire, with a dash of vinegar or verjuice, and serve.

Calf's Liver on the Spit. Lard the bottom with strips of bacon seasoned with salt, pepper, fine spices, powdered basil and thyme, chopped parsley and scallions. Marinate in an earthenware dish with parsley sprigs, scallions cut in 3 or 4 pieces, bay leaf, a little thyme, a little salt, and olive oil. When you are ready to put it on, stick 4 or 5 skewers through it lengthwise, heat the spit almost red hot in the middle, and slip the liver over that spot. It will attach itself and not slip as the spit turns. Wrap in buttered paper. Baste with the marinade. It should turn on the spit about ¾ hour, depending on its size and the heat of the fire. When it is done, unwrap it, glaze, and serve with a good poivrade sauce on top.

Veal Sweetbreads à la Dauphine. Peel 5 sweetbreads. Soak in several waters. Blanch lightly to firm a little. Into the bottom of a pot put veal scraps, onions, and carrots. Line the sides with slices of bacon. Put your sweetbreads in so they touch but are not squeezed. Add consommé, but not enough to wet the bacon. Cover with buttered paper. Bring to a boil. Bake to a good golden colour, passing under the broiler if necessary. This will take about 45 minutes. Drain the sweetbreads, glaze them, serve on a ragout of blanched endive.

If you have no glaze handy, strain the liquid from the braising, reduce it, and use that.

Calf's Liver Loaf. Remove the membrane from half a calf's liver. Chop the liver very fine. Chop an equal amount of bacon, mix the two, crush together in a mortar, seasoning with salt, spices, and finely chopped parsley. Dice 2 onions and brown in meat fat or butter or in grated bacon. Mix the whole, add a slice of ham, a bit of bacon and 3 truffles, all diced, and 3 raw egg yolks. Mix. Beat the whites of the eggs very firm and stir them in. Shape the liver into a loaf, put it into a casserole over slices of pig's caul. Cover with bacon. Bake. After baking, remove the bacon, drain off the fat, arrange your loaf on a platter, and coat with a chervil sauce. (Recipe from C. Durand, of Nimes.)

Veal Birds. Take a piece of rump, slice very thin, beat and flatten. Cut into pieces about 3 by 4 inches. Lard lightly on one side. (Slip thin little strips of bacon into slits you will make in the meat.) Lay them bacon side down.

Make a forcemeat of chicken livers, truffles, and mushrooms, diced, mixed with egg yolks, a little fine spices, salt. Put this on the veal strips, roll them, fasten with skewers, fasten to the spit, wrap in paper. Baste with butter during the broiling. Serve with a spicy italienne sauce.

Blanquette of Veal. When you have enough veal shoulder roast left over, cut the meat into small pieces. Trim off the roasted surfaces. Flatten the pieces of meat, cut into thin slices. Reduce a *velouté* and add these slices. Heat, but do not let boil. Thicken with egg yolks. Add a dash of verjuice or the juice of a lemon, a little piece of butter, and some chopped parsley and scallions if you desire.

Veal Cutlets à la Provençale. A tourist travelling southward through France, when he has passed Valence and reached Mornas, will sense a new flavour in his food. It is garlic. Since in most cases the only difference between Northern and Southern cooking is the garlic flavour, it is scarcely worth while to write a special cookery-book on Provençal cookery. It is sufficient to indicate how much garlic to add to each dish.

For example, for veal cutlets *à la provençale*, slice 5 to 6 white onions and colour them in lard over a hot fire with 1 clove of garlic. Season with salt and pepper. Sprinkle with a little flour. Add wine and gravy and cook 10 or 12 minutes on a slow fire. Meanwhile, fry 7 or 8 seasoned and floured cutlets on both sides, drain off the fat, add enough bouillon to half cover them, bring to a boil, and set on moderate heat. Cover and leave until the liquid is reduced to a thin glaze. Mix the onions in, season with a touch of cayenne, sprinkle with chopped parsley. Two minutes later, arrange the cutlets in a ring on a platter and pour the ragout into the centre of the ring.

Creamed Veal Fillet. Cut into small pieces. Lard each flat-ways with strips of bacon, season with salt, fine spices, chopped parsley, scallions, and mushrooms. Heat with a little butter, add a good pinch of flour blended with a little white wine and bouillon. When the veal is cooked and the sauce sufficiently reduced, thicken over the fire with egg yolks mixed with cream.

Breast of Veal with Green Peas. Cut the breast into pieces. Blanch in boiling water. Heat in a pot with butter, add a good pinch of flour moistened with bouillon, season with pepper and a *bouquet garni*. Do not add salt, for the bouillon is already salted. When the veal is half cooked, add green peas with 1 or 2 leaves of savory and a very little sugar. Just before serving, thicken with 4 egg yolks.

Galantine of Shoulder of Veal. Bone a shoulder of veal. Cut the meat, using about half of it, into a wide, long, thin strip. Chop the other half fine with an equal amount of bacon. Spread a layer of this on the strip. On this arrange strips of bacon, thin, narrow strips of tongue *à l'écarlate*, and the same of truffles. Repeat until all the chopped meat has been used. Roll the meat, tie it up well, cover with slices of bacon, wrap in a cloth, and cook like a fricandeau [which see]. Let the cooking liquid jell. Trim the galantine and serve cold with slices of the jelly on and around it.

Roast Leg of Veal. Marinate 2 days in white wine with pepper, salt, and aromatic herbs. Lard. Roast on the spit. When it is well done, serve with a ravigote.

Marinated Veal for Hors d'Oeuvres. Let a rump of veal hang in a cool place, 4 days in winter or 1 in summer. Skin it, remove the fat and the tendons. Cut in 4 pieces. Rub very well with fine salt. Put it into a stone crock with sliced onions, sprigs of parsley, thyme, ginger, garlic, 12 juniper berries, crushed black pepper, and 3 anchovies crushed in a mortar. Stir all about in the crock. Cover with a cloth. After 4 days, turn the veal over. Let it stand another 4 days. Drain off ⅔ of the accumulated liquid. Put the rest into a pot with the veal. Add 1 bottle of very good white wine. Bring to a boil. Set aside to simmer. You can tell when it it is done by testing with a fork. It should be very tender. Put it back into the crock and let it cool. Put the meat into glass jars, cover with good olive oil, seal with parchment, and use as required, as you would marinated tuna. Veal prepared in this manner is sold commercially as "preserved tuna."

Stuffed Calves' Ears. Singe off the hair, clean. Cook in white veal stock. Fill with a cooked forcemeat. Smooth the stuffing with the blade of a knife. Beat a few eggs and dip the ears in them, then in bread crumbs. Repeat. Lay them out in a pan, sprinkling bread crumbs over them. Just before serving, fry in deep fat. The fat should not be too hot, or the ears will brown too fast and the stuffing will not be heated through. Arrange on a platter, points up. Sprinkle with chopped fried parsley and serve.

Marinated Calves' Ears. Prepare and cook in stock as above. Cut into 4 pieces lengthwise. Marinate in vinegar, salt, and coarse pepper. Drain. Dip in a very light fritter batter. Lay in hot fat in a skillet quickly enough so they will fry evenly. Turn them over.

When they are a good golden colour, remove and drain on a cloth. Arrange on a platter and garnish with fried parsley.

Veal Shanks. Choose thick shanks. Lard with thick bacon strips rolled in salt, pepper, and other fine spices. Cover the bottom of your pot with slices of bacon. Place the shanks on these. Start on a slow fire so that the veal will render its juices. Then raise the heat gradually to brown the shanks lightly on all sides, which will be helped along with a sprinkle of flour. Then add bacon fat and brown well. Remove the bacon fat. Replace it with bouillon. Add a little parsley and scallions and let the shanks cook slowly. Stir egg yolks and a little verjuice into the sauce and serve.

White Veal Stock. Voltaire, who was not only always somewhere but always at someone's place, and wherever he was wrote letters with an idea that they would be published, wrote from Cirey to his friend Saint-Lambert: "Come to Cirey, where Mme Duchatelet won't let you be poisoned. There is not a spoonful of gravy in the kitchen. Everything is made with white veal stock. We shall live to be a hundred and never die."

Here is Mme Duchatelet's recipe, as given to her by the famous Tronchin:

Put into a casserole slices of veal and chicken giblets with a little butter or lard, onions, carrots, and a *bouquet garni*. Add 1 tablespoonful of bouillon and reduce, but don't let it get dry or stick. Cover with bouillon, bring to a boil, and skim, then set aside to simmer gently 2 hours. Make a white *roux*. Put mushrooms in it and stir a few minutes, then pour the liquid from your meat into it, stirring constantly so that it is mixed without lumps. Bring to a boil. Skim. Simmer 1 full hour, skim off the fat, strain.

VENISON. Roast Haunch of Venison. Macerate with good oil, red wine, parsley, spices, and a few slices of onion. Then remove the membranes. Lard with thin strips of bacon. Wrap in buttered paper. Spit and roast. Serve with a poivrade sauce.

Civet of Venison. Lard both sides of the breast with thick strips of bacon. Sear in a pot with lard and parsley. Add a bouquet of *fine herbes*, salt, pepper, bay leaf, and lime. Cover and braise. When it is done, thicken the sauce with browned flour, add a dash of vinegar, a handful of capers, and a few pitted olives. Serve with croutons.

Roast Leg of Venison. Trim well. Lard with thin strips of bacon. Marinate several hours with salt and olive oil. Roast one hour on the spit, basting with the marinade. Make a sauce with the marinade and juice pressed from shallots.

VERJUICE. The juice squeezed from green grapes. The best is made from immature berries. It can be kept for a while by adding salt or a few drops of vinegar.

To Keep Verjuice. Remove unripened grapes from the stems. Crush in a mortar with a little salt. Squeeze out the juice forcefully. Wet a piece of fustian, cover with flour on the fuzzy side. Hang up like an open bag, flour side up. Pour the verjuice through it several times, until it comes out clear as spring water. You will have rinsed some bottles meanwhile, or you will have new ones on hand, so they have no flavour of their own. Sulphur them as follows:

Take a cork that will fit all the bottles. Pass a piece of iron wire through it so that it extends halfway down the bottle, with a hook on the end. On the hook put a piece of sulphured wick such as is used to sulphur wine casks. Light it. Insert in each bottle one after the other. As soon as each bottle is filled with vapour, remove the wick, cork the bottle. After a moment, uncork, pour in your verjuice, and recork well. Store, standing, in the wine cellar. When you come to use, discard the deposit that will have formed in the neck of the bottle.

You can use this verjuice in place of lemon, and even make punch and fresh liqueurs by adding some wine brandy and lemon zest to it.

VUILLEMOT, DENIS-JOSEPH. French cook, born at Crépy, in Valois (Oise), about 1811, of English origin. His paternal grandfather was a member of Parliament. His maternal grandfather was maître d'hôtel for Mlle de Lescure, cousin of Louis XVI, at her Château de Bressuire, in Poitou. His parents wanted to make a lawyer of him, but his natural instincts turned him to the art of his grandfather and of his father, who at that time kept the Hôtel de la Bannière at Crépy. Yielding to this inclination, he came to Paris and went to work for M. Véry, a friend of his father's, at the Palais-Royal. He stayed there two years, after which he went into the king's household under the patronage of Pierre Hugues and Desmonay, of the royal house, old friends of the Vuillemot family.

Later, Vuillemot, burning with the sacred fire, met the illustrious Carême, became his pupil, and received his culinary education from him.

In 1837, Vuillemot took over his father's place at Crépy. In 1842 he acquired the Hôtel de la Cloche at Compiègne, and was there for fifteen years in association with Morlière.

I had known him at Crépy, at his father's. One day, dead tired and dying of hunger, I came to the Hôtel de la Cloche.

"Have you no cartwheels with sorrel or whiffletrees *à la Sainte-Menehould* to serve us?" I greeted mine host.

"Sir," said Vuillemot from inside his cage, having recognized me, "we have nothing left but tiger chops and snakes *tartare*."

At that I recognized him, and from that time on we have been close friends. It was at Pompadour, which Vuillemot had leased from the state, that I finished my *Monte Cristo*.

I am deeply grateful to Vuillemot for the precious assistance he has given me in the preparation of this book, through his contribution of original recipes of which he was the inventor, and through his practical advice.

WATER. Persons who habitually drink water become as fine gourmets on the subject as wine drinkers on wine.

For fifty or sixty years of my life I drank nothing but water, and no Grand Lafite or Chambertin ever gave a wine lover more pleasure than I have had from a glass of fresh spring water. Very cold water, even if artificially iced, is an excellent tonic for the stomach, causes no irritation, and even calms any that might already exist.

But this does not hold for melted snow or ice. This water has no air, and is heavy. Shake it well, and it will soon lose its harmful qualities.

Formerly, all Paris drank from the river that passes through the city. Today, our water comes from Grenelle. Pipes bring it to Sainte-Geneviève, from which it is distributed throughout Paris. For the last five or six years it has been joined by water from the

Dhuis, which goes down the opposite hillside from Belleville, Montmartre, and Buttes-Chaumont.

Seine water was so calumniated, especially by provincials who came to spend a few days in Paris, that it tired of slaking the thirst of two million ingrates. But when Seine water was properly purified, taken from above the Jardin des Plantes and from the middle of the stream, no water could compare with it for limpidity, lightness, and palatability. It was especially saturated with oxygen, from being subjected for two hundred leagues of sinuous flow to the action of the atmosphere. Besides, from its source all the way to Paris it flows over a bed of pure sand, and to this gourmands attribute the superiority of Seine fish to those from other rivers.

WHALE. The largest mammal. Some reach a length of more than two hundred feet. The interior of the whale's body resembles that of land animals. Whales are warm-blooded. They breathe with lungs, so that they cannot stay underwater more than fifteen minutes at a time. They couple like other viviparous animals, and nourish their calves with milk.

The whale has only one mammary gland, placed in the middle of its chest. There has been much speculation about how the calf drinks its milk. Does it swim on its back and suckle? The procedure is really much simpler than that. The calf butts his mother hard, the nipple pours out a stream of milk that the calf drinks along with the water that mixes with it. He immediately expels the water through his vent, retaining all the milk.

It was a whale which settled the difficult problem as to whether there was an underground passage from the Atlantic to the Pacific at the Isthmus of Panama. A whale, mortally wounded in the Gulf of Mexico, was found dead two hours later in the Pacific. The harpoon, still in the wound, bore a number that checked with the one on the log of the harpooner's vessel in the Gulf of Mexico.

Whale meat is red, and resembles beef. It is so healthful that whale fishermen and maritime peoples attribute their excellent health to eating it.

WHITEBAIT. Certainly one of the most popular dishes in

London. I recall being invited by a friend to eat whitebait at Greenwich — without any other excuse or occasion but just to eat whitebait. The invitation was so intriguing that I hastened to accept.

Whitebait is a tiny fish called *yanchette* in Italy, *pontin* at Nice, and simply *poisson-blanc* at Bordeaux. It was the high point of a three-course meal, all fish. I was curious to see the preparation of this dish, for which people came two or three hundred leagues.

The fish were washed by the handful in ice water, drained on a cloth, and set over ice for 20 minutes. Just before serving, they were rolled in white bread crumbs, put into a napkin with a handful of flour, shaken, and poured into a sieve so fine only the extra flour could get through it. The sieve was shaken and then plunged with the fish into very hot fat. A minute was sufficient to cook them. When they turned golden, they were removed with the sieve, sprinkled with salt and a little cayenne, arranged on a folded napkin, and served immediately.

I regret I did not keep the menu of this meal, which was composed of forty-eight dishes, twelve of them fish and each seasoned in its own special fashion.

WHITING. A fish of the cod family, on the market in December, January, and February. In those months it is fat and firm, and has milt and roe beginning in October. There is no meat healthier than whiting. It is flaky, tender, and light. It is even prescribed for convalescents. The finest whitings are caught in the Mediterranean.

Fried Whiting. Scale or, rather, wipe with a cloth, pressing on the flesh; the scales will come off by themselves. Cut off the fins from tail and sides, clean, and eviscerate. Put the liver back inside. Make slanting knife slashes on both sides, flour, fry to a fine colour, but so the fish are still firm. Drain. Sprinkle with salt. Serve on a napkin in a platter.

Grilled Whiting. Prepare as above, but instead of frying, put in a reversible grill, so they can be turned over without breaking. Grill on slow heat, turning over once. Turn on to your platter and serve with a white sauce finished with butter and capers.

Fried Whiting à la Provençale. This is a very popular dish in Provence, and is served especially on Christmas Eve.

Heat 4 or 5 tablespoonfuls of oil in a skillet, add 2 tablespoonfuls of flour, and stir over medium heat to a light colour. Add 2 tablespoonfuls of chopped onion, cook a few seconds. Take off the fire and stir in slowly ½ hot water, ½ wine. Bring to a boil, stirring, and simmer 10 minutes. Add a bouquet of parsley and bay leaf, season, and reduce, stirring constantly, until it begins to thicken. Add 2 tablespoonfuls of Madeira and strain through a sieve into a flat casserole.

Meanwhile, cut 5 or 6 slices of fresh whiting, salt and flour them, and fry in oil. When they are a good colour, drain and place them in the sauce. Simmer gently 10 minutes, Finally, sprinkle the whole with a pinch of chopped parsley and 2 tablespoonfuls of whole capers. Arrange the whiting on a hot platter and coat with the sauce. (Recipe from Urbain-Dubois, chef to the King of Prussia.)

Whiting à la Cherbourg. Take the tail half of a large whiting. Scale, trim off the fins, wash well, dry, and cut into thick pieces. Heavily butter the bottom of a wide, shallow casserole, sprinkle with 2 handfuls of chopped mushrooms, and arrange the whiting pieces on this so that they are tight against each other. Salt lightly. Add a *bouquet garni*. Just cover with a mixture of the juice of 36 steamed oysters, juice of 2 lemons, and white wine. Cover. Cook briskly 8 or 10 minutes. The liquor should be reduced to half at this point. Remove the bouquet, arrange the fish on a platter, reduce the broth further. If it is too thin, thicken with a piece of butter mixed with flour and let come to a boil. Strain, add 2 ounces of butter in little bits, then the oysters, mix, and serve over the fish. (This recipe is also from Urbain-Dubois.)

WINE. Wine is the intellectual part of a meal. Meats are merely the material part.

"One does not age at the table," says Grimod de la Reynière.

The arts of eating and drinking are not learned overnight. When Alexander the Great wanted to add the title of Gastronome to his name, after the title of the Victorious, he took his degree at Persepolis and Babylon to be named Doctor of Eating and Drinking. The fame of his orgies has echoed down two thousand years.

According to Isidore of Seville, the word "wine" derives from *vis*, meaning strength. Pindar called it "Venus' milk," and the

Romans the "milk of the good goddess." It is believed that the
Egyptians taught the Greeks how to make wine. But we know that
the Greeks perfected their methods. One of their most flavourful
wines was made from grapes that were spread out on screens six
or seven feet above the ground and there exposed to the sun for a
week, being taken in at dusk to avoid the dew. Called *diacheton*,
it was an excellent wine, with the aroma of raspberries.

As soon as wine began to be shipped, the Romans imported the
product of Chios, the best wines of Greece. Both Virgil and Horace
sang their praises, and particularly of those that came from the
environs of Psyra. They were recommended for certain illnesses.
Caesar, who had the world's harvest to choose from, served his
friends the wines of Chios to celebrate his triumphs and for the
feasts of Jupiter. Athenaeus says that Greek wines aid digestion, are
nourishing and generous, and that the best come from around Arius,
where three kinds are made.

The best Roman wines came from the Campania, a province
now part of the kingdom of Naples. The names of Falernus and
Massicus were most renowned, and often recur in Horace.

The wines of Mt. Pausilypus were renowned for their lightness,
and Pliny boasts of their bouquet and their sweet generosity. Sophocles calls them Zeus because, he says, like the king of gods they give
health and pleasure, the finest gifts the gods can give.

The vineyards of Alba also enjoyed a great reputation. Their
wines were at the same time strong and light, and they kept well.
Strabo compares them to the finest wines of Greece and Italy, and
Horace, who lived in that part of Italy, says they were in no way
second to the wines of Tenedos.

When civilization disappeared with the barbarian invasion, wine,
the measure of civilization, disappeared too.

The first drinks mentioned in the annals of gastronomy after the
passage of the barbarians were cider, then beer. Then, little by little,
came the first wines. *Clairet* was a clarified wine in which spices had
been infused. Hippocras was a wine sweetened with honey.

The various qualities of wine were recognized one by one as
gourmands had opportunity to appreciate them. No one yet had
mentioned champagne when Wenceslaus, King of Bohemia, came
to France to negotiate a treaty with Charles VI, and arrived at

Rheims in May 1397. There he tasted the wine of the country and found it so good that he spent three hours each day, from three to six, getting drunk. Finally, the time came when he had to busy himself with the treaty, and this worried him. After it was signed, he asked permission to remain in the city he had found so hospitable. He remained another year. He had spent a year waiting for the treaty, a year discussing it, and a year resting from the fatigue of all this diplomatic labour.

When he left, he told the Dauphin the secret of his lengthy visit. The Dauphin tried the wines and found them excellent. The reputation of champagne dates from this time.

The wines of Bordeaux took a long time to overcome the prejudice against them. Saint-Simon tells of a little gentleman from near Bordeaux who had just arrived at court, and drank the wine of his country. This phenomenon continued for twenty-four years without anyone being able to explain it. But one day Louis XV asked for elucidation from Marshal Richelieu, an expert in this sort of thing.

"Tell me," he asked, "is any potable wine harvested by the Bordelais?"

"Sire, there are *crus* of that country whose wines are not bad," said the Marshal.

"What do you mean by that?" asked the King.

"There is what they call white sauterne," said Richelieu, "which is not so good as Montrachet or so good as the wine from the low hill slopes of Burgundy, not by a good deal. But it isn't small beer, either. There is a certain Graves that smells of brimstone like an old carbine, and which is similar to Moselle, but keeps better. Besides that, you could die laughing to hear the Bordelais praise two or three red wines from Médoc and around Bazadais. According to them, they are the finest beverages on earth, and nectar for the table of the gods. And yet these are not Upper Burgundy or Rhone Valley wines, to be sure. They are neither generous nor vigorous, but the bouquet isn't bad, and they have an indescribably sinister, sombre bite that is not at all disagreeable. Besides, you can drink as much as you like of them. You'll go to sleep, but that's all. This is what I like best about them."

To satisfy the King's curiosity, Richelieu brought some Château

Lafite to Versailles, and the King found it passable. But until then, despite the cardinal's great predilection for them, no host had the idea of serving Bordeaux wines to his guests unless they were of that country.

Today, it is said, nothing is rarer in Paris than a Bordeaux of the first *crus* and a good year, because the English buy them all up.

Italy furnishes some famous wines, but, generally speaking, they have more reputation than worth. In the first rank must be placed Lachryma Christi, the vineyard of which was engulfed by the lava from Vesuvius. It was called by this poetic name because it flowed from the grape like tears even before picking. The rare bottles of this wine that survive are vermilion in colour, pleasant, and penetrating.

Spain furnishes its contingent: Alicante, Benicarló, sherry, Pajarete, Rota, Malaga – these grace the finest tables. The Greeks still furnish us with the wines of antiquity, but spoiled by the introduction of resin. This comes from an old superstition, a final homage to Bacchus, whose sceptre was a thyrsus tipped with a pine cone.

Saint Georgy wine, from Hungary, is what is marketed in Paris under the name of Tokay. It is very like Tokay, but a gourmet would not be fooled by it. At Saint Georgy and at Ratchdorf, two qualities are harvested. One is used to make vermouth. The other is sold in Europe. As to the real Tokay, since the vineyards from which it is harvested belong half to the Emperor of Russia and half to the Emperor of Austria, it is evident that only through a revolution in which the cellars of these monarchs were pillaged could common lips aspire to touch this nectar of the gods.

The wine of Constance, happily less rare, is its rival not only in reputation but in real excellence. And both must yield to the Persian wines harvested in the environs of Shiraz and named after that city. Upon the death of the Bailli de Ferrette, ambassador at Paris for the Order of Malta, there were sold from his estate seven or eight flagons of Shiraz at 285 francs a half bottle.

The custom of consuming or testing several sorts of wines at the same meal is often unhealthy, especially when sweet wines follow acid, or heavy wines light, and above all after too heavy a meal. But light and sparkling wines, old, generous, dry wines – that is to say, those which contain little sugar or colouring matter – do not have this inconvenience, because their mission is to accelerate digestion.

WOODCOCK. The queen of the marshes. For its delicious flavour, its volatile principles and delicate flesh, it is sought after by all classes of gourmets. But it is eaten only during three or four months out of the year. Woodcocks on the spit are, after the pheasant, the most distinguished of roasts. This precious bird is so venerated that it is rendered the same honours as the Grand Lama: toast moistened with lemon juice receives its drippings and is eaten respectfully by the fervent gastronome.

Elzéar Blaze, great hunter and great cook, has this to say about the woodcock:

"The woodcock is excellent game when it is fat. It is always best during severe cold. It is never eviscerated. A delicious purée is made by crushing the woodcock in a mortar. Top this purée with larded partridge wings, and you have the highest product of culinary skill. When the gods came down to earth in olden days, they subsisted on this dish exclusively.

"The woodcock must not be eaten too soon after shooting, before it develops its full aroma. The flesh would be tasteless and without flavour. Prepared in a salmis, its aroma blends very well with the truffle. Wrapped in bacon and spitted, it must be watched carefully by the hunter. An overcooked woodcock is good for nothing. But a woodcock cooked to a turn, served on golden toast juicy with its drippings, is one of the most delicate and savoury dishes a gentleman can eat. When he takes the precaution to wash it down with an excellent Burgundy, he can flatter himself that he is a superb logician."

Though the flesh of the woodcock is excellent, it is not for the man with a weak stomach or one who is bilious or melancholy, but for those who exercise. Everything in a woodcock is good.

Woodcock on the Spit. Pluck and singe 4 woodcocks. Skin the head. Tie the feet together and stick the beak through them. Lard if thin, tie up in bacon slices if fat. Pierce with a skewer fixed at both ends so it will not slip off. Season pieces of toast with oil, pepper, and lemon juice, and place them under the birds to receive the drippings. Broil for 30 minutes. Serve on the toast.

Another Method. Eviscerate and stuff half full with a mixture of grated bacon, parsley, shallots, scallions, coarse pepper, and salt. Sew up again. Broil as above. If this is to be served to an Englishman, accompany with bread sauce.

Salmis of Woodcock des Bernardins. Take 4 woodcocks roasted rare on the spit. Divide them according to the rules of the art. Cut the wings, the legs, the belly, and the breast each in two.

"On the platter on which the dissection has taken place, and which must be of silver, crush the liver and other entrails of the birds, adding the juice of 2 good-sized lemons and the finely chopped zest of 1. Arrange the pieces of woodcock on this platter, season with a few pinches of salt and powdered fine spices (if you haven't the four spices in powdered form, use a little fine-ground pepper and nutmeg), 2 tablespoonfuls of excellent mustard, and ½ glass of the best white wine. Put this platter over a spirit lamp and stir so that the sauce will penetrate each piece, and none will remain sticking to the platter.

"Great care must be taken to prevent this ragout from boiling. When it reaches almost that temperature, sprinkle with a dash of virgin oil, lower the flame, and continue to stir. Then take the platter off and serve immediately, without ceremony, for this salmis must be eaten very hot.

"It is essential to use forks on this occasion, for fear of devouring one's own fingers if they have touched the sauce." (*Almanach des Gourmands*, 1806.)

ZEST. The yellow skin of lemons, oranges, and citrons. The essential oil to which these fruits owe their aroma is concentrated in the zest. The white part underneath has none, and is disagreeably bitter besides, which is why the zest should always be separated from it.

Index of Recipes

Lightning Source UK Ltd.
Milton Keynes UK
UKHW020250290121
377879UK00004B/47